LR61971 30∞

Henri Rousseau

Translated by Joachim Neugroschel

Phaidon · Oxford

Yann le Pichon

The World of
HENRI
ROUSSEAU

"In his simplicity, Henri Rousseau, to our great fortune,
was convinced that he ought to show what he saw.
What he saw was love, and it will always
leave us wide-eyed with amazement."
PAUL ELUARD

Contents

About the Life and the Legend

Foreword by Jeanne Bernard-Rousseau 10

Preface I by Jacques Lassaigne 13

Preface II by Michel Hoog 15

Author's Preface 18

Introduction 21

1
The Mysteries of Love and Marriage 27

2
Childhood Scenes, Family Life 45

3
The Landscape Portraits and Their Symbolism 65

4
The Flight from the City and the Return Home 85

5
The Obsession with the Jungle 133

6
Allegories and Dreams 175

7
The Myth of War and Death 213

8
The Soul of Still Lifes, the Language of Flowers 231

Biography 247
Selected Bibliography 278
Sources of Illustrations 282
Acknowledgments 285

About the Life and the Legend

I have always been disturbed and sometimes even paralyzed with embarrassment when art lovers and critics ask me about my memories and impressions of my grandfather the Douanier Rousseau, for they are trying to force me to remember things that would amplify his legend. I finally decided to do what my mother had done: I stopped mouthing other people's words, and I intend to abide by my decision. The things I might have told those people are part of the intimate and personal background of my childhood. Grandfather and I were linked by a joyous bond of affection and complicity. . . .

During his lifetime, what fun it was to be the granddaughter of such an original painter! Every stroll with him was a festival. I was moved by the very sight of him, despite his bow tie and his hat, because he was almost more childlike than I!

When he died, my paternal grandmother was angry because I didn't cry. What could I do? I couldn't help recalling the way he walked through the streets of Angers singing "Auprès de ma blonde, qu'il fait bon dormir." And I also figured that he would be reunited with Grandmother, whom my mother had lost when she was twelve. Besides, Mother was going to give me the little bronze angel that he loved so much.

At school, whenever I was bored I instinctively drew in my notebook, sketching the same wild plants and the same huge herbs that he had depicted. He was with me, beyond life and his burgeoning legend: a light and mysterious presence that contrasted sharply with Mother's suffering when she recalled the six years she had spent with her father and younger brother. Her father never received his due, and he had to endure the humiliation of wounding sarcasm at the Salon of the Independents.

"Someday, you'll be getting over one hundred thousand francs for my paintings!" he would tell us proudly. He was convinced of his genius, but his family didn't understand the mystery of his gift. We were particularly bemused with regard to his portraits. My affection for him is the dominant note of my profound rapport with him, but it took a long time for me to comprehend the mystery of his genius. And, oddly enough, it was a child who helped me! When the son of my friends the le Pichons came to me for piano lessons, I let him leaf through the album of Wild Beasts, which Mother had given me as a souvenir of Grandfather when she came back from his funeral in Paris. Young Yann le Pichon was deeply attracted to the work of the Douanier Rousseau, and one of the first things he discovered was that my grandfather had gotten most of the exotic subjects of his paintings from this album. Next, he tried to systematically track down my grandfather's sources and inspirations. I let him peruse our archives, our documents, and all the souvenirs from Grandfather's studios. In time I asked Yann le Pichon to defend Rousseau's true memory.

First and always, the Douanier Rousseau remains "my grandfather," and I always feel that, as such, he never leaves me and never stops helping me.

Have I perceived his genius in its entirety? I'll know the answer to this question only when I find my grandfather again.

Jeanne Bernard-Rousseau

Preface I

by Jacques Lassaigne
Honorary Curator at the Museum of
Modern Art of the City of Paris

Something new about the Douanier Rousseau!* Yann le Pichon has already distinguished himself by discovering a reference album of wild beasts,† published by the Galeries Lafayette, the creatures in which served as models when Rousseau painted animals—though he might also have seen the animals at the menagerie in the Jardin des Plantes, in Paris, which he visited regularly.

Yann le Pichon studied music with Rousseau's granddaughter in Cherbourg, where she lived. The granddaughter had reliable memories of the Douanier, whom, incidentally, she resembled in a number of ways. The furnishings in her home included the famous Louis-Philippe sofa that Rousseau had not hesitated to place in the jungle for one of his most illustrious paintings. In the granddaughter's waiting room, a visitor could view the album, which contained two hundred pictures of animal life accompanied by an instructive text, as well as postcards depicting the Douanier's youth in Laval. That was all it took to make Yann le Pichon one of the foremost specialists on the Douanier Rousseau.

Le Pichon soon realized that he could pursue this research and discover Rousseau's secrets by finding the sources of his inspiration. They were the humblest of sources: postcards, photographs, reproductions of works he might have seen in the Salons of his era; academic works, but also canvases by Cézanne and Gauguin, whom he admired, just as he was intimately familiar with the works of such contemporary poets as Apollinaire and Jarry.

This book is thus the result of a passionate effort at reconstruction; and, indeed, it is immensely interesting.

The various chapters cover the familiar themes of the painter's most notable works. We also find his lesser efforts, each with its subject matter: from the landscapes around the Beucheresse Gate of Laval, where the Rousseau family resided, to the Parisian landscapes of Plaisance, where the painter himself subsequently lived, and the tollgate where he worked as a customs inspector for a long time. Soon, however, Rousseau began dreaming; no subject seemed too remote for him, too bizarre or exotic, even jungle beasts. The critics systematically ridiculed him, but this merely spurred him on to produce one surprise after another.

Rousseau skillfully invented the appropriate environment for each subject he treated; he conceived veritable portrait landscapes. These landscapes are not so much invented as they are recognized by him, rediscovered in his memories yet verified by documents, with reality and the unconscious working together.

Rousseau had no qualms about using allegory. One of the merits of this study is the very thorough biography at the end, based on Rousseau's own canvases. The reader need not get tangled up in anecdotal details, but future lovers of Rousseau will not be able to work without this basis. Might we not also dream of an exhibition to illustrate the lessons from this book?

---

* Henri Rousseau was known to everyone simply as "the Douanier," the customs inspector, a post he gave up in 1885 in order to devote himself entirely to painting.
† This album was reprinted in the journal *Arts*, February 15, 1961, for the Rousseau jubilee at the Galerie Charpentier.

Preface II

by Michel Hoog
Curator of the Musée de l'Orangerie, Paris

Employing a highly personal method of working, the Douanier Rousseau gathered the elements for his paintings from numerous sources: engravings in illustrated magazines, all sorts of paintings, photographs, and advertising catalogues furnished a detail here, the posture of a person or an animal there, or even a compositional structure. Yann le Pichon, one of the first to point out these visual sources, has gathered them here in an impressive dossier, as it were—a dossier, indeed, that is probably not yet closed.

Any number of artists have been inspired by photography or the works of their predecessors. But rare is the painter who used these sources as often as Rousseau did. Was it a lack of confidence in his own imagination and inventive mind? Did he wish to paint "realistically" (the unabashed intention of so many artists back then)? Did he feel so unsure of himself in rendering gestures or attitudes? What he lacked in this highly codified domain was the long studio apprenticeship of painting from models—a training from which most of his contemporaries benefited, even the least-conformist painters. Did he, perhaps, by "quoting" good "authors" in certain cases, hope to take refuge behind their authority? On closer inspection, Rousseau does not lack imagination. He employs real elements, whether observed or copied, but subjects them to his fantasy, changing the scale, making "mistakes" in the proportion, offering improbable situations—all of which permitted him to achieve a superior coherence, just like the Surrealists, such as Max Ernst, who admired him thirty years later.

However, the relationship between Rousseau and his contemporaries or immediate predecessors does not boil down to borrowings that one can interpret as collages pulled together with the Douanier's own language. In the closing years of the nineteenth century, the art of painting was renewed perhaps more profoundly than at any moment in the previous four centuries. Rousseau's *oeuvre* was by no means isolated, untimely, or fixated on academic or backward models. In the course of time, Rousseau became aware of a painting of *rupture*, launched by Edouard Manet and the Impressionists. This transformation was elaborated through the years, and Rousseau took a greater part in it than he is generally credited with.

The Salon of the Independents opened in 1884, and Rousseau exhibited there regularly. He enjoyed some success; his paintings were noticed and commented on, not always derisively. He familiarized himself there with the works of innovative artists. And, no doubt, the mere existence of a Salon "without a jury or prize" allowed Rousseau to express himself unrestrainedly by authorizing him to create huge canvases in full freedom and with the certainty of being able to exhibit them.

Thus, in many paintings, particularly in the tropical landscapes, Rousseau coped with a problem very much on the minds of most artists toward the end of the nineteenth century: the challenge to traditional perspective. Need we recall how profoundly the Impressionists, and then Cézanne, Gauguin, Toulouse-Lautrec, and countless others, challenged the received ideas of depth and relief, or, rather, challenged the traditional pictorial methods for depicting depth and relief? On this point, Rousseau was no more awkward, no more backward, than his contemporaries in seeking new means of spatial representation.

Incidentally, we must abandon once and for all the idea of the Douanier Rousseau as an artist who was naïve (in the pejorative sense) and unpolished. Even before devoting himself entirely to painting, Rousseau came to know the museums and visited exhibitions. He was familiar with the artworks of all eras, at least through photographic reproductions (which were more widespread than is believed). Before him, van Gogh had dealt with many such reproductions at Goupil's gallery.* Even though he never received any academic training, Rousseau, albeit awkwardly and incompletely, knew and assimilated the principles of such instruction. Also, countless how-to-paint handbooks were in circulation, teaching the principles of art and perspective, of landscapes and portraits. Rousseau got hold of such manuals, as proved by many of his canvases, notably the views of Paris based on a precisely calculated manipulation of planes and vanishing traces. One even feels that Rousseau is trying to flaunt newly acquired knowledge here. Likewise, certain vast skies in which the clouds are delicately nuanced with grays, browns, and steely blues are really pastiches of skies by Nicolas Poussin or seventeenth-century Dutch landscape artists. It is now certain that Rousseau did not join the French expedition to Mexico (1864–66). His supposed participation was a legend spread by Guillaume Apollinaire. Frequenting the Jardin des Plantes in Paris, studying picture albums, especially *Wild Beasts*, and illustrated newspapers—all this was enough to feed Rousseau's exoticism.

Rousseau's palette is neither indifferent nor interchangeable. Canvases with multiple figures, like **The Representatives of Foreign Powers** or **The Centennial of Independence,** burst in a rich variety of colors, while in the landscapes the gamut is generally quite restricted. **War** is almost exclusively black and gray, down to the leaves on the trees; the rare touches of red suggest the wounds of the corpses; green and yellow, the colors of hope, light, life, are just about absent. The ancient codes of color symbolism were so widespread, even in highly popularized works or in dictionaries, that Rousseau had to be aware of them, if only unconsciously. By

---

* During the past few years, we have come to take for granted the importance of the image, as opposed to print, in the mental universe of our contemporaries. The new vectors of the image are certainly quite pervasive; however, the existence of an abundant *figurative* culture parallel to the *printed* culture is not new. The multiplicity of widely distributed illustrated periodicals, illustrated popular editions, and installment publications dates back to the mid-nineteenth century in France and Western Europe. Older painting and academic art benefited from this development; and original illustrations (whether creative or reportorial) obeyed the canons, patterns, and stereotypes of traditional art. Rousseau's methods have to be viewed within this context, knowledge of which is indispensable for explaining, say, Cézanne's work as a reaction.

adapting the color scale, sometimes even the treatment, to the subject matter, Rousseau redis-covered—though most likely in all innocence—Poussin's method of using "modes."

In short, Rousseau possessed and cashed in on an artistic (and probably literary) education, often incomplete and poorly assimilated, but serious—as a self-taught background often is. It is wrong to see him as a sort of "savage genius" or "naïve ignoramus." Demonstrating his pictorial knowledge, exhibiting his works and having them noticed, even selling them—for this minor functionary, such things meant true upward mobility, the affirmation of a self-acquired intellec-tual background.

There are other examples of Rousseau's profound rapport with certain preoccupations of his contemporaries. One of the most important and beguiling aspects of his work is his depiction of tropical flora, with people and animals usually reduced to silhouettes. (The great exception here was **The Snake Charmer,** the savage child recalling Gauguin's paintings, with which Rousseau was acquainted.) This profuse, pervasive vegetation, permitting but meager space to living crea-tures, completely hiding the sky, unfolding without density in a single plane, can be found at approximately the same time, 1900, in Gauguin, but in many other artists, too. One need merely cite *The Black Castles* of the later Cézanne, the *Water Lilies* of Claude Monet, the landscapes of Renoir, Klimt, Augusto Giacometti, as well as Odilon Redon's decorations at the Abbaye of Fontfroide. Such a convergence within a few years would call for an explanation.

In opposition to the realistic or naturalistic obsession which was forced upon nineteenth-century painters and writers by what amounted to intellectual terrorism, these landscapes derive from the world of dreams, the imaginary, the reinvented. They define a universe beyond every-day urban life, beyond time, a cosmic and slightly pantheistic nature. An uprooting toward the exotic and the fantastic is an obvious aspiration of urban life, which, in the late nineteenth cen-tury, was already marked by the machine. Colonial expeditions and religious missions, with their accompanying movements in opinion, the success of such writers as Jules Verne and Pierre Loti, not to mention their countless epigoni, bear further witness to this trend toward exoticism.

Thus Rousseau, seemingly entrenched in his studio, participated in some of the most auda-cious research in contemporary painting. This was probably one reason for his success with other artists (we know that Picasso, Robert and Sonia Delaunay, Brancusi, and Kandinsky were among his first admirers). But by reintroducing the values of the imaginary into the art of his pe-riod, he went beyond one of the needs of his time—and ours.

Author's Preface

The Douanier Rousseau painted for over thirty years, but did not begin to be truly appreciated until the final years of his life, and then by just a few art lovers. This means that not all his works have come down to us, unfortunately. Some have vanished; others were destroyed; still others are unfairly treated as suspect by several art critics who are trying to prove their impromptu expertise by pronouncing these works too perfect or too mediocre. And, finally, certain collectors, distrustful and possessive, are hiding some very beautiful and thrilling works by the painter.

I am happy to present most of Rousseau's work here, although I regret not having enough space to reproduce and analyze the Douanier's entire known oeuvre. With the greatest possible rigor, I have strived to represent the true range of Rousseau's art, which is more varied than we commonly believe. I have refused to leave out old, minor, or too hastily executed pieces, as long as they reveal the genius of this Naïf and his orientations. Nevertheless, this book should not be considered a catalogue (something that still remains to be done).

The choice of photographs, drawings and sketches, paintings, vases, and sculptures presented for the reader's attention and admiration was not made at anyone's wishes or under any pressure, moral or financial. I quite independently and voluntarily assumed the responsibility of making this sometimes delicate selection. I would like to thank my publisher for allowing me to do so, and for so effectively facilitating my research with regard to collectors. (The prices for Rousseau's paintings, rising nonstop, have reached record highs, so that his works are quickly put on sale and then we lose track of their new, speculating owners.)

Any mistakes in interpretation, comparison, or even attribution were not intended by me, and I am willing to admit to them, provided, obviously, that I am shown definite and objective evidence.

If any readers have new information, unknown paintings, or original documents and are willing to help defend and embellish the memory of Henri-Julien Rousseau, they are cordially invited to write me in care of my French, British, or American publisher. I promise to reply with all due discretion—just as I have kept the secret of the whereabouts of certain paintings—and I thank these readers in advance for their confidence. Such new contributions could enrich a second edition of Henri Rousseau. Above all, they would help in establishing a true catalogue raisonné, which I, along with so many art historians and art lovers, fervently desire. An exhaustive inventory of Henri Rousseau could only be the fruit of assiduous collective work that is both international and free of any partisan spirit! If this project were begun, I would not hesitate to make available everything I have received from the painter's family, as well as my personal archives and knowledge.

Some details on the makeup and editing of this book must be presented here, for the sake of a better understanding of its aims.

Although slightly arbitrary, the thematic classification of Rousseau's works allows a better analysis of his biographical and iconographical inspiration.

The illustrations are not always—indeed, may be anything but—the direct sources of his paintings. They are sometimes offered as indirect influences, as documents on Rousseau's ambience, sometimes ulterior, but as close as possible to the painter, his life, his mentality, the people surrounding him.

Whenever Henri Rousseau supplied titles, these complex—even erroneous—titles of his works are given in the captions to the reproductions. Otherwise, the most appropriate titles have been chosen from among those so far invented (including some rather whimsical ones). The titles reserved by collectors, museums, or photographers have been inserted in the list of photographic credits, which include, when authorized, the names of owners and the size of each painting.

The dates for works are given only if inscribed by the painter. The dates of the exhibitions by the painter at the Salon of the Independents or at the Salon d'Automne are indicated in the commentary and the biography. I refused to make up arbitrary dates, the establishing of which would be imprudent because Rousseau's painting evolved very little. He remained a prisoner of his handicaps and habits; he demonstrated regressiveness in the patterns of his workmanship and in his reversion to earlier themes.

For lack of space, I had to reduce my large bibliography to essential books and articles and forgo pointing out any obvious errors in these works. I have not, however, omitted works announcing discoveries of iconographic sources, most of which, incidentally, I already knew.

For reasons of courtesy, I was careful not to enter into any of the violent polemics engaged in by several contemporary French authors—to the detriment of their objectivity—and besides, I wished to preserve my Rousseauist quietude. May those other writers likewise respect it! I do not enjoy quarrels of jealousy. Moreover, the Douanier Rousseau, who delighted in remaining an Independent, is no one's property. He belongs to us all. From up there in his little clouds, he must be laughing at the coteries that keep yanking him in all directions, some singing the praises of certain of his canvases that others consign to the scrap heap—and vice versa.

I dedicate Henri Rousseau *to my wife
and our children, Gwenaëlle and Tugdual,
and I hope that its poetic spaces will
make up for all the time that it so
possessively deprived them of.*

Introduction

**The Douanier Rousseau Rediscovered
Through His Biographical and Iconographical Sources**

*A deeper understanding of the various
levels of meaning in a work of art
increases our enjoyment of it.*
Maria K. Kramer

The French use the idiom "a violin of Ingres" to mean a hobby. Now the Douanier Rousseau had a real "violin of Ingres": his violin. He taught elementary and advanced music to his neighbors' children in the Parisian quarter of Plaisance, where he lived. I knew about these lessons, so I felt even more admiration for my piano teacher, Mademoiselle Jeanne Bernard-Rousseau, his granddaughter, who resembled him physically and mentally: she had the same playful and easygoing character, the same prodigality, the same aptitude for "gathering one's rosebuds," no matter what the weather.

She said she would help me rediscover, along with Mozart, Beethoven, and the Douanier, the enchanting melody played on a transverse flute by Rousseau's **Snake Charmer** (in a print above the granddaughter's piano). I was so impatient that I arrived ahead of time for our appointment.

While waiting for my lesson in the parlor on Rue Loysel in Cherbourg, I sat down on the Louis-Philippe sofa that the Naïf transplanted into the middle of the jungle in his **Dream,** and I leafed attentively through his album of *Wild Beasts* (published by the Galeries Lafayette). I realized that spontaneous generation does not exist in art any more than in biology as the spoonbill tamed by the snake charmer popped up again to my astonished eyes. On the yellowed pages of this album, which was meant to capture the imagination of children, the painter's fingerprints, in the dominant colors of his palette, provided me with the evidence of his irresistible borrowings.

These monkeys, these beasts, these birds from zoological gardens reminded me of the ones I had come upon with my father in the bush of the remote Annamite mountains of Vietnam, where my father initiated me into life—real life, far from school. Rousseau, in the privacy of his Paris studio, had freed these animals from their cages and restored them to nature by projecting them into his visionary painting.

The photos were revealing. In the house at the Beucheresse Gate (through which the Laval woodcutters once passed en route to the woods and the countryside), those photos had aroused visions of a cruel Eden in little Henri Rousseau. Haunted by the visions, the boy grew more attentive to his great-aunt's tales about wolves, the adventures of Robinson Crusoe and his imitators, and of Paul and Virginie, than to the drudgery of the three R's.

It soon dawned on me that the imagination might be simply a mental reorganization of reminiscences of early determining impressions, restored by random images that are found or patiently sought after. And I arrived at the hypothesis that if the emotional origin and profound inspiration of artistic expression were investigated, they might turn out to be the idealized, heightened, and magnified transcription of childhood fantasies reconstituted in an effort to escape the harsh laws that reality inflicts on the adult, and from which he tries to take refuge in an aesthetic attitude.

Hence, might an artist's sublimation of his original psychic instincts not be just as much a determining factor as his genetically acquired characteristics? This question obsessed me.

Whether they are musicians, poets, painters, or sculptors, aren't creative people ultimately just men or women who, in their souls and their unconscious, are far more sensitive to the precariousness of our human condition? If they drew upon their ancient, residual frustrations for the affective energy necessary to transform and exalt those frustrations, to let us share them, then might not the reason be that these artists had not recovered from their frustrations?

"Whom do we call an artist? Unwittingly, any man to whom an art is necessary," says André Malraux. Malraux also feels that "artists do not attribute to their art any values superior to those of life; they experience them as such, just as that which concerns Christ has an irreducible value for a Christian merely because it concerns him."

I no longer believed in the divine right of geniuses. Did they not choose art for the sake of the art of living differently? Did they not impose themselves upon the common run of mortals with their own superhuman deviations, which were aroused by their despair at being inadequate? I now saw their parries as caused by their paranoia.

A Law of Nature

T hus, I had already reached the conclusion that we are anything but free in front of a work of art," says Marcel Proust in *Remembrance of Things Past*, "that we do not create it at will, but that, since it is pre-existent to us, we must discover it, because it is both necessary and hidden, and as we would discover a law of nature." Proust—whose character Elstir the painter, curiously enough, had certain traits in common with the Douanier—managed to recover time if not health.

I announced my discovery of the album entitled *Wild Beasts: Approximately 200 Amusing Illustrations Drawn from the Life of Animals, with an Instructive Text* in the French journal *Arts* (February 15, 1961), which was celebrating the great exhibition organized in Paris by the Galerie Charpentier for the fiftieth anniversary of Henri Rousseau's death. At the same time, I pointed out that here we had the modest iconographic source of the painter's most celebrated canvases, an obvious indication of the way his creative imagination worked. Encouraged by several articles in the international press (particularly *The New Yorker*, March 4, 1961, and *Der Spiegel*, April 5, 1961), I undertook a systematic analysis of this subject and decided to extend it to all of Rousseau's paintings. I found my investigation all the more interesting because Rousseau was viewed during his lifetime, and is still viewed today, as a crude and limited autodidact who found within himself the miraculous inspiration and novel themes of his so original paintings. How was this possible? To what patterns did he bend "reality," which he claimed to scrutinize so closely? What was his brush describing? What Muses had leaned over his cradle?

"Man sees and moves in what he sees, but he sees only what he dreams," said Paul Valéry.

Yes, what did the Naïf see? Why did he look at what he saw in such a way? What was he dreaming of—this so-called primitive painter, to whom so many naïve painters owe their success? What was he remembering? Where were they born—the dreams of this oneiric painter who became the grandfather of Surrealism (just as Cézanne became the grandfather of Cubism), and who fascinated the great Picasso, unsettling him and marking him? What metamorphoses took place in this man, at once constrained and liberated, who in the heyday of academism so deeply renewed instinctive art that, in spite of himself, he scandalized or befuddled most of the contemporary art critics? Yet he was greatly admired, in passing or in returning, by painters as diverse as Signac, Pissarro, Vallotton, Redon, Gauguin, Renoir, Delaunay, Picasso, Léger, and even Kandinsky, one of the first creators of abstraction ("I have always looked for a chance to buy a Rousseau," wrote Kandinsky on October 28, 1911, one year after the Douanier's death, to Robert Delaunay, whom he asked for help in finally acquiring some Rousseaus).

This lowly customs inspector was systematically ridiculed by the visitors to the Salon of the Independents, where, every spring for twenty years, he showed his paintings as an apple tree produces its blossoms. How and why did he seduce Alfred Jarry and Guillaume Apollinaire, who were at the source of his mythical renown? Poets know and divine! Why, finally, did such poets as Max Jacob, Léon-Paul Fargue, André Salmon, Philippe Soupault, Jean Cocteau, Paul Eluard, Tristan Tzara, André Breton, and André Malraux make him one of their own, feel kinship with his genius?

It is time to unveil the mysteries of an art that still provokes us now, almost a century after it entered the lists, and that has never stopped amazing the world.

Pilgrimages to the Source

The object of this study, to which I have devoted more than twenty years of research, comparisons, and reflection, is to try to answer these key questions. I hope I may thus help people toward a better grasp of Rousseau's painting: the public who is discovering him, the art lovers who collect his canvases or reproductions, the art critics who do not always know how to view him, and the curators of museums in which his works are dispersed. Does not "grasp" mean take hold of, take along, make one's own, and hence love?

"People came from everywhere to admire me!" he dreamed once during the year of his death. At the time he was talking to a journalist, who smiled; but this is now the case in Prague, Moscow, and Leningrad, in New York, Washington, and Philadelphia, in Los Angeles, Tokyo, and Göteborg, in London, Zurich, and Hamburg, in Basel, Berne, Lugano, and so on and so forth.

Who would have believed it back then?

I have made pilgrimages to these sources, and even though I have often identified with him, I obviously cannot claim to have loved the people and things he loved, to have endured everything he suffered, to have lived his life. However, despite any artful dodges he may have employed to gain appreciation for his works, his perfectly sincere *oeuvre* has frequently confirmed the memories of his daughter and his granddaughter, these contemporaries and last witnesses to his life; and, finally, confirmed my own intuitions, too.

Henri Rousseau nearly let himself die of grief and gangrene in 1910, the year he exhibited his **Dream** (a naked woman lying on her couch in the midst of virgin forest), and the year Sigmund Freud, the author of *The Interpretation of Dreams,* published his remarkable study *Leonardo da Vinci and a Memory of His Childhood.* Since then, art historians have been neglecting, forgetting, or suppressing the fundamental psychoanalytical discoveries about the reactivations of infantile desires and distresses, the graphic and sculptural projections—so often narcissistic—of the imaginative life of artists. Such oblivious critics seem to me like Galileo's detractors, for whom our world, created once and for all by God, remains immutable. And yet it does turn, the wheel of our memory turns, even our eyeballs turn in their orbits!

It was not enough, I felt, to seek out the pictures, the engravings in books and illustrated magazines, the color prints and vignettes, the photographs and postcards, the reproductions of paintings, the sculptures and tapestries, the landscapes and monuments that set off the processes of pictorial re-creation in Rousseau's mind. I also, with all the prudence and circumspection required when dealing with probable mental phenomena and unquestionable epiphenomena, have tried to pinpoint these images' influence on Rousseau's inspiration and craftsmanship. For I would tend to agree with what Sarah Kofman says in her book *The Childhood of Art:* "the work of art is a confession by its maker." And to achieve a better reading of Rousseau's autobiographical paintings, I had to find the wonders that had provided an escape for the child who became the father of naïve art.

"If not childhood, then what was there that is no more?" asks Saint-John Perse in *Eloges.* What is left if not the vision that childhood maintained?

By presenting Rousseau's world as it was revealed to me in the life stories of him and his family, in the direct testimonies of his closest relatives and staunchest friends, and in the indirect and direct sources of his paintings, and by uncovering the influence that his works may have had on other painters, I hope to contribute to a better approach to artistic creation.

At the close of this intensive analysis, which led me to examine one of the most fruitful and dynamic periods in the history of painting, I wonder whether art is not the sublime road to the personal unconscious, where the underground paths of the collective memory converge. To trace the route and clear the approaches, it now seems to me, would consist in deciphering the symbolic archetypes through which man inscribes the history of his progressive awakening to consciousness, to civilization, and to the comprehension of his destiny and his ambition: namely, his efforts to overcome the death and oblivion of his origins and thus make his identity less ephemeral.

The Nostalgia for Childhood

André Breton, one of the people who best knew Rousseau, magisterially said in his book *Surrealism and Painting,* "The late nineteenth century in Europe witnessed the blossoming, with the Douanier Rousseau, of an entirely new branch, destined to become a stock, of a marvelous tree that had been thought dead. At first defiant and ironic, the reception of his works, especially in America, became more and more understanding, more and more deeply emotional. Nothing outside his paintings—whether highest intellectual ambition or supreme craft—can deprive them of this prerogative: his works rest on the cornerstone of ingenuity, and if this ingenuity could do nothing other than gratify our nostalgia for childhood, it would deserve to be regarded as an unequaled grace. However, by their very ingenuity, these works put us in possession of a further key: strolling through them . . . we are allowed to seize in living flesh, as it were, the process of enriching and renewing humanity's treasury of legends."

This is true: the Douanier Rousseau lives within us. This book, dear reader, invites you to acknowledge that, if you still remember your childhood.

*"Do you believe I wouldn't be happy
to feel more often the sensations of love?"*
HENRI ROUSSEAU
to his beloved Léonie

1 The Mysteries of Love and Marriage

The heat of passionate love lies in its reactivation of deep, ancient strivings, somewhat like a volcano exploding because of the decompression of molten matter. Passion is the episodic or exhaustive outlet for those aspirations, just as dormant craters that suddenly spurt vapors, ashes, and lava from the depths of the globe recall the forgotten history of the earth. And the deliriums that deliver man from the pressures of his past are also the most confidential rumors from that past; they force the historian to focus on the soul of a man.

Henri Rousseau hinted as much in some of his divagations: his passion for painting originated in his passion for his first wife, Clémence Boitard. Under her encouraging gaze, or thanks to his persistent memory of her, he drew the strength to express, in his pictorial *oeuvre*, his mnemonic attachment to the beauty of the world around him, to the beauty of the universe, which transported him beyond the visible. "Beauty is simply the promise of happiness," said Stendhal. To paint beauty is to seek happiness.

Rousseau's family and others who observed him offer tender or dazzled testimony, and their statements concur in one point: it was his fervent affection and his approach to happiness that constituted the foundation of his artistic calling. Of these witnesses, Wilhelm Uhde was the most impressive.

"A Pure Sacred Union"

Rousseau's passion for work, tenaciously vigorous will power, and awareness of his own validity raise him above the common run of men. He was a model and a source of serenity. Old people came to him, haunted by misery and on the verge of despair; they had faith in life when they saw how strong and unshakable this old man was. Sitting before them, painting one of his great landscapes, he would suddenly doze off: the afternoon was hot. Then they saw him move his brush across the canvas again, a strange expression on his face.

"Didn't you see my hand move?" he asked.

"Of course, Rousseau, you were painting."

"No," he replied. "My poor wife was here, and she directed my hand. Didn't you see her or hear her? 'Don't worry, Rousseau,' she told me, 'you'll see it through!'"

He steadied himself in his chair, we are told, and painted until sundown.

That is how intimate painting was to him!

Equally intriguing was the letter that the Douanier wrote on December 19, 1907, to the examining magistrate at the civil court during the investigation for his trial. (This trial was faithfully reported by Maurice Garçon in his study *Le Douanier Rousseau: Accusé Naïf.*) The reader must carefully weigh Rousseau's chaotic words to understand the true origin of the ills he was complaining about, for through them he evokes other ills, both disturbing and ancient.

"Today, when I feel better in my head and my heart, which make me suffer so much when I am to appeer [*sic*] before you, Your Honor, I see that today I cannot stand the pain anymore. And, Your Honor, this is not astonishing. Married the first time to a wife I adored, and she likewise, unfortunately she was consumptive, we had seven children, we lost six. After that, it was my poor wife who left this earth, which is arid for some, after twenty years of a pure sacred union living only for each other as our parents said themselves, in that way we made each other happy mutually. Ah yes those twenty years were the happiness of my life, also I had courage. . . . Fortunately I loved everything surrounding me and for good cause. . . . If my parents had known that I was gifted in painting, as our dear, departed Clément himself told them, who did the portrait of Paul Arène and who was director of the Ecole des Beaux-Arts of Lyon, who was my neighbor at 137 Rue de Sèvres; that I ought to be the greatest and richest painter in France today . . ."

I

A Password in Two Names

In thus delivering himself to the judge in order to get out of prison, the Douanier allowed some glimpses into the crannies of his unconscious, revealing some of the flashing glows that illuminate the deep sources of his art and his motives.

Clamoring equally with truth and meaning are Julia Rousseau's unpublished recollections of her father's passion for Clémence. Even sixty years later, when talking to intimates, she recalled the dreadful jealous rages that Rousseau inflicted on his wife. It did not take much to set him off. Perhaps a man passed them as they were strolling to the Hippodrome or through the Bois de Boulogne, and if this passerby cast an envious glance at Clémence's charms, Rousseau instantly launched into anxious reproaches. This artist who could never paint the shadows of creatures or objects and their interdependence in chiaroscuro, who did his best to detach creatures and objects from any mutual influence, from any confusion on his canvases—this artist could not help taking offense at what he imagined as his wife's bonds with anyone but himself. She could belong only to him.

In the evenings, at dinner, he harassed her with such tenacious spite (the more obstinate for being inappropriate) that little Julia got scared and would tremble with both nervousness and indignation. At such times, Clémence, calm and lucid, leaned over and murmured to her, telling Julia to count the little flowers painted around the edge of her plate. The mother thereby hoped to distract the child from the jealous husband's persecution, but this mysterious whispering, alive with complicity, merely increased the husband's distress, now intensified by fatherly possessiveness. (And we are not even considering Julia's possessiveness: after Clémence's death, she could not stand the intrusion of "models" in their home, and she complained particularly about a certain Gabrielle.)

Let us probe this excess emotional zeal (jealousy is, quite literally, etymologically the derivative of such zeal). The husband's affect might supply us with the password to his vocation as a painter. This password is linked to two names: Clémence and Clément. Two names crystalizing twin feelings of jealousy, which is defined in the dictionary as "anxious love by a person who fears that someone else is preferred to him" and "a feeling of envy aroused by a rival's glory, prosperity."

Two feelings triggered and maintained by an intolerable inferiority complex, a sense of not being loved . . .

If only his parents had known that he was gifted in painting, they might have loved him more and better, those parents who lived only for each other, as they themselves said.

J The Transition to the Pictorial Act

ealousy is always born with love; but it does not always die with love," said François de la Rochefoucauld. Indeed, the lover's demand does not even give in to the loss of the beloved by whom he has so ardently wished to be loved exclusively. Neither distance, nor his mother's death, nor his first wife's death, nor his second wife's death, nor the failures of his love life ever quenched Rousseau's hope for achieving the "pure sacred union." Hope involves doubt; otherwise it would be faith. The more Rousseau doubted, the more he tried proving the contrary to himself, so he might finally believe that happiness had come.

How did his basic jealousy change into his fruitful passion for painting, which he experienced in the years following his marriage to Clémence? How did he achieve the transition to the pictorial act that brought him serenity, and how can we explain this soothing outcome?

In *Love Is Much More than Love*, Jacques Chardonne says that "jealousy is the vice of possession. For lack of possessing the real person, the jealous party exhausts himself creating a fictitious presence that is continually vitalized by the notion of losing it." He provokes this presence in order to evoke it concretely and pigeonhole it. He invokes it in order to evoke it fictitiously, impose its immutable dependence on canvas, imprison it within the frames of his paintings.

Having lost the pious image of his mother—who was guilty, in his eyes, of having preferred his father to him—then his younger brother, with whom he broke all ties, Rousseau was unable to resolve his internal conflict, which was caused by his guilt at rejecting his mother. Or, rather, he could solve it only by means of a "transference" relationship with his wife. However, his wife could not compensate for this loss. She was only an illusory compensation, doubly unfaithful to the original model, a false alter ego! He therefore resorted to real images of his mother, through those of Clémence, in order to re-create the fusion he had been denied. (Substitution equals possession.) He imagined Clémence as she ought to be; first on the basis of disappointing photographs that were inadequate to catch her, to preserve her as he saw her; then by comparing her to playful and romantic visions that he depicted under her approving eyes, just as he had drawn during his childhood under his mother's vigilance.

The twosome, the couple, a binary rhythm mark these paintings with their dominant and painful theme. He reassures himself and blossoms by reaffirming—fictitiously, but almost credibly—an impossible union, a communion he so much desired.

An Inalienable Egotism

Creating this union, he believed that one and one can only make one. Yet he did not even succeed in fusing men and animals with one another or with plants, in joining their completely autonomous colors, in wiping away nuances, in diluting a light of coherence upon them, a light that Rousseau divided, the way rain divides the hues of a rainbow. He wanted to mend himself, but he continued to separate. And he even supplied a necessary if insufficient reason for this, as reported by Vollard in *Memories of an Art Dealer*.

"One morning, we were standing in front of one of his paintings, which certain critics had treated as a magnified postcard. It showed a nude woman dreaming on a red sofa in the middle of a primeval forest. I said to him: 'Tell me, Monsieur Rousseau, how did you manage to make so much air circulate among these trees?'

" 'By observing nature, Monsieur Vollard!' "

Could not Rousseau just as easily have replied, "By observing my own nature and under the sway of my inalienable egotism"?

"All these paintings," said Philippe Soupault, "are relics of a state of mind of a painter who is sure of himself and of his eyes. Nothing—neither the smiles of his friends, nor the criticism of his neighbors, nor the insults of journalists—will turn his head. He clutches his brush with all his might and stares straight ahead." He does not compare, he takes possession.

He was an "Independent": he did not suggest, he affirmed. He was an *"Isolé"* (the title of one of his canvases), consoling himself by affirming his presence in the world. And if the man was an apprentice, if solitude remained his mistress, no one would know him without seeing, in his work, the persistent hope of joining the Other in order to be recognized at last, the unsurpassable dream of being joined by the Other in order to become unique at last.

Separated from One Another

In **The Present and the Past,** Rousseau depicted the faces of former wives or husbands in the clouds over a newlywed couple. The words commenting on the painting say a great deal more than one realizes at first sight. Regrets and wishes, rejections and attractions secretly mingle. Pay heed to the word order and the spelling errors!

Etant séparés l'un de l'autre   *Separated from one another*
De ceux qu'ils avaient aimé [sic]   *From those whom they loved*
Tous deux s'unissent de nouveau   *Both of them unite once again*
Restant fidèle [sic] *à leur pensée.*   *While remaining faithful to their thoughts.*

This widower and this widow, uniting in a new marriage—symbolized by the ivy that connects them and the bouquet in their left hands—are not separated independently but *from* one another, from those they loved. On the other hand, are they not also isolated by the singular rather than plural form of the past participle *aimé* (loved) and the adjective *fidèle* (faithful), both of which would require a final plural *s* in standard French usage? Might these spellings be, not orthographical or grammatical errors, but involuntary mistakes of inattentiveness to the other person? In other words: while trying to unite again and still, doesn't he remain separated from his second wife by his loyalty to the thought of those he loved and who must have loved him?

In his volcanic letters to his various loves, Rousseau demanded this love, proved that he deserved it and was worthy of it, even assured them that he was loved by them. He "put the cart before the horse," as they say in the countryside. He projected himself into the future in order to confirm the past and strengthen the present.

"I would like to talk to you, be there next to you, place a gentle kiss on your rosy lips and on your hair, your lovely ebony eyes; I love you, you know I do, I love you straightforwardly, I, too. I wish it were Thursday evening already, my adored angel; how long time will seem to me; and now to you, too, isn't that so, my darling little wife? If you can, come, and we will meet at the wine dealer's, by the main gate of the cemetery, which you know. . . . I love you, my Josephine, I love you! I kiss you millions of times, on your rosy lips, let your whole face be covered with my burning kisses, to wipe away the marks left by the tears that I unhappily caused and for which I beg your forgiveness; which I think you will grant me in the name of your love and affection for me. I kiss you again many times, until as soon as possible, until Thursday evening; I suffer so deeply, if nothing held me back I would go and find you." (Letter to Josephine, June 21, 1899.)

If nothing held him back! If nothing held *them* back!

"We Have to Procreate"

Do you believe I don't suffer, do you believe I wouldn't be happy to feel more often the sensations of love one feels when two people love each other the way we love each other, natural sensations, and neither a woman nor a man should deny themselves [*sic*] the right to feel them, since nature made us like this, created us for one another. Christ said: Any tree or any being that does not produce is not useful. Hence, we have to procreate, but at our age we don't have to fear this. Yes, you make me suffer deeply, for luckily I still feel. Let us unite and you will see whether I am incapable of serving you. . . . It is true that this is not the reason why people get married at our age, but after all, neither of us has spoken his last word. . . ." (Letter to Eugénie-Léonie, Saturday evening, August 19, 1910.)

Unable to convince his loves to say their ultimate words to him, give themselves totally to him, he exorcised his solitude by painting couples and weddings. He was no longer able to procreate, so he created. He made these trees of Eden blossom and bear fruit—trees as idyllic as those of the Italian primitives, the trees that God granted to the first man before offering him his helpmeet. Rousseau celebrated being replanted in this earthly paradise, where man felt "sensations of love" that were perfectly natural and free of any restraints, where the woman could strip naked without false modesty, just like flowers and leaves, oranges and bananas, the sun and the moon.

"The thing that distressed Rousseau," said Fernande Olivier, "was that his fiancée [Léonie] did not want to go against her father's wishes. 'One can still love at my age without being ridiculous. It's no longer the same love as for you young people; but must a man be resigned to living alone just because he is old? Going back to a lonely home is terrible. Yet at my age, a man has the greatest need to warm his heart. . . .' He said all these things in a soft, tender, mellow voice." A child's voice demanding a caress.

The more Léonie resisted, the more obstinate he became, even drumming up his friends, asking them to supply him with proof of his talents as a painter. Since these efforts did not suffice to move her, he drew up a will, calling her his wife.

"To Mademoiselle Eugénie-Léonie V., widow of her first husband Monsieur Auguste V. . . . (and second wife of Monsieur Henri Rousseau, artist-painter), my best friend, to whom I owe a debt of eternal gratitude, I leave my entire estate, including my furniture, jewelry, money, paintings. Furthermore, I authorize her to claim a share of twenty percent from the proceeds of any art dealers and others who sell my paintings. I would like my dear Léonie to grant half of what she will have to my daughter, Julia Rousseau, the wife of Bernard, residing in Angers, in the department of Maine-et-Loire, Paris, the . . . 1909."

1. An Inexhaustible Source of Love

Léonie wouldn't give in. Rousseau visited friends to warm his hands on their ardent friendship: Jastrebzoff, otherwise known as the painter Serge Férat, and his sister Hélène d'Oettingen, otherwise known as the writer Roch Grey, to whom he sold several paintings.

"He came a long distance," Roch Grey recalls. "He always arrived late. Before having dinner with us, he always stopped in front of the Economie ménagère, waiting for her to come out—the hard, ungrateful woman he loved. . . . Sometimes, he sat for a portrait that would never be completed. . . . Preoccupied with his love, certain that he would still inspire her, he wanted to be drawn younger and more martial-looking under his white mustache, which drooped a bit mournfully. When sitting for the portrait, Rousseau grew drowsier and drowsier, fighting off sleep. He sometimes half-opened his eyelids, making excuses, asking the others not to whisper, for this was what made him fall asleep. Once he was awake, youth kindled in the depths of his eyes, a lust for life, gaiety, the inexhaustible source of love that flourished in his stunning lotuses, in his virgin forests. . . . When he left, always at fifteen minutes past midnight, so as not to miss the last métro, we would walk him slowly to Place Pereire. We spoke about Léonie, the future that was being delayed; he very obstinately asked us to invite her over, to prove to her the necessity of their marriage, the wonderful life awaiting her. . . . Once, when he was in a great hurry, I took our automobile and drove him to the Economie ménagère; the speed amused him, the ease of locomotion made him pensive. When he got out of the car, he paused on the sidewalk, gesturing to us from far away. Pink and white in the jostling throng, he vanished inside the wide doorway of that place, which is the ugliest of all the cheap stores in Paris. I wondered how he managed to harmonize his so rare, so precious tastes for dream plants and unknown animals with this passion that he flung at the crooked feet of a nasty and brutal little shopgirl."

Drowsiness and Sublimations

Such were the mysteries of love, the transfigurations, that he inspired in those who aspired to perfect happiness. Such was the power of purification and paroxysmal enchantment that the Douanier Rousseau drew from his dark disappointments, like an alchemist amid his stills in the penumbra of his laboratory, transforming lead into gold, refining a substance—the shadows bright, and youth inalterable.

When his disillusionment came over him again and a flash of lucidity struck down all hope, he gave in to his drowsiness. When he was half asleep, old strivings were precipitated, and their centrifugal quality was reanimated. When he awoke, he was exalted by this return of compensatory energies; he picked up his paintbrush in order to channel these energies onto the reassuring screen of his paintings. At such times, his face was awash with serenity. His painting had restored him to himself.

Henri Rousseau: **Henri Rousseau as Orchestra Conductor.**

"Clémence: Waltz with an Introduction for Violin or Mandolin," by Henri Rousseau.
Published by L. Barbarin, 17 Boulevard de Clichy, Paris.

Rousseau's art was born under the sign of his passionate love for Clémence Boitard, whom he married on August 14, 1869. He liked taking her to the races at Longchamp, after which they strolled under the acacias along the bridle paths in the Bois de Boulogne. At the Au Bon Marché department store (which opened on Easter Tuesday, 1872, at 22 Rue de Sèvres, five hundred meters from their home), Rousseau purchased his brushes, paints, and canvases while Clémence chose the fabrics for the fashions she created. To woo her, he resorted to his talents as a former musician (for his regiment): he wrote her a waltz, published and paid for by the Literary and Musical Academy of France.

*"The Bois de Boulogne in Autumn.
Avenue of the Acacias. Bridle Path."*
Postcard.

Henri Rousseau: **The Promenade.**

34

The Little Rabbits Maintain a Friendship.
Advertising vignette for Ibled Chocolate.
Lithograph by Vieillemard.

Henri Rousseau: **A Carnival Evening.**

Antoine Watteau: Gilles. Louvre.

The painter Félix Clément, Rousseau's neighbor on Rue de Sèvres, got him a pass from the Minister of Public Education and Fine Arts, which allowed him to enter and "work" in the museums. The delighted Rousseau thus went to the Louvre. Watteau's Gilles made a deep impact on him. Such grace and simplicity in his posture! But Gilles was all alone. So Colombine escaped from an advertising vignette and joined Gilles on a moonlit night near the gardeners' shack on the Avenue of the Acacias. The Naïf showed this painting at the first exhibition of the Society of Independent Artists in 1886. Pissarro instantly admired "the preciseness of the hues and the richness of the tones." On the other hand, the Soleil critic was stupefied: "A Negro and a Negress in disguise are lost in a zinc forest one carnival evening, under a full, round moon that shines without illuminating anything, while the most bizarre constellation, made up of a blue cone and a pink cone, is pasted on the black sky." The painter, very proud of being mentioned in newspapers, glued this clipping into a school notebook.

Henri Rousseau: **Happy Quartet.**

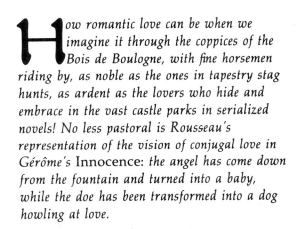

ow romantic love can be when we imagine it through the coppices of the Bois de Boulogne, with fine horsemen riding by, as noble as the ones in tapestry stag hunts, as ardent as the lovers who hide and embrace in the vast castle parks in serialized novels! No less pastoral is Rousseau's representation of the vision of conjugal love in Gérôme's Innocence: the angel has come down from the fountain and turned into a baby, while the doe has been transformed into a dog howling at love.

Henri Rousseau: **The Acacias.** Crayon drawing.

Jean-Léon Gérôme: Innocence. Official illustrated catalogue for the centennial exhibition of French art from 1800 to 1889 at the World's Fair of 1900 (no. 322).

"Bois de Boulogne. Avenue of the Acacias. Paris." Postcard.

Detail from Royal Hunt: The Quarry. Gobelin tapestry, 1733. Compiègne Castle.

Henri Rousseau: **The Rendezvous in the Forest.**

Rousseau held on to his **Country Wedding** until 1910, after showing it in 1905. He had himself photographed in front of it and dedicated it to his daughter, thus emphasizing his fidelity to the memory of his first marriage.

Painted on a canvas almost as tall as Rousseau himself (1.63 meters), this wedding was probably based on a photograph of people thrust between two rows of trees. These trees play the same role as the artificial settings of professional photographers of the era, who tried to add range and depth to their portraits. Comparing Rousseau's composition with the postcard of an Auvergne wedding or Dagnan-Bouveret's pompous and humorous painting, we can appreciate the decisive influence of photography on the Douanier's art. This influence is obvious in the symmetry, the stiffness of the subjects, the rigidity of the design, the black-and-white contrasts, and the pure invention of bold colors.

"The imagination imitates; it is the critical mind that creates," said Gide. Rousseau devoted his full critical mind to the highly simplified selection of attributes and the evocative power of the signs. The figures are arranged symbolically: the men next to the horse-chestnut trees and the women next to the acacias. The father, at the left, sitting on an oak trunk, holding a stick in his right hand and the marriage contract in his left, represents order and authority; the mother, on the other side, holds the bride's veil. The bride, wearing orange blossom, radiant with purity, holds her husband's hand tight in her right hand and, with the other, clutches her white missal against her abdomen. In the front, the squat, black, staring dog is the emblem of fidelity.

Dagnan-Bouveret: The Wedding Party in the Photographer's Studio, *1878–79.*

"Picturesque Auvergne. An Auvergne Wedding." Postcard.

Henri Rousseau: **A Country Wedding.**

Henri Rousseau:
The Present and the Past,
1899. The Barnes Foundation,
Merion, Pennsylvania.

*Photographic portrait
of Clémence Boitard,
Rousseau's first wife.*

*Henri Rousseau's letter to
Joséphine Nourry, widow
of Le Tensorer, two
months before Rousseau's
marriage to her:
"Paris, June 21,
1899. My beloved. It is
seven in the morning, and
I am doing what I
planned to do when
coming home yesterday,
but I was tired. Even
though I had no desire to
sleep, I preferred resting
my Body and not my
Mind. I barely slept a
wink, I jumped up, calling
you, looking for you, I'm
stiff all over and I've had
a headache since
yesterday. We've hurt
each other a lot, yes
certainly and why, for
futile reasons. Ah, how
deeply this question of
conviction hurts, we love
one another, certainly,
etc."*

Henri Rousseau: **The Environs of Batignolles.** Painting on cardboard.

"Vincennes. Restaurant at the Yellow Gate." Postcard.

40

Henri Rousseau: **The Artist Painting His Wife.**

ersevering in his effort to stop the passage of time, to hold on to the past and the present, to reconcile his first and second marriages, to unite Clémence and Joséphine, to remain faithful to his thoughts ("I don't want us to be separated any more," he wrote to Joséphine), the Douanier composed a painting that he glossed with a quatrain full of highly significant mistakes in grammar and spelling. "It's a philosophical painting; it's a bit spiritual, isn't it?" he later said about this work. The clouds with the floating faces of previous spouses and the ivy linking the two sexes are not the only symbols here. By using his first and second wives as models in parks and in the country, Rousseau was probably trying, unconsciously, to evoke the distant but still-haunting image of his stiff and serious mother, whose love does not wane.

Notice the "Japanizing" effect of the tree in **The Environs of Batignolles.**

"Saint-Cloud Park. Town of Avray. The Small Pond. Artist's view. Mirage." Postcard.

41

Robert Tatin:
Homage to the
Douanier Rousseau.
Sculpture.
Robert Tatin Museum
in Cossé-le-Vivien.

Henri Rousseau: **Portrait of the Artist with a Lamp.**

Henri Rousseau: **Self-Portrait.**

Henri Rousseau: **Portrait of Clémence.**

42

Henri Rousseau: **Portrait of Rousseau's Second Wife with a Lamp.**

Henri Rousseau: Untitled female portrait, certified by Armand Quéval. Photograph.

Picasso told Jakovsky and Penrose that he felt the need to test the quality of his own paintings by confronting them with Rousseau's lamp portraits, with which he never parted. Like Picasso, the naïve sculptor Tatin always associated the Douanier with the idea of the couple. Whether exalting them and framing them like daguerreotypes before his first wife's death, or illuminating them with kerosene lamps during his second wife's illness, Rousseau sought a household equality in these portraits. After being widowed a second time, the artist pursued his dream of a new marriage and looked for a third wife.

In the style of the Pont-Aven school, Rousseau sketched a small profile portrait of a woman, whose features are seen again in **Beauty and the Beast.**

Henri Rousseau: **Portrait of Monsieur Steven.**

Henri Rousseau: **Portrait of Madame Steven.**

43

*"I wish you a great deal of happiness,
and may you always be very studious,
and I hope you win lots of fine prizes."*
HENRI ROUSSEAU
to his granddaughter Jeanne Bernard-Rousseau

Childhood Scenes, Family Life

If it is true that a painter seeks himself and finds himself, loses himself and finds himself again in his paintings, if it is true, as Buffon observed, that *"le style est de l'homme même"* ("style is of the man himself"), then it is a painter's work that best reveals the fundamental traits of his temperament—of his "soul," as people used to call it.

If we had to sum up Rousseau's fundamental traits in a word or two, we might say: credulity and obstinacy. A virtue preserved from childhood and linked to his mother's religious devotion, plus a fierce attempt to identify with his severe and stubborn father!

In the past, we are told, credulity grew out of misfortune. Unable to deal with the natural calamities they endured or the catastrophes they themselves provoked (cataclysms, ferocious animals and enemies, famine and disease, fire and death), men supposedly appealed to superior forces: their fathers and their leaders. The fathers and the leaders, in turn, to comfort their frightened charges and to prove their own power, invoked transcendental powers, spirits and gods, as well as sacred intermediaries, the sorcerers and priests. The latter gradually became the "heads" of their societies, by codifying the invocations and incantatory formulas of their simple faith. (In French, such a simple faith is idiomatically known as a *foi de charbonniers*, a faith of charcoal-burners—who, black with the soot of their wretchedness, fix their feverish gaze only on the sparks from their fireplaces, following these sparks as they drift up to the sparkling stars.) It is said that the sorcerers and priests constituted the first stab at an edificatory primitive art.

"Surgunt indocti et rapiunt coelum—they rise ignorant and seize hold of the sky," said Saint Augustine. Creating would thus be a form of resistance to the chaos of abandonment and the anguish of disappearance, a hope for indulgence and a faith in felicity. "The painter's apprenticeship is nothing," said Nicolas Poussin, "if it is not guided by fate!" His own fate and that of the world.

The figures in children's drawings come from the same impulse—the symbolic figures that children draw in clay, on sand, slate, walls, or paper, asserting their own existence and that of their precious parents, their need for protection against the frailty of their lives, and their haunting fear of being deserted by their parents. Through their figurines and scribblings, children, too, have to *face* (in the literal sense of the word) the threatened ruin of their entity, they have to entrench themselves in a hermetic and hostile environment, or at least in what they imagine as such. Sartre believed that existence precedes essence, that man exists first and then defines himself. Doesn't man also define himself the better to exist and resist? Doesn't he become what others agree upon or disagree with?

The Struggle for Life. This is the eloquent title of a painting that Rousseau exhibited in 1898 and that he used again, in 1905 at the Salon d'Automne, to evoke his **Hungry Lion.** He was particularly fond of this painting, despite the cruelty of the critics who guffawed at his "infantile daubing . . . which surpasses anything that one might dream." They compared him, once again, to a primitive. "His tenacity in the infantile genre is marvelous, his treatment is so dry and primitive as to arouse the jealousy of the Stone Age painters." This line had been written earlier by a critic who didn't believe he could truly compare. No smoke without fire! As "smoky" as these disproportionate judgments may have been, they did not lack acumen. For the inspiration and preservation of ideograms in our new primitive derived from almost the same state of mind as that of the cave sculptors and cave artists, who, in creating their effigies, were forced to scrupulously respect the ritual order, without which they feared that their appeal to the supernatural might be ineffectual. Could not the supernatural be the result of an excess of the natural?

"In Rousseau, the same laborious application persists throughout his life. . . . With the coming of age, his technique is perfected, becoming more effective. That is certainly true. But his technique does remain the same." This statement by Pierre Descargues confirms the conclusion of most critics of the Douanier: the treatment of his canvases is repetitious. The flagrant contradictions among the posthumous datings of his works, as cunningly devised by certain critics on the basis of his "manner," are an amusing proof of this.

Descargues also points out the lack of expression in Rousseau's figures. "Whether adults or children, they never look at us. They are shut up in themselves. . . . They are neither sad nor gay. They pose. And posing for a painter takes a lot more time than posing for a photographer."

I

An Archaic Notion of Art

t is not so much the posing of his models as the pause in the history of art that constitutes Rousseau's irruption. This strikes us in the masks of his subjects, in their hieratical postures, and in the sacralization of their settings. Was it for no reason that the most mediocre journalists and the finest poets of Rousseau's time noticed the primitive virtues of his creations and respectively denounced or praised them, not hesitating to liken him to Memling, Giotto, Uccello, Fra Angelico, or Fouquet? A list that might be completed with King René's Master of the Smitten Heart . . .

What binds Rousseau to these earlier painters? What are his affinities with them?

Until the start of the Renaissance in Western Europe, and even today in the so-called primitive cultures (also known as "backward" to the extent that they care more about reproducing their oral, initiatory, and ethical traditions than about trying to conquer science and technology, which would imperil their familial, social, and tribal structures), art, essentially sacred, derives from conventional and orthodox iconographic codes.

"The naïve religious consciousness of the multitude did not require intellectual proof in matters of faith: the mere presence of a visible image of holy things sufficed to demonstrate their truth," writes Johan Huizinga in *The Waning of the Middle Ages.* He also points out that "especially in fifteenth-century works of art . . . the dignity of the subject and the goal of the work were more important than the appreciation of beauty."

The theories of "art for art's sake" are the result of artistic inventions of the Quattrocento. Earlier art was exemplary, in the sense of the Latin word *exemplum.* It was functional, and its function was essentially to edify the people—to build and to convert to piety. It was a matter of consoling the people, reassuring them, safeguarding their social cohesion. And artists were simply the craftsmen for the partisans of this necessary exemplarity.

"In the figurative image of the late Middle Ages, the elements thus did not constitute immediately representative signs of sensory experience; they were a medium of traditional culture. On the one hand, the latter implies a reference to a body of texts; but on the other hand, it refers to the material realities rooted in current experience. It implies a collective memory that demands the presence of the conventional support of certain of its objects." (Pierre Francastel, *La Figure et le lieu: L'Ordre visuel du Quattrocento.*) And the author adds that "illusion dominates all our activities and all our imaginings. We are fascinated by both the shadow of reality and the shadow of God."

Actually, we are, above all, frightened by the precariousness of our lives and the ephemeral character of our civilizations, just as Pascal was terrified by the eternal silence of the infinite spaces in which our origins and our destiny vanish. But, thank God, to take our mind off this fear, sometimes all we need is to take a look at the sheer beauty of the things or beings that surround us, and that do so much more than divert us. For this look instantly convinces us that we dare not despair.

Picasso would soon be leading a number of artists to an iconoclastic ardor so revolutionary, and to a figurative regression so suicidal, that these artists would end up making their last stand and destroying themselves. In contrast, Rousseau, who called himself "modern," returned to a completely archaic notion of beauty. His *oeuvre* exudes a bitter fragrance that grabs your throat, like the scent of wild flowers that feed on decaying compost. Rousseau's works have this effect because they cannot hide either the distress of their creator or the bliss to which he aspired.

"To the extent that Rousseau's mind instinctively followed a route parallel to that of the primitive painters, one can justify the deep cause of his kinship with them. Like them, he adjusted the signified vision of his notion to the values of traditional observation. . . . But this is no longer a matter of religion in him; all the rationalism of the centuries separating him from the Middle Ages stamped his mind with popular common sense, the highest expression of which is the romantic pantheism at the very basis of his philosophy." Thus writes Tristan Tzara in an unforgettable article, "The Role of Time and Space in the Work of the Douanier Rousseau."

Rousseau became a Freemason and an anticlerical—partly as a jealous reaction to his mother's piety, then his first wife's piety, then his daughter's. However, he never gave up his faith in the ubiquity of God. In one letter he wrote to the woman who was to become his second wife, he was trying—in vain, as it turned out—to convince her not to get married in church.

"God is everywhere," he stated, "he sees everything, he knows that we're in love, that we're united by the same affection and we care for each other. He did not ask that men style themselves his representatives on earth, for he sees everything, he knows our innermost thoughts, he knows that one can rise up to him without ostentation and even confess to him alone! He prevents those who love him from doing evil, because they fear him, just like all the other spirits who are around him, who is the Spirit superior to all, the Spirit par excellence. This God doesn't ask that we kneel before another man who is the same as we, but who has no other goal than to keep weak and fanatic minds under some kind of yoke. . . ."

This profession of faith in God's immanence in the world, written in a highly personal letter at a highly decisive moment of Rousseau's life, is perfectly sincere. It accurately explains his regard for the harmony of nature, as a continual work of the Creator, the sovereign Mind, in which the minds of men participate. The same thought was uttered in a different way by the French poet most comparable to the Naïf, Francis Jammes: "The primitive is a sage who doesn't realize what he knows." The evocative strength of Rousseau's paintings is based not on his knowing a lot but on how much he made out of what he knew. Inspiration rules over fabrication. And if we know of only two modest paintings that he did on religious themes (**The Holy Family** and **Flight into Egypt**), it may simply be because he sanctified everything that his brush touched.

Agnosticism and materialism were the beliefs of many of his contemporaries, who were seduced by the prospects of mastering the universe which the new scientific discoveries offered. But neither agnosticism nor materialism had any more purchase on Rousseau's mind than the quest of those same contemporaries for a new artistic expression—more analytical than synthetic, more objective than subjective, more descriptive than imaginary. None of these things affected his sensibilities in any way whatsoever. He never analyzed, he catalyzed; he never decomposed, he composed.

The Douanier Rousseau was firmly convinced that he was taking the right path toward the future of painting, that he might survive the prevailing disintegration only by passing through the realism of a "*regretté* Courbet," "the Courbet whom I miss" (as he referred to him, and as he wrote in his scrapbook of news clippings), to the symbolist crystallization of the imaginary, as produced by the primitives and their heirs, the popular picture-makers.

Fernand Léger, the first painter of industrial and urban civilization, said that Rousseau (from whom he borrowed the inspiration for his *Nudes in the Forest*) remained a worker while Cézanne was a "lowly engineer"!

The Influence of Popular Imagery

"For Léger, according to the conversations we had," says Pierre Descargues, "Rousseau was exemplary for two reasons: he came from the common people (Léger always believed that such a background could provide access to profound truths); and he painted precisely, no fancy work, no Impressionism, no superficial play of light or color, for he painted as straightforwardly as David."

In reality, if there was any profound influence on the Douanier Rousseau, it came from the graphic expression of the traditional illustrators of popular imagery since time immemorial. When Alfred Jarry and Rémy de Gourmont invited him to work for *L'Ymagier*, they understood the originality of his inspiration as much as Jean-Léon Gérôme, who had realized he could give Rousseau only one bit of advice: Maintain your naïveté. By counseling him to remain himself, Gérôme had sent him back to his first visual impressions: pious images and church banners, Epinal engravings (an early form of strip cartoons), romantic illustrations in small moralizing works presented to schoolboys as prizes, shop signs and county-fair calicoes, commercial advertisements and labels (whose anonymous makers had simply taken the anagogical road of the abbreviated symbolism in frescoes and stained-glass windows, illuminated manuscripts and tapestries, wood carvings, and medieval sculptures).

The "grand" aristocratic and middle-class painting born in the Renaissance had eclipsed the idioms of this pictorial language, which now could find expression only in the votive offerings of seaside and country chapels, where popular fervor took refuge. In his genius and glory, the Douanier Rousseau resurrected those idioms. With him, painting once again became the obedient daughter of poetry, imagination, credulity. It was not until the 1937 exhibition of Popular Masters of Reality (organized under the patronage of the French Ministry of National Education, the general manager of the School of Fine Arts, and the City of Paris) that viewers were finally allowed to realize what had happened.

Rousseau wrote that he was "encouraged by already famous painters such as Monsieur Gérôme, Cabanel, Ralli, Valton, Bourguereau," and Clément. He also borrowed certain themes from their academic compositions. For these reasons, critics have written that Rousseau owed his technique to some of the artists he mentioned. Dora Vallier, for instance, says, "Strange as it may seem, the evolution of Rousseau's painting passed through Gérôme's *oeuvre*." A minor similarity detected between the laurel branches in the Orientalist's *Cock Fight* and the Naïf's jungle flora does not prove in any way that the earlier painter inspired the later one. Let's not fool ourselves: we mustn't confuse themes with designs, figures with treatments.

Henri Rousseau's painting has no kinship with that of the academics and Orientalists, the portraitists and hacks, whom he listed, by and large, for purely opportunistic reasons. It's obvious that his technique has nothing to do with theirs. Rousseau's **Happy Quartet,** for instance, owes nothing but its subject to Gérôme's *Innocence*; Rousseau transposes it into a style and context that are totally different, earlier—in a word, primitive. And this is so true that none of his contemporaries could have pointed out such borrowings, which, if revealed, would surely have caused a scandal!

The Douanier Rousseau saw only what he believed, because he looked only at what he had imagined and premeditated. He distinguishes only things to which the eyes of his memory are accustomed.

"Rousseau knows very little about the people surrounding him, he doesn't know what they busy themselves with, what they're up to, what they're thinking. He instinctively seeks out a man's good side, he dwells on these good sides, and ignores anything else. . . . Once, I happened to make a comment that one doesn't make at my age. At this moment, I was thirty years older in his eyes; he was talking about the days when we were both young, and he asked a woman only slightly younger than I whether she was my daughter, and a young man long out of adolescence whether he was my son. . . . He was not at all astonished when Puvis de Chavannes—an elderly gentleman whom wicked pranksters had asked to play a joke on him—came to visit him and talk about painting to him. He took it for granted when he saw his name as the recipient of a silver medal in a newspaper, or when Gauguin told him that he, Rousseau, had been awarded a government commission, or when he, Rousseau, was invited to a soirée by the president of the Republic. Likewise, he was stupefied upon learning that the man who received the medal was some other Rousseau. . . ."

This observation by Wilhelm Uhde, confirmed by other witnesses of Rousseau's mental state, would lead us to think that the Douanier misunderstood his critics' worst denigrations and mistook them for praise. "I was also told that I was not of my century," Rousseau explained. What did he care! He stuck to his own little path, like a child who wanders off during a stroll and is called a dreamer by his family. Henri Rousseau was a contemplative man, and a primitive who, as pointed out by the reviewer in *La Patrie* (April 23, 1911), was influenced by Daguerre's invention.

Three Golden Rules

Rousseau had an innate sense of fine order: his was the taste of a child who instinctively arranges things. This gift of spontaneous synthesis was linked to his loving observation of details. He was as impressed by the architecture of a tree as by the sight of its foliage, a precious adornment which he transposed into a delightful stylization. His color harmonies were simple and as elementary as his draftsmanship was naïve," wrote Adolphe Basler.

If one looks closely at Rousseau's "fine orders," one sees that they follow three golden rules instinctive to children and primitives: interiorize by immobilizing, ennoble by stylizing, amplify by simplifying. "He was an unemployed primitive," wrote André Lhote in *La Nouvelle Revue Française*, "in an era when people had eyes only for the most falsely refined depictions of worldly adventures. In the Middle Ages, he would have delighted the crowd and offered a rough-hewn but noble image of saints and donors."

In the Middle Ages? Why, then, do we love him so much today? Is it, as Jung believed, that the "final vestiges of the collective soul, while disappearing, repeat in our dreams the eternal primordial content of the human soul"? And might it be that we too want to resist their disappearance?

A child's minor chagrin, his minor joy, immoderately exaggerated by an acute sensibility, will ultimately become the principle of an artwork in the adult, even without his realizing it." Charles Baudelaire: "The Child's Genius" in The Artificial Paradises.

Elle fut bâtie par André de Laval, Maréchal de France, en 1433, elle servait autrefois de porte de la Ville et contenait des cachots entièrement privés de lumière

76 - LAVAL - La Tour Renaise

Artaud-Nozais, Nantes

14 LAVAL — Le Jardin public - La Perrine
Au loin, le Château et les Ponts sur la Mayenne

LAVAL (Mayenne) — Un sous-bois à la Perrine

16 LAVAL — Une Allée du Jardin Public - La Perrine

Artaud et Nozais, Nantes

Laval — Jardin de La Perrine - G. F., PARIS

LAVAL. — Le Quai Paul-Boudet, le Pont Vieux et la Mayenne.

ND. Phot.

73

Du Nouvel An, fêtant l'aurore,
Ils vous offrent l'ample moisson
De fleurs, que pour vous fit éclore,
Ma bien sincère affection.

CARTE POSTALE

Two of the postcards that Rousseau selected and mailed to his granddaughter in Angers.

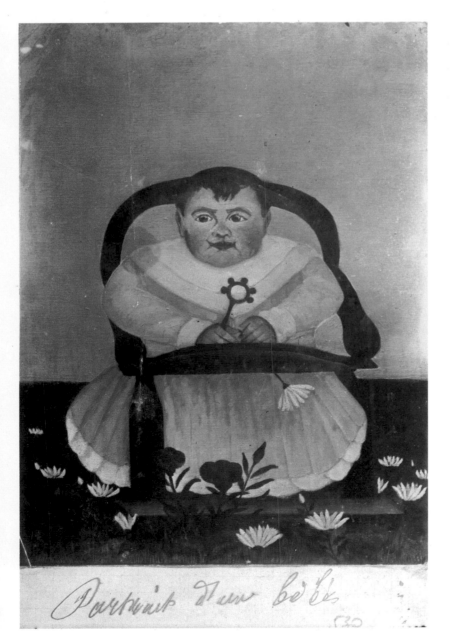

Henri Rousseau: **Portrait of a Baby.** Photograph of a painting that disappeared; Rousseau signed and put the photograph in a notebook.

ittle Jeanne, I'm sending you these two charming little clowns, and I wish you a great deal of happiness, and may you always be very studious, and I hope you win lots of fine prizes. Your grandfather who kisses you, H. Rousseau.''

The Douanier's tenderness and sympathy for his granddaughter, for babies and children in general (he showed some ten portraits of them at the Salons of the Independents, though without winning a prize), find their most poignant expression in this encounter with **The Abandoned Child in the Countryside near the Bridge of Saint-Cloud.** The subject of this poetic painting, whose authenticity has been considered somewhat suspect by certain art critics, seems to have been inspired by the small photographic portrait of Rousseau's granddaughter. In any case, this is a rather suggestive encounter—of the painter with his childhood.

Photographic portrait of Jeanne Bernard-Rousseau, the painter's granddaughter, by H. Thillier, photographer, 22 Boulevard de Saumur, Angers.

Henri Rousseau: **The Abandoned Child in the Countryside near the Bridge of Saint-Cloud.**

Henri Rousseau: **Mother and Child,** June 29.

Henri Rousseau: **Girl Knitting.** Pencil drawing.

"Montmartre. On the Fortifications." Postcard.

Henry Rousseau: **View of the Fortifications.**

The Fortifications. *Photograph by Atget.*

It's summer. The men are napping, their wives sewing, knitting, or cuddling their most recent babies, while the children are frolicking in the grass all around. These family outings at the gates of Paris, these picnics with friends and neighbors on the capital city's fortifications, where people strolled, gave the painter a chance to make a few sketches, bucolic views (like today's instant snapshots), to preserve those dazzling hours.

At first a "Sunday painter," the retired customs inspector went on to dress his paintings in their "Sunday best."

Henri Rousseau:
Old Juniet's Carriole, 1908.

Henri Rousseau: **Old Juniet's Carriole.**

Photographs of Claude Junier's carriole,
taken near the woods of Clamart by his wife, Anna.

Henri Rousseau: **View of Montsouris Park.**

To vary his Sunday strolls on the fortifications, in the public parks of Paris (such as Montsouris Park), or the nearby suburbs (like Malakoff), the Douanier joined some good neighbors, who took him off to the country, the "great outdoors." Claude and Anna Junier (not Juniet) ran a grocery store, where Rousseau shopped. They became friendly, especially because of the painter's affection for their niece Léa Junier. During an excursion to the Clamart forest, Rousseau asked Anna if he could photograph their carriole. He wanted to paint it with their white mare, Rosa, and their dogs, including Marquis, their superb sheepdog. Utilizing the two photographs as best he could, Rousseau depicted himself under his boater, to the left of old Junier, who was holding the reins. However, the Douanier placed Anna in the back, between her nieces, and he shifted the dogs. The vehicle is parked. Everyone is looking at the painter, who has replaced the photographer. However, the shopkeeper can't help glancing at his cherished mare. The only movements in the landscape: a few clouds, and a small dog leading the way, while the leaves of the trees, obscure in the photographic view, seem to quiver with pleasure.

Henri Rousseau: **The Promenade to the Manor.**

Henri Rousseau: Sketch for **View of Malakoff.**

Henri Rousseau: **View of Malakoff.**

Henri Rousseau: **Montsouris Park, the Kiosk.**

"Paris. Montsouris Park." Postcards.

PARIS — Parc Montsouris

Henri Rousseau: **The Baby's Baptismal Celebration.**

Rousseau sees a child only in isolation, separated from its parents—even when the latter are celebrating its baptism.

We know that Henri Rousseau regretted that his mother was so pious. What was he unconsciously reproaching her for? Her austerity, her rigor, or the fact that she was dividing her love? The solitude of this child left on harsh rocks is so anguishing! The severe density of the black of its hair and eyes, of its booties and bathing costume, owes less to possible influences by Uccello, Goya, Courbet, or Manet than to the photographs that Rousseau used as models. But perhaps he was also mourning: for his illusions of earthly and family happiness.

60

Henri Rousseau: **Portrait of a Child.**

Henri Rousseau: **Portrait of a Child.**

Henri Rousseau's concentration on the striking facial features of the children of his friends and of the grocers he wanted to please, and the dislocation of their bodies placed awkwardly in space (well symbolized by the baby's articulated Punchinello), prefigure the distortions of Picasso's Expressionistic Cubism. However, accustomed to affected, conventional portraits such as those by Emile Munier, who worked with Bouguereau, the parents were shocked by Rousseau's work. They couldn't stand the unbecoming bulk of their cherubs' thighs, despite the springlike freshness of the backgrounds in these paintings.

Pablo Picasso: Portrait of Maya, 1938.

Reward. *After E. Munier.*
Catalogue of the Salon of 1881.

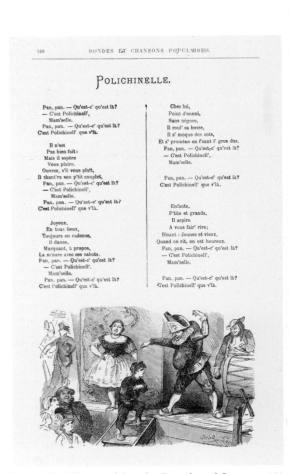

"Punchinello." Illustrated Popular Rounds and Songs, p. 168.

Henri Rousseau: **Portrait of a Child.**

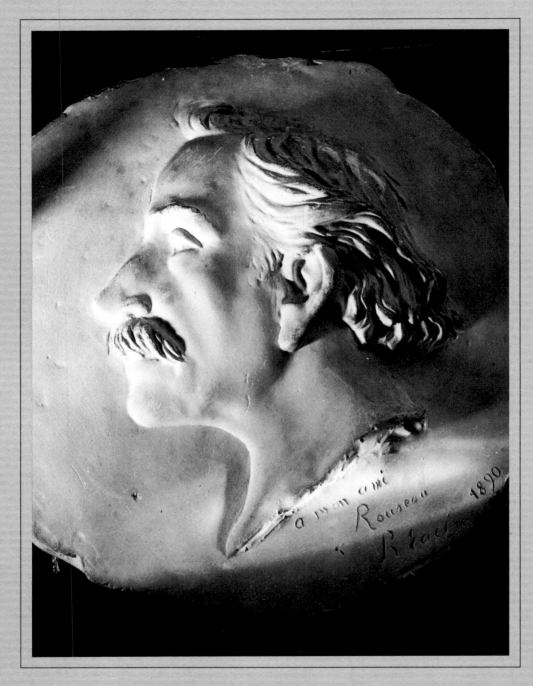

"I am the inventor of the landscape portrait."
HENRI ROUSSEAU
to the examining magistrate, Boucher

3 The Landscape Portraits and Their Symbolism

There are two ways of understanding a portrait: history and fiction. The second way, peculiar to the colorists, is to turn the portrait into a painting, a poem with its accessories, full of space and reverie. . . . Here, the imagination plays a greater part, and yet, since fiction is often truer than history, a sitter may be more clearly depicted by the rich and facile brush of a colorist than by the pencil of a draftsman.''

This definition of the fictional portrait, presented by Charles Baudelaire in his *Salon of 1846*, applies just as readily to ''landscape portraits,'' which Henri Rousseau prided himself on inventing. The scandalous effect produced on the Salon journalists by Rousseau's portrait of Guillaume Apollinaire and Marie Laurencin sufficiently demonstrates the aptness of that definition.

''When the painting appeared at the Salon of the Independents, the entire press rejoiced at my portrait, which was reproduced in *Comoedia*,'' recalls the poet Apollinaire. ''The journalists were unanimous in their conclusions: this portrait bore no resemblance whatsoever to me. Now, if the portrait didn't resemble me, how could they possibly have recognized me? I had asked the Douanier not to indicate my name: he must have broken his word! But I had to pay tribute to his honesty when, upon consulting the exhibition catalogue, I saw that the painting bore only these words: **The Muse Inspiring the Poet**. . . . I had to admit that this portrait was such a striking and novel likeness that it dazzled in spite of themselves all those who saw the resemblance but wouldn't believe it. Painting is the most pious art. In 1909, we witnessed an act of collective suggestion parallel to those that gave birth to the purest religions.''

"A Philosophical Thought"

To what was this resemblance due—this resemblance that the poet inspired in the Naïf? What caused this osmosis allowing viewers to recognize both the painter and his subject? What linked these portraits to their landscapes? What did the painter mean?

In a letter written from Santé Prison to the examining magistrate Boucher, the Douanier Rousseau stated that he was the inventor of the landscape portrait. ''In all my works,'' he added, ''one notices sincerity, which I have always sought in both my actions and my work.'' Then he proposed an honest transaction: "So, I am deeply distressed, and, seeing that I am now in this cell between four walls, I am afflicted with dizzy spells, and sometimes I nearly fall down upon seeing everything whirl. Oh, I suffer deeply, Your Honor! If, in your goodness, you could grant me my freedom, I would paint a fine portrait of you in any composition and size that you would like. . . ."

Its own prisoner, his art endured no bars but his: the trunks of trees. Touched by the artist's distress and his sincerity, Boucher nevertheless remained completely insensitive to his "unbelievable" talents as a landscape portraitist.

Having trotted about the galleries of the Louvre, Henri Rousseau knew perfectly well that he wasn't the first artist to place his sitters or historical, mythical, or religious figures in a landscape or to embellish them with rustic trappings. This was not the original aspect of his contribution. His invention was to introduce "a philosophical thought" into his paintings: that is, one or two symbolic accessories representing the personal and social role and the sex of his subjects. He himself cannot be dissociated from his painter's beret, his palette and brush; anymore than Apollinaire from his big Muse in a peplos, his goose quill and poet's narcissus; or Frumence Biche from his sergeant's uniform and his sword; or Edmond Frank (Loti) from his cat and his fez; or Charlotte Papouin from the stone blocks of her quarryman father; or Jarry from his owl; or the little girls from their dolls, their Punch and Judy, and their flowers; or men from their cigarettes; or women from their fashionable dresses and their umbrellas or parasols. Sometimes, Rousseau pinpoints the accessory in an inscription that emphasizes the originality of the painting:

Avec le portrait de madame Izard
Fait sur la petite photographie
On la voit l'année du mariage
Et l'ombrelle donnée par son gai mari.

With the portait of Madame Izard
Based on the small photograph,
We see her in the year of her marriage
And the sunshade she got from her merry husband.

"Spiritist" Convergences

The attributes did not just serve to increase a resemblance that the painter feared he had not effectively caught, assimilated, and rendered. He ascribed to them a mysterious, fetishistic, quasi-totemistic value.

His "philosophical thought" also extended to the choice of landscape, the surrounding in which he felt he ought to place his figures, and the minute and pious preparation of the canvas that was to receive them. He accorded all this a significance comparable to the care with which the portrait photographers of the nineteenth century, in order to immortalize married couples, picked the finest backdrop to flatter them. If he acknowledges his models, if he writes that he is eager to have them come to his studio for the sitting (the sitting of himself, the master, in front of them), if he changes an appointment, apologizing for standing them up, announcing that he will be out at a certain time and even offering an excuse, such as a visit to a friend, a violin or drawing lesson he has to give, errands he has to run—it is not *only* because he is short of money. ("Today, I have a few sous left for food," he wrote to Apollinaire, asking him for an advance. "I don't know how I'll manage. I also have thirty-five francs to pay for an article of clothing that I need, since I don't have anything proper to wear; and you know I have to go out; my shoes are also worn, etc.")

He was in a hurry to paint his models, above all because he had prepared, inwardly and intensely, to receive them—to cull the quintessence of their likeness, which was already fixed in his mind. Tied to them in a "spiritist" way, he feared any relaxation of this bond, this intense convergence, this real tension.

On June 26, 1894, he wrote to Jarry, "I brought back the Japanese lantern, which won't look bad in the trees; today I began, having waited for you; and I'm going to work hard on it, so that I can continue with you when you come. . . ."

Similarly, on December 27, 1908, it was Apollinaire whom he called to order: "I am writing a few lines to you in haste, since I couldn't see you Thursday. I am still waiting for your charming Muse to pose at least once. Otherwise, everything is going well; I have found some poet's narcissuses. . . ."

"Work hard . . . continue with you . . . pose at least once." The words outstrip his thoughts, harking back to his unconscious.

Portrait Landscapes

The "landscape portraits" are first and foremost portrait landscapes. Rousseau invents the environment he feels is most appropriate to the sitter even before the sitter arrives. The sitter will have to find his place here, in the location assigned to him. In this regard, an experience reported by Max Weber is revealing about the way Rousseau composed before he had his model pose. Noticing a blank space for the dog in **Old Juniet's Carriole,** Weber asked the Douanier whether he might not be painting the dog too big. The Naïf, smiling at his canvas, replied, "No, that's the way it has to be!" Man, too, has to integrate himself into Rousseau's nature.

Despite his predilections for blossoming gardens and flowering trees, Rousseau sometimes, if more rarely, would pick an austere nature. He did so for the child among the rocks and the woman's portrait in the former Picasso collection. In these paintings, Rousseau made reference to Leonardo da Vinci's *Mona Lisa* and *The Virgin of the Rocks*, retaining the mountainous background and trying to capture the divine smiles that made the Italian master so famous. Rousseau refused to admit any connection here: "Come, come, don't you recognize the fortifications of Paris? I did these things when I was a customs inspector. . . ." He said this to Picasso's mistress Fernande Olivier, who thought she recognized the mountains of Switzerland.

What analysis would we need to unveil (as Freud revealed the vulture* inscribed in the robe of Leonardo's Virgin) a secret childhood memory concealed in such an enigmatic smile? As Picasso said, "Psychoanalysis is very nice, but we've still got to draw it!" Isn't this what painters do?

A Mathematical Rigor, a Euphoric Jokester

There he is, getting down to work, rigorous, maniacal, very intent on expressing once more his notion of the painting, recopying the face and body of his patient, feature for feature, form for form. And in so doing, he exalts himself, becomes euphoric, and starts to sing old humorous and nostalgic refrains, whose grotesque lyrics are not devoid of profound meaning.

Apollinaire reports: "Above all, he measured my nose, my mouth, my ears, my forehead, my hands, my entire body, and then he transported these measurements very accurately to his canvas, reducing them to the dimension of the stretcher. Posing is very boring, and so, in order to entertain me, Rousseau sang me songs from his youth.

" 'Oh, I don't like big tabloids
That talk a lot of politics.
Who cares if the Eskimos
Have gone and ravaged Africa.
What I need is *The Little Paper,*
The Gazette, my mother's cross.
The more drowned bodies in the river,
The greater my reading pleasure.'

"Or else:

" 'Oh, me, oh, my! My teeth do ache!'

* It was not a vulture but a kite. Freud misread his German translation of Leonardo.

"And I remained motionless, admiring the great precautions he took to prevent any other fantasy than the one characterizing his personality from coming and destroying the harmony of his mathematical design, which was similar to the human face he wanted to depict. . . . And this painting, which he had meditated on for such a long time, was attaining perfection. The Douanier had just completed the folds in the magnificent robe of my Muse, he had just tinted my attractive black jacket, the black that Gauguin declared inimitable; he was about to finish my work, which is painting without any literature. . . ."

Devoid of any literature, the Douanier's painting nevertheless does not lack turgidity or minor trickery. Indeed, there is something playful in Rousseau's relationship with his model. By means of this ritualistic and ceremonial staging, he tries to fascinate his sitter, convince him that he himself is a serious professional artist obeying the rules of art, the demands of figurative likeness, these processes of making of which he alone guards the cabalistic secrets. He thus hopes to obtain suitable fees. He needs the fees badly to fill his purse, to buy presents for his loves, and to maintain his reputation as a painter among literati, as well as among both big art dealers and the small shopkeepers in his neighborhood (his debts with them make them doubt his true abilities and his chances of paying his bills).

I Schematic Reductions to a Purifying Simplification

It is also true that although Rousseau was no bookkeeper, geometrician, or academician, he managed (paradoxically, because of his innate inability to do imitative drawing) to do *portraits,* in the etymological sense of the Latin verb *protrahere:* to pull forward. Rousseau pulls toward himself, he throws into relief, he extracts the essential features of the sitter's character, the sitter's very soul, which is concealed beneath his habitual outer appearances. Rousseau appropriates the soul. He brings it out into the open. He sets it into the world, with a chromatic boldness that is all the more pure in that his plastic awkwardness must be covered up with attention to compositional balance, an attention that is particularly insistent because the artist doesn't know how to indicate the visual order or planes in space.

"Probably from his childhood on," writes Roch Grey (one of Rousseau's most sensitive admirers, according to Adolphe Basler), "Rousseau admired everything that was well done, well executed, smooth, even: an old sideboard glossy with wear and tear, the surface of a motionless fountain at twilight, the mechanism of his father's watch, like a pewter onion. Leafing through old almanacs, gazing at advertisements for perfumes, for liqueurs, he developed a taste for drawing."

After reading this very acute theory of Roch Grey's, we might add a confident assumption that the Douanier Rousseau, whose first portraits were simply colored versions of graphic reproductions of daguerreotypes and photographic calling-cards, was impressed by the centered composition, the hard gazes, the overweening stupor in photographic portraits. Indeed, Rousseau made use of them until the end of his days, whenever models were unavailable or had preceded him into the grave and he wanted to resurrect them.

Whatever their psychological or pictographic origins, Rousseau's landscape portraits, by virtue of their schematic reductions, their clarifications, and their lack of any opportunistic mannerism, upset and renewed both the concept and the very art of the portrait, so that its academic and veristic traditions were suddenly rendered obsolete.

"The art of this divine and primary man, in perfect harmony with his character," observes Adolphe Basler, "is isolated by its very chastity from all the disarray, all the professional competence, all the cerebral or sensual perversities of pictorial modernism. His careful procedures left nothing to chance. Everything on his smooth and lovely surfaces combines to form a fullness of expression. The rigorous wielders of perspective, the routine slaves of drawing will always reproach him for a pathological infantilism. However, because of the spirituality that brought them forth, his naïve and imperfect creations are more coherent and more impressive than many works of automatic perfection and any material produced by scholarly disciplines."

Not the least of the singular portrait features given to us by Rousseau and allowed to stay by their models (some sitters destroyed or removed them) is their troublesome resemblance to the artist who painted them. Art historians would no longer have to track down the identities of the figures in his paintings if they truly understood that each figure partakes of the artist, and that all of him is in all of them. "Every portrait painted with the soul is a portrait not of the model but of the artist," said Oscar Wilde in his *Picture of Dorian Gray.*

And could Rousseau have had any other model but himself? His head swollen with so many memories and so much ambition, he gazed at himself in his palette as in a mirror. But this mirror told him that nature and its constantly renewed colors were more beautiful than he. He then respectfully grouped the colors on his virgin canvas with his brush. He made his tubes ejaculate voluptuously—yellow ocher, Naples yellow, chrome yellow, yellow-green, lake and emerald green, mineral blues, cobalt and ultramarine, ivory black, burnt siena, vermilion and red, Pouzzuoli, or silver-white. And he inhaled these ethereal and resinous fragrances. He could smell the heady perfumes of woods and gardens wafting from the depths of his adolescence, the sweet scents of grass and moss where he lay on his back, drifting with the clouds. Clouds that were soon wounded by the setting sun, whose streaks of blood he would someday recapture.

"Rousseau is the dreamer of reality. . . .
He remains under the sway of his inner demon, a sense of ingenuity and poetry,
a power of dream and imagination, which impel him to conceive
and create with life something different from what he would like.
He is madly in love with nature and intoxicated by the reality
that nature lays out before him. He sees it, to be sure;
but above all, he dreams it."
ALBERT SARRAUT

"The figures are as calm as the gods who direct eternity.
They are exempt from pain,
sheltered from worry and care, from all frustration."
CHRISTIAN ZERVOS

"I was thinking of my grand old friend Henri Rousseau,
that Homer in a concierge booth, with his prehistoric
dream that sometimes brought me very close to the gods."
MAX BECKMANN

"This art is not defined by what he sees . . .
but by the pictorial quality of what he dreams. If **The Customs House** *is worthy of Uccello,*
it is also a haunted landscape. . . . Like the eternal song,
Rousseau expresses the arrival of the seasons, the fine outline of the branches against the sky,
and the accumulation of the russet leaves on the ground,
with the same seemingly disarmed efficacy
with which primitive people express their religious feeling.
Aside from his talent, it is his flight from history,
a flight we perceive as a deliverance, that connects him to a resurrection."
ANDRÉ MALRAUX

The entire composition of **Myself.
Landscape Portrait** is stamped
with fairly deliberate symbolism.
The painter's levitation toward the clouds,
whose two-cornered forms resemble his beret.
The jutting prow and the mast of the boat,
whose spanking flags decorate the artist. The
erection of the Eiffel Tower and the rise of
the balloon that floated overhead during the
famous World's Fair of 1889. The house
chimneys on the Left Bank, the street lights
on the Carousel Bridge and the tree on the
Quai de Louvre. Rousseau's assertive
presence at the Port of Saint-Nicolas, next
to the customs booth where he frequently
stood guard. The immediate proximity of the
Palace of the Louvre, which he hoped to
enter some day, and where Marie Foucher,
with whom he was very much in love,
worked as housekeeper for the chief architect.
Marie's first name on the palette, penetrated
by his finger, next to the name of his first
wife, Clémence, who died on May 7, 1888.
(He subsequently covered her name with that
of Joséphine, his second wife to be.) His
immense brush pointing toward his
signature. The fictitious decoration in his
buttonhole. The flagrant disproportion
between his body and the silhouettes of the
midget gawkers . . . Everything combines to
edify him, to produce an orgasm of his pride
and desire, to glorify him!

In 1926, the naïve painter Rimbert did
a painting glorifying Rousseau, whom he
watches (from his window) rising to the
heavens, where he will find Cézanne, Ingres,
Delacroix, Courbet, and Renoir. Right after
the Douanier's death, Delaunay composed
his City of Paris on the same site as
Rousseau, whom he replaced with one of the
Three Graces from a Pompeian fresco.

René Rimbert: The Douanier Rousseau Rising Toward
Glory and Entering Posterity, *1926.*

Robert Delaunay: The City of Paris,
1910–12. Left-hand view of the painting.

*Photograph of customs
inspectors working at the
Port of Saint-Nicolas,
Paris, in front of the
Carousel Bridge.*

Henri Rousseau: **Myself. Landscape Portrait**, 1890.

Henri Rousseau: **Sergeant Frumence Biche.**

Photograph of Frumence Biche in uniform.

Photograph of Marie Biche to the right of her produce cart at the corner of Rue de Médicis and Boulevard Saint-Michel.

The portrait of Frumence Biche at the time of its discovery in the attic of his daughter Cécile Cheneau's cottage in Davray, Aube.

Marie Foucher turned down the Douanier in order to marry a policeman, Frumence Biche, on March 3, 1891. Biche died in May 1892. Rousseau tried his luck again, and, in his attempt to conquer the widow's heart, he offered to paint a portrait of the deceased after a photo of Biche all decked out in his sergeant's uniform. The artist faithfully respected the details, even reproducing the number 35 (Biche's artillery regiment) on the collar. However, Rousseau placed Biche in a lunar decor beyond the grave. Marie Biche took the painting to the farm of her parents-in-law in Aube, where it remained until 1961. Marie became a produce vendor near the Luxembourg Gardens. She remained Rousseau's best friend, and he also greatly loved her daughter Cécile. Hunger often drove him to her cart, and she was delighted to offer him her vegetable soup and her fruits.

Henri Rousseau: **The Muse Inspiring the Poet,** 1909.

The Offer of the Heart. *Arras tapestry, fifteenth century. Cluny Museum.*

Henri Rousseau: **Portrait of Guillaume Apollinaire and Marie Laurencin with Poet's Narcissus.**

Photograph of Rousseau completing the second version of **The Muse Inspiring the Poet.** *Left:* **Portrait of Monsieur Brummer.**

Photographic portrait of Apollinaire.

Marie Laurencin: Apollinaire and His Friends, 1909. Center: Apollinaire.
Right: Picasso and his mistress Fernande Olivier. Foreground: Marie Laurencin.

Emile Binnet: Saint-Germain-des-Prés, 1948. Left to right: Boubal, Boris Vian, Jacques Prévert,
le Bonapartiste, Jean Genet, Juliette Gréco, Jean-Paul Sartre. Foreground: Duncan (seated) and Brienne.

Henri Rousseau did two landscape portraits of the poet Guillaume Apollinaire and the painter Marie Laurencin, his mistress. The first portrait was shown at the Salon of the Independents in 1909, under the title **The Muse Inspiring the Poet.** Rousseau then painted an almost identical replica, in order, as he explained, to replace the gillyflowers with true poet's narcissus. In the long-past spirit of the elegant tapestries of the fifteenth century, he placed his sitters against a backdrop based on a nook in the Luxembourg Gardens. To prolong the pleasure, he had his models come back to his studio several times. He corresponded with Guillaume Apollinaire in order to arrange their sessions and underscore the importance of his work. The first letter is dated August 14, 1908: "I'll have to know your size so that I can take the measurements. . . . We'll be able to do an important and attractive work. . . ." The final letter, on June 25, 1909, announces, "Your portrait is advancing, just a little more patience and soon I'll have the pleasure of delivering it to you." In Comoedia, then in Les Soirées de Paris, Apollinaire tells how the painter took his measurements and about the scandal triggered by the portrait. The Salon

journalists may not have recognized the unidentified poet, but Marie Laurencin was flabbergasted. She, who depicted herself as so fine and distinguished in her self-portraits, protested, "Why, I'm not that fat!" "What do you want," Rousseau supposedly

answered, "Guillaume is a great poet, he needs a big Muse!"

Eventually, the Poet and his Muse "produced little ones," such as the anecdotal pastiche painted by Binnet, who can't deny his Rousseauist atavism.

Henri Rousseau: **Portrait of Pierre Loti.**

Hans Memling: Portrait of a Man.

Photographic portrait of Pierre Loti in Constantinople.

I t's quite simple," said Derain; "hang a Rousseau between two old or modern paintings; two
good paintings; the Rousseau will always make a stronger impression of density and
equilibrium." If he is placed between Memling, to whom Jarry often likened Rousseau, or
Bourdichon, to whom Rousseau is tied by a long tradition of French popular iconography, and Fernand
Léger (who, like the Douanier, admired an exhibit of paintings by Louis David), a strange originality,
made up of restraint and vigor, freedom and rigor, characterizes the works of Rousseau. All the more
receptive for being uneducated, Rousseau condensed a whole network of influences, which are apparent
only to alert eyes. The **Portrait of Pierre Loti,** which Courteline bought in a curio shop for his
Museum of Horrors, is a replica of the portrait of Edmond Frank, a Montmartre writer, that was
exhibited in 1906 at the Salon of the Independents. Frank lived in the castle of the Brouillards, which
overlooked the houses and factories of Saint-Ouen and Saint-Denis. The Douanier depicted him with
his alley cat, near the acacia in his garden, wearing a Turkish fez. The copy that Rousseau
subsequently painted bore such a strong resemblance to Pierre Loti that people thought the famous exotic

Henri Rousseau: **Landscape Portrait** (*Belonging to M.B.*), 1909.

Jehan Bourdichon: Saint Mark the Evangelist. *Illuminated illustration in* The Book of Hours of Anne of Brittany.

writer was the model. Once again, fiction was stranger than truth! Painted at the same time as the Apollinaire portrait ("My face served for a unique experience, which I won't forget," he said), almost contemporary with the portraits of Loti and of Monsieur and Madame Steven, as well as the "girl in pink," the portrait of the antique dealer Joseph Brummer ("This man will propagate Rousseau's glory through all the studios in Paris while popularizing African sculpture," said his friend Basler) follows the same strategy of the gaze as that employed by the father of Cubism, Pablo Picasso. These portraits reveal a comparable attempt to identify the face that is observed, measured, stripped, analyzed by the angst-ridden painter, and to structure and reduce the face to contrasting planes that would soon overlap. "I am the inventor of the cutout portrait," Rousseau should have written.

Fernand Léger: The Leisures, or Homage to Louis David, *1948–49.*

Baronial Life. *Tapestry, fifteenth century, Cluny Museum.*

Henri Rousseau: **Portrait of a Child.**

Henri Rousseau: **Portrait of a Woman.**

Photograph of Charlotte Papouin.

Picasso in his studio at 23 Rue La Boétie, standing in front of Rousseau's **Portrait of a Woman.** *Photograph by Brassaï.*

80

We know that the "girl in pink" was none other than Charlotte Papouin, the eight-year-old daughter of a stonecutter who supported Rousseau with his friendship and modest resources. Though he painted the girl in front of a curtain of flowering trees, Rousseau also wished to evoke her father's profession: he surrounded Charlotte's feet, between a black and a white goat, with blocks of limestone and milestones. This is what he called a "philosophical thought"!

But just who are the models for these two female portraits? Documents and other evidence are insufficient, and this lack has triggered a polemic, both futile and aggressive, among art critics. What does it really matter whether the left-hand painting (which Picasso bought secondhand in Montmartre for five francs and which then presided over the Bateau-Lavoir banquet) and the right-hand painting are portraits, imaginary or real, of Rousseau's second and first wives (which is likely) or of some unknown ladies? It is more interesting to track down the probable iconographic and psychological sources. These two landscape portraits might also be evocations of the Lady, lofty and remote, whose heart knights and troubadours tried to conquer by some artistic or military exploit. These paintings may also be reminiscences of the Mother, distant and domineering, magnified by her tiny son, who feared her because of her whip or umbrella, but yearned for her. A far-fetched interpretation, the adversaries of psychoanalysis would claim. But, given the circumstances, it's true!

Henri Rousseau: **Portrait of a Woman.**

A figure in The Siege of Troy. *Tapestry, sixteenth century. Musée de l'Ancien Evêché d'Angers.*

Le Moniteur de la Mode, *no. 43 (1885). "The illustrated pink periodical. Good taste and Parisian elegance in tandem." Colored engraving by J. David and E. Tailland.*

Photograph of a lady with an umbrella strolling in the forest of Saint-Germain-en-Laye. Sirot Collection.

Julia Bernard-Rousseau lived with her father for eighteen years and vividly remembered her graceful mother, whom she lost when she herself was twelve, in 1888. Julia claimed that the woman in this **Promenade** was her mother. She says this painting depicts one of the Rousseau family outings in the forest of Saint-Germain-en-Laye, where they went on Sundays to visit Clémence's family. Even if Julia's statement is accurate, we may still believe that in order to perform this reconstitution, the painter recalled the style of Renaissance tapestries and also consulted the fashion engravings that his wife, a modest couturière, referred to for her creations. This is how the painter regarbed his memory.

"It is very interesting to find the qualities of his soul in his art," said Uhde, "and to compare his life with his painting. He didn't have the temperament of the peaceful amateur, who cares only about details; his was the spirit of the hero, who is constantly and ardently focused on the whole."

Henri Rousseau: **Promenade in the Forest of Saint-Germain.**

"Would you believe that when I walk through the countryside
and I see the sun, that greenery, those flowers,
I sometimes think to myself: 'All this is mine!'"
HENRI ROUSSEAU
to a *Comoedia* reporter

The Flight from the City and the Return Home

4.

The thing that makes me happiest of all is to contemplate nature and paint it. Would you believe that when I walk through the countryside and I see the sun, that greenery, those flowers, I sometimes think to myself: 'All this is mine!' That's a bit daring, isn't it: all this belongs to me." The *Comoedia* reporter who, on March 19, 1910, quoted these words directly from the lips of the Douanier Rousseau added that "a truly childlike happiness burst out in his laughter." Laughing at the boldness of his intimate revelation, "I possess the landscapes that I paint," the Naïf experienced a sort of jubilation, blending the pleasure of recovery with the provocative joy of revenge on his isolation and poverty.

A significant fact: when Henri Rousseau received an important commission, he sometimes felt the need to do a second version of the painting that he would soon have to release—a second version, as though to safeguard his property. *Bis repetita placent:* things repeated, things asked for again, are pleasing . . . especially to their creator! By reproducing nature, doesn't he duplicate himself?

"Pictorial" Projections

What does the painter's revelation relate to? Jan Gordon made an interesting point in *A Step Ladder to Painting:* "In painting, one of the basic sources of inspiration is the bizarre sentiment that the subject is yours. You have enclosed it in your mind, you have spiritually absorbed it and you are about to transform it into art." But one would have to go back to the origin of this desire for assimilation and ask, as Marion Milner does in *The Unconscious and Painting,* whether one of the functions of graphic art might not be the restoration and re-creation of what the painter desired, loved, identified with, but also lost when he was taught, through the rigorous and methodical process of acquiring intellectual knowledge and learning abstraction, to distinguish between the object and the subject, the self and the non-self. Like any child, might he then not have gotten rid of his mania for drawing and coloring? Was he turned off, dis-gusted (in the etymological sense of "losing his taste")? And now, as an unwilling adult, does he feel a profound regret, an insurmountable nostalgia?

When Rousseau complained, at fifty-one, of having been "obliged to initially follow a different career from the one my tastes summoned me to," he pointed out that this was because of his parents' "lack of fortune." It's a common story—the family tragedy of the liquidation of a hardware store, the father ruined by his real-estate speculations, the auctioning off of the wonderful family home ("How could we help having medieval ideas in the family, since we were born in a medieval tower?" his brother wondered). These devastating events were painful to little Henri Rousseau. It was hard to take—this liquidation, which frustrated him like a premature weaning. He had first seen the light of day in this home, he had played here and dreamed here. The dispossession, the wrenching from the nest where he had known the primary pleasures of being nursed by his mother, could only arouse an insatiable desire in him to alter his relationship with the outside world through a healing and sustaining retreat to painting.

One could investigate at length the obvious correspondences between the appetite for painting and the desire to eat, to absorb, to drink. Such a study would take us from cave drawings to the still lifes of the most refined painters, from prehistoric caverns to the inns loved by so many painters or daubers, who gladly decorated their dining rooms. For instance, there is a still life in Marie Henry's place at Pouldu: onions accompanied by the eloquent assertion "I love onions fried in oil"!

Provisioning and Preserving

Inns, taverns, cafés were the cradle of French painting from 1848 to 1918, and in a work I am preparing on this theme, I plan to show how the painters who frequented these places and influenced one another there were dependent on their food-bearing hostesses. I intend to discuss the inn of Père Ganne in Barbizon, Mère Toutain's Saint-Siméon Farm in Honfleur, the Pension Gloanec in Pont-Aven, and Marie Henry's (alias Marie Poupée's) seaside pub in Pouldu, Mère Fournaise's restaurant in Croissy, the Café Guerbois, the literary cafés of Batignolles, the open-air taverns along the Seine and the Marne, the pubs and bars of Montmartre and Montparnasse, and other establishments where painters so often toasted the new style of painting and its godmothers. Like most of these artists, the Douanier Rousseau did not escape the emotional regression produced by the anxieties of separation and creation.

It would not be preposterous to state that the hunting and the hunger of wild beasts in Rousseau's exotic art, and the fishing in his rural landscapes are the prime themes of his painterly projections.

His family home, which was just a fortified gateway in Laval, was historically a place of both inward and outward passage for its inhabitants. Through this gateway people once passed to go out to the fields or on a journey, through it they came back when they returned home.

When will I see, alas, the chimney smoke
In my small village, and in what season
Will I see the yard of my poor house,
Which is a province for me and much more?

These lines were written by Joachim du Bellay in the sixteenth century (*The Eternal City*).

Henri Rousseau chose to become a customs inspector in Paris, where he checked the arrivals and departures of various merchandise, including wines and liquors. Would it be unfair to ask whether his choice might have been determined by his nostalgia for being in an intermediary position between the town and the country, an indecisive state between security and adventure, a transition between order and freedom, reality and imagination? In short, between house and forest, between provisioning and preserving?

In the late nineteenth century, the suburbs of the City of Light were still "country." A map of the landscapes that the Douanier liked to paint is revealing in this regard. The customhouse, the fortifications, the Gate of Bas-Meudon, the bridges of Sèvres and Saint-Cloud, Point-de-Jour and the viaduct of Auteuil, the bridge of Grenelle and the footbridge of Passy, the Lyon railroad bridge at Charenton, the carriages on the Quai d'Austerlitz, the tree-lined paths in the Bois de Boulogne and Bois de Vincennes, the villages south of Paris, but also the quays of the Seine, the banks of the Oise and the Marne, the canals and sluices—all these things were invitations to voyages, to satisfy "that least desire" evoked by Baudelaire:

The setting suns
Drape the fields,
The canals, the entire city
With hyacinth and gold:
The world falls asleep
In a hot light. . . .
There, all is but order and beauty
Luxury, calm, and voluptuousness.

To go back there, to the countryside, to rediscover the areas and eras of certainty and sweetness on Place Hardy, between Beucheresse Gate and the cathedral, where the child took his first steps, guided by his sister Anatolie: such is the painter's lovely dream, to wander through his memories.

If the Douanier did flee the city, he never fully left it. At most, he traveled to the home of his daughter, then his granddaughter in Angers, or to his son-in-law's parents' home at Saintes (in Charente-Maritime) during vacation; or he accompanied his friends the Papouins to Brittany. But he didn't paint in these places. It was in the suburbs of Paris and on the quays of the Seine that he wore out his shoes. He let the clouds (so often tinted by the colors of the sunset), the dirigibles, and the first airplanes travel for him. He captured them in the sky! And even his impressionistic sketches of outdoor "views" are quite hasty, as if he were hurrying to go back and complete them in his Paris studio (sometimes on the basis of engravings, photos, or picture postcards), incorporating his image of them, the imaginary colors that best suited them and that he had foreseen.

I The Rediscoveries of the Man and the Child

always see a painting before doing it, even when it's very complicated. Only while I paint it do I find things that surprise even me and give me pleasure," he confided to Arsène Alexandre in an interview.

Just what pleasure does he mean? Might it be the same kind of pleasure as one feels on running into a cherished person whom one has lost sight of? "Well!" one cries. "What a small world! What are *you* doing here? Who would ever have thought . . . ?"

> For the child in love with maps and prints,
> The universe is equal to his vast appetite.
> Oh, how big the world becomes in lamplight.
> How small the world to the eyes of memory.

These lines from Baudelaire's poem "The Voyage" could have been written by the Douanier Rousseau. "The child sees everything as new," Baudelaire wrote in 1863 in an article entitled "The Painter and Modern Life" (published in *Le Figaro*). "He is forever intoxicated. Nothing is more like what is known as inspiration than the joy of a child absorbing form and color." (Note here, too, the words "intoxicated" and "absorbing.") And this art critic, enlightened by his experience as a poet, adds, "Genius is nothing but childhood found again at will, childhood now gifted with, as means of self-expression, virile organs and an analytical mind that allows it to put in order the sum of involuntarily amassed materials."

Just think of the rediscoveries of the man and the child he used to be, the child he never really stopped being. "Nothing is as mysterious as those muted preparations that await man at the threshold of life. Everything is played out before we reach the age of twelve. Twenty years, thirty years of fierce work, a whole lifetime of drudgery will not make, will not unmake what has been done, what has been undone once and for all, before us, without us, for us, against us," Charles Péguy remarked in *L'Argent*.

Certainly, the Douanier's pictures existed prior to the paintings he did and redid from 1872 to 1910. They are reappearances!

"Verily, I say unto you, if ye cannot be as children, ye shall not enter the Kingdom of Heaven," Jesus told his disciples, just as he promised them in his evangelical Sermon on the Mount (in the very heart of nature): "Blessed are the poor in spirit, for theirs is the kingdom of heaven." It already belongs to them!

Wasn't it through the humility of his gaze and through his virginal comprehension of the world that Rousseau (the "angel of Plaisance," as Apollinaire called him) regained the very green paradise of his childhood loves? And wasn't this why "the savor and enchantment that escape from his works have not stopped moving us," as Tristan Tzara has said, a poet who understood him and loved him (which boils down to the same thing)?

H Intimations of Ancient Landscapes

ow was this paradise regained? In a chapter entitled "Preserving What One Loves," Marion Milner indulges in a "deeper reflection on the phenomenon of sending the imaginary body to assume the shape of that which one is looking at." Milner intelligently wonders about the power of painters to "spread something that was part of themselves around the objects of the exterior world": might this power be a "means of trying to deal with the primary human difficulty of the disillusion caused by separation, jealousy, and the loss of love"? Jealousy, which I have discussed in the chapter on "The Mysteries of Love," was maintained and preserved by Rousseau, perhaps since the unthinkable birth of his younger brother, Jules, with whom he eventually broke.

By confronting the landscapes he chose to paint and superimposing them on the outskirts of Paris—those of Laval and Angers, of Mayenne and Maine-et-Loire, the landscapes that struck the child's and then the adolescent's eyes—one is astonished to see that the earlier landscapes are implicit in the later ones. Pastures grazed by peaceful cows, rivers crossed by bridges and viaducts, aquaducts and footbridges, quais lined with fishermen, streams encircling factories, farms, houses, and villas, roads meandering in between hedges and gates, clearings and undergrowth, where the petits bourgeois stroll and picnic in their Sunday best, shady paths in parks and public gardens, castles on slopes, mills along waterways, villages lost in verdure, sudden sawmills and quarries among the flowers of the fields—these all evoke the world he discovered and wondered at during his early years.

Thus Rousseau moved away from the trials that harassed him: grief and debts. The more afflicted he was, the more fertile his creativity. After the deaths of his first wife, his grown son, his second wife, after the frustrations of his final loves, he sent more and more works to the Salons. The Douanier Rousseau donned the mantle of suffering by finding himself again in his Sunday retrospectives, in the promenades of the past.

"The art of Henri Rousseau," observed Roch Grey, "was born and took shape on Sundays. In childhood, he grew accustomed to viewing this day as devoted purely to fun." Hating school, he made painting his vacation. He worked very hard at painting—as conscientiously as a good pupil does on his slate and in his notebooks. Yet Rousseau produced such an aura of emancipation in his landscapes that they radiate the sheer pleasure of living. Renoir loved paintings that make one feel like going for a stroll. This is true of Rousseau's paintings: his art, as Apollinaire wrote, is "quite simply, healthy and worth stopping for."

A Pantheistic Symbiosis

Within this context, it comes as no surprise that Rousseau preserves the "awkwardness" of any child's playful drawings: irrational perspectives, lopsided groupings of houses pierced by black rectangles, gigantic trees, Lilliputian stiffness in men but prestigious vastness in mother-women, phallic forms of factory chimneys and Eiffel Towers, smoke and clouds in cottony plumes, serpentine roads, halts at barriers and hedges, thick shrubbery, black marks to stress relief, frontal views of leaves and flowers, silhouettes of animals, suns and moons drawn with compasses, sharp, distinct colors, and so forth. Often comparable to the projections of magic lanterns, these landscapes are as symmetrical and simple as those affectionately inscribed picture postcards that show the places where we were reconciled with ourselves and hence with others.

Rousseau's painting is orderly: it obeys him. Apollinaire said, "I often saw him working and I know how careful he was about all the details, how anxious to maintain the primitive and definitive conception of his painting until it was done. I also know that he left nothing to chance, certainly nothing essential." Rousseau's painting repeats the "faults" that are simply the other side of the childhood coin: excess spontaneity, frank egocentricity, an emphatic taste for the anecdotal, a caricatural simplification of the subjects, lack of mastery over proportions and volumes, inability to render depth and perspective, faulty color contrasting, laborious details. And, like a child, Rousseau wants to belong to nature, to be on the receiving end of nature.

His erudition is completely unintellectual. His true sources are in popular imagery. And, despite his references to certain uninspired academic painters, all he seeks in them is the expression of a theme, which he will strip of any excessive refinement, any allusive subtlety, any aestheticism. Yet this does not at all prevent him from being touched by grace and possessing the great distinction of the most assured authenticity.

"The complete sincerity of Rousseau," said Robert Delaunay, "who, with the purest sensitive means, was in contact with an intense love of life, achieves a balanced sensitivity that seems made up of ease and happiness. His art comes from the depths of the people. . . ." We can agree that Rousseau was primarily natural, in the full sense of the term, and that he was never distrustful about being natural.

We take his painting seriously though it aroused the mirth of so many of his contemporaries. We take it seriously not because of its unintended revolt against the academic routine of the nineteenth century, a revolt by a man whose persevering courage brought him solidarity with several young painters. Rather, we take his art seriously because it offers us windows, hedonistic appeals to live once again in harmony with nature, as in the time when, by means of a pantheistic symbiosis, we formed an integral part of the universe.

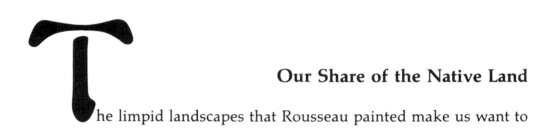

Our Share of the Native Land

The limpid landscapes that Rousseau painted make us want to be in nature:

> To be in nature like a human tree,
> To spread desires like a foliage deep,
> And feel, in peaceful nights and thunderstorms,
> The universal sap flow in my hands!

This, the ardent wish of Anna de Noailles, was what Rousseau lived in his painting. He brings us back to our origins, reminds us of our roots, our beginnings.

In this sense, he well deserves the nickname of the Naïf (from Latin *nativus*, innate, natural, native) and the qualifier "ingenuous" (from latin *ingenuus*, born free). For his art is imbued with innocence, it invites us to be reborn to the world, to take the full measure of our share of the native land. His genius, born of an invincible fixation on his household lares and a euphoric attachment to his memorable coming into the world, engages our affectionate complicity with its astonishing lyrical power. Rousseau makes us regret our denials and repudiations.

No, the Douanier is not an anarchist. Marked by his atavism, he stayed faithful to his roots. Although unusual, his *oeuvre* drains the pictorial qualities of a whole line of forerunners, who, from Romanesque frescoes to Renaissance tapestries, from books of hours to the simplest popular images, handed the spirit of the French family down to him: a spirit of clarity, acumen, and good humor, order and lightness—in a word, harmony.

Incidentally, Rousseau was not so lost in our civilization as he may have seemed during his lifetime. The admiration he receives from ecologists, the inspiration he provides for advertising artists, the frequent use of reproductions of his paintings by book and record publishers, the international success of his exhibitions, and the journalistic myth of the miraculously inspired, simple, good-natured fellow—all these things confirm, if necessary, the timelessness of his art.

"The genius doesn't create, he retraces. . . . Poets are the truest of all men," said Lamartine. But the profound truth that they express doesn't always seem likely to their contemporaries, who overreact to the sheer appearance of their new and original work. What poet could more effectively express, in just a few verses, the truth about the Douanier Rousseau than Guillaume Apollinaire?

A tiny bird
On an angel's shoulder
Sings the praises
Of gentle Rousseau

The movements of the world
The memories pass
Like a boat on the billow
And regrets in the deep

Gentle Rousseau
You are that angel
And that bird
Of your praises

You walk across Paris very slowly
The breeze in the mauve sail Are you there mother?

I whirl around,
A crazy beacon,
My nice boat
Has sailed away

They say she was beautiful
Near the Mississippi
But that the Paris fashion
Makes her more beautiful. . . .

The evocation of this bird "on an angel's shoulder" is all the more touching because the Douanier Rousseau seldom returned from a walk without bringing back a bird that had fallen from its nest, a stray dog, some confused, abandoned creature. "Rousseau feels a natural need to love and be loved," said Uhde. And in an article in *L'Amour de l'Art*, Philippe Soupault claimed that in order to paint, Rousseau dipped his brush into his heart. Isn't this a fine way to evoke his elephant-calf memory and the revivals of his memories as a possessive child who, starved for affection, permanently recomposed the world of enchantment that offered him dispensation from suffering?

LAVAL. - Porte Beucheresse

LAVAL. Vue sur Avesnières et la Mayenne. ND Phot.

MAYENNE. - Moulin de la Roche Gandon

34. - LAVAL. - Le Pont Vieux et le Château au clair de lune

LAVAL - Le quai Jehan-Fouquet et le vieux pont

Childhood memories are the warp and woof of Rousseau's paintings. These views of Laval and Mayenne, places he knew in every detail, in which one sees a striking similarity to the landscapes of his mature years, indicate his favorite subjects. Passage gates, arches and bridges, calm rivers pierced by fishing lines, villages, factories and homes framed by trees, uninhabited castles, moonlight among the clouds, intrigued horse and dogs—all the things he didn't want to forget.

Henri Rousseau: **View of Vanves
to the Left of the Gate of Vanves,** September 1909.

Henri Rousseau: **Old Tower of Avranches.**

"Gate of Vanves, Fourteenth Arrondissement." Postcard.

The Douanier Rousseau, employed by the Customs Office from 1872 to
1893, often stood guard, both day and night, at the gates of Paris, on
the fortifications, and along the banks of the Seine. This photograph
by Atget and these picture postcards allow us to imagine him at his post.
"Unfit for any difficult work, credulous and not very talkative, he never joked
with his colleagues; instead, he sat down somewhere all alone and painted. . . .
One night, in the wine market, they set up a skeleton among the vats and they
manipulated it with the aid of a string. They had a good laugh, watching
Rousseau politely addressing the skeleton and asking him whether he was
thirsty." (Wilhelm Uhde, Henri Rousseau)

Halt, go no farther! Uncouth as his **Customs House** may be, mystery
haunts it among the black silhouettes of the inspectors, the trellis, and the
gaslights. At the border between town and country, this medievel keep in
Avranches, which Rousseau might have seen in traveling to Brittany, must
have recalled his childhood home, Beucheresse Gate, with its ground-floor shop
and its dark windows. The visible effort to balance the mass of the keep and
its roofs, the slightly risky attempt at perspective in the rising road add an
impenetrable strength to the astonishing presence of this Old Tower.

The Fortifications. Gate of Arcueil. *Photograph taken in June 1899 by Atge*

Henri Rousseau: **The Customs House.**

Henri Rousseau: **Strollers in a Park.**

First shown at the Salon of the Independents in 1895, the **View from an Arch of the Bridge of Sèvres** *effectively renders Rousseau's fascination with openings and passages that lead out into a promising beyond of rustic and woodland joys. In his obstinate quest for bird's-eye views, which allowed him both to express the attraction space had for him and to master the fear in which he held it, the painter comes up against a foreground that is virtually his "strait gate." Does happiness ultimately lie beyond the portal, the arch, the porch? As Graham Greene wrote in* The Power and the Glory, *"In our childhood, there is always a moment when the door opens and lets the future in."*

Like Rousseau, Utrillo, who was often inspired by picture postcards, found his path in an immediate, straightforward art. Utrillo likewise shares Rousseau's nostalgia for the home, which lingers and concretizes their family attachment.

Maurice Utrillo: The Ravine of Presles.

"The Bridge of Sèvres." Postcard detail.

"The Bridge of Sèvres." Postcard detail.

96

Henri Rousseau: **View from an Arch of the Bridge of Sèvres.**

Henri Rousseau: **Landscape with a Dirigible.**

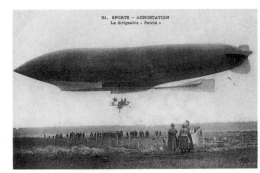

"Sports Ballooning. The Dirigible Patrie." Postcard.

"Billancourt. Banks of the Seine and Bridge of Sèvres." Postcard.

30 Villeneuve-Triage — La Passerelle du Canal

"Villeneuve-Triage. Canal Footbridge." Postcard.

Flying machines lighter than clouds—what miracles! Even before the Belle Epoque, the subject was in the air. Rousseau had seen a reproduction of Goya's Balloon, read Jules Verne's ''A Voyage in a Balloon'' in the periodical Le Musée des Familles, and gone around Bartholdi's Monument to the Aeronauts of the Siege of Paris. The Aeronautics Grand Prize in 1900, Santos-Dumont's dirigible

Henri Rousseau: **View of the Bridge at Sèvres and Saint-Cloud with Airplane, Balloon, and Dirigible.**

adventures in Saint-Cloud in 1901, the flights of the Lebaudy dirigible in 1905 and of the Patrie over Meudon in 1906, the exploits of Blériot, Voisin, Farman, and Delagrange excited the press, as well as the painter who claimed to be "modern." Balloons, dirigibles, and airplanes invaded postcard landscapes, to which photographers often added them, and from which the Douanier extracted them to slip them into his former "views."

12. BELLEVUE — La Boucle de la Seine — Panorama sur Sèvres
St-Cloud, Boulogne, Surusnes et le Mont-Valérien

"Bellevue. Bend in the Seine. Panorama of Sèvres,
Saint-Cloud, Boulogne, Suresnes, and Mount Valérien." Postcard.

Thérond: General View of the Viaduct Bridge of Point-du-Jour.
Drawing in Le Magasin Pittoresque *(1886).*

"Paris. The Viaduct of Auteuil." Postcard.

"Paris. Point-du-Jour." Postcard.

uilt for the Exposition of 1867, the viaduct of Auteuil, "the work of Monsieur de Bassompierre, is marvelously framed by the surrounding site," wrote Le Magasin Pittoresque. The Quai du Pont-du-Jour soon became a high point for strollers. Café boats moored there, and restaurants drew the tipsy Parisians. Near a sand pile on the Left Bank, the Douanier Rousseau stood and gazed at the viaduct during sunset, then painted it in his studio. His painting, shown at the first exhibition of the Society of Independent Artists, in 1886, is probably one of the finest and most representative of his landscapes. It did not have the good fortune to find favor with the shortsighted art critics. After pulling **A Carnival Evening** to pieces, the Soleil journalist wrote: "The other canvas depicts a view of the Quai du Point-du-Jour at Auteuil. In an attempt at art, inexperience is no crime; but one would do well, I think, to entrust such a viaduct, such a train, such trees to the most discreet of one's cardboard boxes, waiting to show it when a period of progress arrives."

Henri Rousseau: **View of Point-du-Jour. Sunset.**

The Port and the Bridge of Grenelle. Photograph.

Henri Rousseau: **The Bridge of Grenelle Under Snow.**

47. PARIS — Pont de Grenelle et Statue de la Liberté   C. L. C

"Paris. Bridge of Grenelle and Statue of Liberty." Panoramic France letter card.

Shivering *under the snow in* **The Bridge of Grenelle Under Snow** *and outlined in autumn behind the Passy footbridge, the replica of the statue of* Liberty Enlightening the World, *presented by France to the United States in 1886, is obviously accompanied in these paintings by a patriotic flag. But, like the Eiffel Tower in other views, the statue is perfectly integrated by the painter, who places it almost on the same level as his small figures, themselves like statues, in landscapes that are both familiar and frozen. When viewing them, one can't help singing the poem that Apollinaire wrote about the nearby Pont Mirabeau:*

Let night come the hour strike
The days go I stay
Love goes like this flowing water
Love goes
How slow life is. . . .

Rousseau, too, had the gift of arresting life and slowing it down.

The Statue of Liberty at the Bridge of Grenelle. Photograph.

Henri Rousseau: **View of the Footbridge of Passy.**

Henri Dochy: Night over the City. *Engraving.*

"Banks of the Seine, Quai du Louvre."
Postcard for Crème Franco-Russe.

"Paris: the Seine, View of the
Bridge of the Saints-Pères."
Postcard.

The moonlight, the starry illumination of the street lamps on the
Pont des Arts, their reflection trembling in the Seine, the unsettling
shapes of the tarpaulins on the barrels, the desertlike space of the
quai and the shadows of the customs inspectors, the spires of Notre-Dame
and Sainte-Chapelle with the pennoned masts of the boats create the
mysterious serenity and "dark light" of this seraphic painting. Completed
several months before the death of Rousseau's first wife, Clémence, it was
shown at the Salon of the Independents in 1888, although under the wrong
title. This is actually a view of Ile de la Cité from the old Bridge of the
Saints-Pères (today the Carousel Bridge), as proved by these postcards and
the Dochy engraving. In the foreground: Port of Saint-Nicolas on the Quai
du Louvre, where the Douanier placed himself in **Myself**, two years later.

Henri Rousseau: **View of Ile Saint-Louis from the Port of Saint Nicolas (Evening).**

Henri Rousseau: **The Washerwomen of Melun.**

"Melun. Pont aux Moulins." Postcard.

When he was growing old, the Douanier Rousseau displayed a supreme stripping-down and extreme modesty in his landscapes, especially the paintings of Notre-Dame and Ile Saint-Louis. Perhaps this development was due to his haste to capture them, and to a self-assurance gained from the growing number of commissions for paintings. All he retains in these landscapes are the dominant colors and the essential features: he seizes only their essence, affirming their sui generis character. If he describes more than he invents, it may also be in reaction to the deliriums he undertook in his exotic paintings. This lesson in sobriety and humility seems to have been learned in their own fashion by certain later painters, such as Utrillo or Marquet. The latter, incidentally, was quite familiar with Rousseau's works, since he also exhibited at the Salon of the Independents from 1901 on, and the Salon d'Automne from 1904 on.

Henri Rousseau: **Notre-Dame Seen from Port Henri-IV,** 1909.

"Paris. Port Henri-IV." Postcard.

Albert Marquet: The Seine in Paris, *1934.*

Henri Rousseau: **View of the Luxembourg, Chopin Monument,** Composition 1909.

"Paris. Luxembourg Garden. Monument to Frédéric Chopin." Postcard.

"Paris. Luxembourg Garden." Postcard.

The Park of Saint-Cloud. Postcard.

Henri Rousseau: **The Avenue, Park of Saint-Cloud.**

Crossroads at Pré Catelan. Postcard detail.

Ah, the Belle Epoque, when the women showed off their fancy wardrobes under the foliage of the summer paths in gardens and public parks. They wanted to honor their husbands, to excite their ardor or jealousy, or, even better, to arouse the envy of their rivals! What painter could render as simply as Rousseau the stiff charm and petty vanity of these coquetteries? Rousseau views them from above (as if he could fly over the dense trees or through their branches) only to avoid feeling that he doesn't belong and to allow nature its full pre-eminence. We could even say that these figurines, who almost seem to be posing, lend themselves to the painter's mise en scène, as though he were a postcard photographer. For these rosy women in the Park of Saint-Cloud, one suspects that he had in mind Watteau, of whose works he had several reproductions in his studio. We also see a quest for airy lightness, something rare for Rousseau.

Henri Rousseau: **Landscape in Buttes-Chaumont.**

ritish soccer was becoming popular in France, and teams were training in the Bois de Boulogne, where the Douanier observed them on Sundays. Borrowed from contemporary illustrations, but set in a specially reserved place within his autumn landscape, these players have barely enough room to play. They give the stunning and comical impression of flying toward their sunlike balloon. The picture almost looks like a ballet. "The amusing Monsieur Rousseau will not abandon his attempts at infantile art, which recall toys, the laughable shapes of wooden or gingerbread figures," said a journalist in Le Matin. The Douanier's puppet figures, almost intentionally humorous, were like trees hiding the forest: they prevented the art critics from admiring his sharp but sober, sumptuous but simple sense of nature and its seasonal colors. After him, and influenced by him, other painters took up this theme and the contortions of the players: Robert Delaunay in his Cardiff Team (1912–13) and in Soccer (1917), a watercolor on paper; then Pablo Picasso in his bathers playing with a balloon on the beach of Dinard (1928).

G. D. Rowlandson: Soccer Players. Newspaper illustration.

Popular chromolithograph showing schoolboys learning how to play Rugby.

Henri Rousseau: **Soccer Players,** 1908.

Henri Rousseau: **View of Saint-Cloud from the Heights of Bellevue.**

Artist's study in forest of Meudon-Bellevue. Postcard detail.

Lucien Vieillard: Lakeside Village.

Henri Rousseau: **The Stone Quarry.**

"Châtillon-sous-Bagneux. Stone Quarry." Postcard.

In most of Rousseau's paintings, an anecdotal element, whether technical, animal, or human, has caught his attention; the more unusual this element, the more bucolic the painter makes the landscape. These astonishing accessories are merely an accidental pretext: they give him a chance to add mystery to his compositions. The gas lamp in **View of Saint-Cloud** and the mechanical winch in **Quarry** intrigue the painter, who, like a child, wonders: "What's that? What's that doing here?" Since the thing is there, one might as well use it as a foil for the overall harmony. It offers an excellent opportunity for breaking the linear perspectives, constituting space, and attempting to balance the surrounding planes. The totality suddenly takes on a playful, yet strange and poetic character. This is something that so many of his imitators failed to understand.

Henri Rousseau: **The Water Mill.**

Henri Rousseau: **View of a Park.** Pen-and-ink drawing heightened by white gouache on graphite strokes.

"Laval. The Garden of the Perrine." Postcard.

28 — LAVAL.   Le Jardin de la Perrine.   ND. Phot.

"Bois de Vincennes. The Bank of the Lake." Postcard.

845. Bois de Vincennes
Le Bord du Lac

As suggested by several postcards evoking the places that Rousseau liked to haunt, he was particularly attracted by parks and stretches of water, which must have reminded him of his home town on the banks of the Mayenne and the many hours that he fished in that river as a child. What did he regain? A flight from solitude, a dash toward the future, the dreamed-of opportunity to translate onto canvas a perspective effect as applied to a stream. At times, the Douanier is such an attentive observer that he even tries to render a few timid shadows, reflections of imperious light, the fine, bold slenderness of a branch sticking into the sky. One may well be astonished by the quality of the drawing at the Art Institute of Chicago, for nothing else in Rousseau's oeuvre equals its refinement. And yet all the mysterious naturalism of his genius recurs in this painstaking exercise!

Henri Rousseau: **The River.**

"Champigny. The Banks of the Yonne." Postcard.

Henri Rousseau: **Banks of the Marne.**

Henri Rousseau: **The Pond.**

"Park of Villeneuve-l'Etang." Postcard.

Whether he pauses on the banks of the Marne or the Oise, studded with factories closed on Sundays, with mute, simple homes, with distant farms or coquettish, isolated villas; whether he walks a bit to discover the solitary bend in a stream or halts at the reed-choked edge of an old quarry that has turned into a pond, the Douanier is sensitive primarily to the calm of these stretches of water. His paintings of them reflect this peace, which is often confirmed by the tiny fishermen whose rods seem to draw from the very source of this quietude.

Whether smeared with gray, dotted with rose or mauve clouds, or showing a remnant of blue as limpid as water, the sky is brought to our attention by a factory chimney, some windswept trees, or a few pointed and thickset poplars. And silence reigns.

Henri Rousseau: **The Fisherman.**

Henri Rousseau: **Landscape on the Banks of the Oise.**
Villa Mathilde, territory of Champoval.

Banks of the Marne at Alfort. Postcard.

117

Henri Rousseau: **Landscape with Water Mill and Cart**, 1879.

"The Sites of the Morin. The Lassault Mill at Couilly-Saint-Germain." Postcard.

"Cernay-la-Ville (Seine-et-Oise). Interior of the Grand Moulin farm." Postcard.

ousseau's paintings reveal the pleasure felt by a truly naïve spirit in the simplest things; his works betray this fascination. Preoccupied by these things to the exclusion of all else, he assigns them the most meaningful life, devoting all the resources of his imagination to this world. Christian Zervos, in Rousseau, exclaims that "A thrilling sweetness, a joy preceded by surprise emanate from his spellbinding works." Starting with his very first works, the painter seems to have been spurred by a blend of sureness and delight: self-confidence. "I took a chance and showed my first efforts to Monsieur Gérôme, telling him that I was self-taught, but that I would be proud to get his advice," Rousseau said to Arsène Alexandre, who describes "his good, trusting face, which was not without malice, and his easy, rustic attitude."

"Your brush stroke is very bold," replied Gérôme. "Go home and observe nature very closely." The **Mill**, signed in 1879, already showed the concision, economy of details, general balance of forms, precise outlines, and airy perspective that are admired in all the works of Rousseau's maturity, such as his refreshing **Tollgate**.

Henri Rousseau: **The Tollgate.**

"The lovely Areas of the Marne.
Joinville-le-Pont.
The Tollgate.
The Fishermen." Postcard.

Henri Rousseau: **View of the Chair Factory and the Seine Quay at Alfortville.**

The Seine Quay and the sluice at Alfortville. Photograph.

Here are two landscapes that typify Rousseau's attraction to pictorial reportage. Choosing two eccentric buildings, he concentrates his composition on them, precisely recalling their utilitarian function: the mill at Alfort and the Chesnoy et Cie Chair Factory. The postcard bearing the inscription Moulin d'Alfort also has the words Bateau-Lavoir, which Rousseau added to another version of this painting. And in a reprise of **The Chair Factory,** he tries to improve the space along the Alfortville wharf. This concern for accuracy and for a "literal copy" of the observed landscape never interferes with Rousseau's natural propensity for capturing the landscape's secret essence and original character. "Rousseau's penchant for realism is unwittingly corrected by an intense poetic feeling that tones down the material and spiritualizes it," said Zervos. Rousseau's anecdotes become antidotes to imitation, to which he never became a slave. He is more natural than naturalistic, more of a dreamer than a realist.

Henri Rousseau: **Banks of the Marne (Charenton). The Alfort Mill.**

Banks of the Marne at Charenton-le-Pont, upstream from the Bridge. Postcard.

Henri Rousseau: Sketch for **The Alfort Mill.**

Henri Rousseau: **The Cliff.**

Gustave Courbet: Detail from The Cliff with Boats.

ousseau respected Gustave Courbet, whose realistic
paintings of models and of the virile beauty of blacks never
lost hold of the Douanier. It was under Courbet's direct
influence that Rousseau did these two genre paintings. The
influence was twofold: it came from the cliffs that Courbet painted
near Etretat from 1889 on, and his Stormy Sea, also called **The
Wave** (shown at the Luxembourg Museum before entering the
Louvre in 1889). In his own **Cliff,** Rousseau schematizes and
simplifies the structure of the rock, pacifies the ocean, gives the
waves cottony edges, adds two fishermen in the boat and lets two
unreal sailboats drift across the horizon in the rosy light of sunset.
(This same light can be found in a **Cliff** of Courbet's.) To imagine
his tempest, Rousseau takes up the image of a cruiser launched in
1896, the **D'Entrecasteaux** (carefully respecting the gap between
the third smokestack and the other two, a feature distinguishing
this cruiser from all its contemporaries). Rousseau, also inspired
here by Courbet's The Wave and the seascapes of painters then in
vogue, chops up the sea and liquefies the sky.

Henri Rousseau: **The D'Entrecasteaux in a Tempest.**

The armored cruiser D'Entrecasteaux. Photograph at the Museum of the Navy.

"The Armored Cruiser Patrie in Choppy Weather. After R. Dumon Duparc." Postcard.

Henri Rousseau: **Landscape with Farm and Cow.**

Henri Rousseau: **Rainy Morning.**

Henri Rousseau: **The Country Road.**

Henri Rousseau: **The Forest Road.**

ENVIRONS DE MONTEREAU — Forêt de Valence
· Carrefour des routes de Paris-Fontainebleau-Provins

Millot, lib.-éditeur, Montereau

"The environs of Montereau.
Valence Forest.
Crossroads of the Roads to
Paris, Fontainebleau, and Provins."
Postcard.

Young Gayal. *In* Bêtes sauvages (Wild Beasts),
Galeries Lafayette.

ousseau was more of a colorist than an architect, and his sense of delicacy won out against geometry. This is one of the good reasons why he often used a path or a road as an effective means of drawing out the linear perspective of his paintings and creating a natural depth. Sometimes he traced his roads with a compass or a ruler, even painting two roads, as in his magnificent forest road, in order to overcome more effectively his handicap as an autodidact. He then filled in the edges of these roads with awkward slopes, stiff low walls, rustic barriers, milestones or piles of rocks, small signposts, a grazing cow (borrowed from his album).

How happy he was to make trees live in these landscapes. After his arduous efforts to make the grass grow, his delicate touch set the beeches and even the poplars trembling with delight. Rousseau's soul entered the painting. Under their blue or grayish skies, these country landscapes became coherent, vibrant, persistent. Very simple new masterpieces, but so moving that we would like to stroll about in them and even live in them!

125

Henri Rousseau: **The Shepherd.**

Charles Jacque: The Shepherd. *Drawing, engraved by Rouget for* Le Magasin Pittoresque *(1862), p. 349.*

"O ma tendre musette," "O my tender musette."
In Rondes et chansons populaires,
a collection of French folk songs, p. 332.

Often called **Summer,** Rousseau's **View of Brittany,** *which he exhibited in 1907 at the Salon of the Independents, directly reproduces a lithograph by Pirodon, based on Camille Bernier's painting Springtime. Rousseau loved the deep-cut roads and underbrush of this unjustly forgotten painter, who had become famous for the Breton landscapes he showed at every Salon from 1879 to 1885. Rousseau did a less elaborate first version of his painting in 1906. This luminous version is by a visionary who makes everything fantastic: the white horse, the oak trunks and their fickle leaves, the blue pool, which replaces the meadow. When the Italian painter Soffici saw this painting at the Salon, he fell madly in love with it. He came back to see the Douanier in 1910, to have him do a second version, whereupon the Douanier painted* **The Pasture,** *quite rapidly, copying one of his canvases from 1907,* **The Pasture. Banks of the Oise.** *Soffici was disappointed and left the painting to Roch Grey and her brother, Serge Férat. Inspired by a drawing by the Barbizon painter Charles Jacque, Rousseau's "pastorale" owes its romantic note to La Harpe's illustrated song in* Rondes et chansons populaires, *"O ma tendre musette." As he painted, Rousseau often crooned the antiquated songs of his childhood.*

Henri Rousseau: **View of Brittany,** 1907.

Spring, Bannalec, Finistère. *Lithograph by Eugène Pirodon, based on the painting by Camille Bernier.*

Henri Rousseau: **The Pasture.**

emale nudes and cows in meadows are the two chief themes in the abundant and conventional pictorial output during the late nineteenth century. It is certainly impressive to leaf through the catalogues of the Salon. Rousseau painted only a few nudes—taking refuge in exoticism in order to conceal his modesty and awkwardness. On the other hand, he tackled cows all the more heartily for having come from a cattle-raising area. Indeed, he enjoyed reinventing lovely rustic landscapes, borrowing typical details here and there: a woman with a distaff, round or conical haystacks, etc. But he didn't take his cattle from the fields; he got them, as we have already seen, from engravings and prints. The bull in Rousseau's **Peasant Woman in the Meadow** and the ox in his **Bagneux** are merely the flip side of his Wild Beasts album. Since this banteng ox, also known as the "white-buttock ox," comes straight from Java, Borneo, and Sumatra, we should not be surprised that when Rousseau added the creature to his sketch of the environs of Bagneux, he had the very logical idea of transforming the church into a pagoda, imagining a small exotic tree, and engaging a Chinese as cowherd. The Douanier really did gather his elements everywhere!

Henri Rousseau: **Peasant Woman in the Meadow.**

Henri Rousseau: Sketch for **View of the Surroundings of Paris. Township of Bagneux.**

Banteng Ox. *In* Bêtes sauvages (Wild Beasts), *Galeries Lafayette, p. 60.*

Henri Rousseau: **The Haystacks.**

Henri Rousseau: **View of the Surroundings of Paris. Township of Bagneux,** 1909.

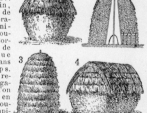

Le cant. a 20 comm. et 14.300 h.
meulard [lar] n. m. ou **meularde** n. f.
Grosse meule.
meulardeau [dŏ] n. m. Meule de taillandier.
meule n. f. (lat. mola). Corps solide, rond et
plat, qui sert à broyer ou à aiguiser : meule de moulin, de rémouleur. Tas de foin, de blé, etc., de forme généralement conique et recouvert d'une sorte de toit de chaume, que l'on élève dans les champs. Tas de bois recouvert de gazon, que l'on carbonise en plein air. Couche à champignons. Tas de fumier provenant des couches. Masse de minerai soumise à l'action du feu. Maçonnerie qui entoure le fourneau des fondeurs de cloches. Pain entier de fromage de gruyère, à cause de sa forme

Meules : 1. Permanente; 2. A courant d'air (coupe); 3. Ronde (temporaire); 4. Longue.

Le Larousse pour tous, *vol. 2, p. 177:*
"I sow at random."

In the Zoological Garden. The Camellia Hothouse."
Supplement to Le Petit Journal, *no. 331 (March 21, 1897).*

Henri Rousseau: **Lady in the Exotic Forest.**

T*he imagination is the eye of the soul," said Joseph Joubert. Is the soul merely the mirror of our memories? What must Rousseau have thought when he saw in* Le Petit Journal *Meyer's color engraving of the camellia hothouse in the Paris Zoological Garden? Did he imagine he had once taken a dream stroll, long, long ago, with his mother in a paradisal forest?*

"Wonders return in the Zoological Garden," said the Petit Journal *article. "This time, we are offered the enchantment of poetry. Imagine the most complete collection of camellias, all of them holding out their countless blossoms in delicately varied colors. . . . When you walk*

Henri Rousseau: **Lady with Umbrella in the Exotic Forest.**

among these splendid bushes, you think you are strolling in Paradise."

This was all it took to propel Rousseau's imagination toward Cythera—or, rather, toward Louisiana and the banks of the Meschacebé, or Mississippi, of which his mother had read him Chateaubriand's intoxicating descriptions in Atala. "Trees of all shapes, all colors, all scents, mingle, crisscross, rise aloft to heights that tire the eyes. Wild vines, begonias, colocynths interweave at the foot of these trees, scale their branches, clamber to the tips of twigs, shoot out from the maple to the tulip tree, from the tulip tree to the hollyhock. . . . From the bosom of these massifs, the magnolia lifts its motionless cone;

crowned by its big white roses, it rules the entire forest, and its only rival is the nearby palm tree, which gently waves its green fans. . . ."

These are descriptions of Rousseau's exotic promenades, whose lovely ladies emerged from the pages of some tedious fashion magazine. All we lack are the colors. Alas, for all my efforts, I was unable to get the original painting! The Barnes Foundation, which jealously guards the lady in her jungle, is so afraid that her pretty colors might fade if she escaped, that we are left only with the pleasure of imagining them on our own.

*"I don't know if you are like me,
but when I enter these hothouses and see
these strange plants from exotic countries,
I feel as if I have stepped into a dream."*
HENRI ROUSSEAU
to a *Comoedia* reporter

5 The Obsession with the Jungle

As a surprise, it was a beautiful surprise. For five years the Douanier Rousseau had been trying, in vain and in his vanity, to capture public attention by exhibiting his views of Paris and outlying landscapes at the Salon of the Independents. He had debuted here in 1886 with four paintings, including **A Stroke of Lightning on the Left Bank of the Seine, over Vanves.** Now, five years later, he tried a new stroke of his own. In 1891, at the seventh Salon, he exhibited an exotic composition entitled **Surprised!** A tiger, leaping through a thick jungle under the blasts of a storm, is electrified by lightning.

According to the journalists, this was the "most unmitigated success" along this line: an almost universal joke. "Monsieur Rousseau grows more stupefying each year," reported the young painter Félix Vallotton in *La Gazette de Lausanne.* "But he is commanding attention and, in any case, publicity. Backs are heaving and mirth resounding in front of his contributions. Furthermore, he's a terrible neighbor: the alpha and omega of painting. . . . Not everyone laughs, and some people who feel like laughing soon stop; it is always nice to see a faith, no matter what sort, expressed so ruthlessly."

To Become What He Has to Be

On July 10, 1895, at the request of Alfred Jarry, Henri Rousseau wrote a brief autobiographical note for *Portraits of the Next Century,* which Girard and Coutance were hoping to publish in their "Essais d'art libre" series. In this note, Rousseau made the following significant confession: "It was after a very rough ordeal that he managed to become known by the many artists around him. He has perfected himself more and more in the original genre that he adopted and is on the verge of becoming one of our finest realistic painters. . . . He will never forget the members of the press who managed to understand him and supported him in his moments of discouragement, and who helped him become what he has to be."

By caricaturing him, didn't these journalists (whose simplistic judgments he conscientiously pasted into his school notebooks) contribute to keeping him in his stereotypes? He had to be what he was. The "original genre" that he adopted, and that Félix Clément or Jean-Léon Gérôme advised him to cultivate, is both singular and original, particularly because (despite the inspira-

133

tions and the models he sought here and there in order to give himself greater authority), his only source was his personal vision of the world and of his arrested life. An "extra-ordinary" world, congealed so that he might escape the harsh reality of his miserable life, his wretched jobs as a bailiff and then a customs man, his family tragedies and amorous disappointments, his official failures as a painter.

"Discouraged, suffering the loss of my purest affection, not being at all materialistic, I found my life had become that of a philosopher who no longer loves anything but nature, the grand and beautiful nature that every sincere artist ought to venerate. Thus, I find myself quite happy when I am in nature," he wrote to his judge, begging him not to keep him in prison, to let him go back to his painting, so that he might "develop the natural intuition which was in me and which even my parents were unaware of."

Although calling himself a realist, the Douanier Rousseau detached himself from reality, ignoring it and making up for it by means of the psychological phenomenon of dissociation, which restored his infancy to him, along with its initial and initiating images.

The Real and the Imaginary

A esthetic contemplation is a dream stirred up," writes Sartre in his thesis on *The Imaginary*, "and the passage to reality is an authentic awakening. . . . People have often spoken of the disappointment of returning to reality. . . . In point of fact, this malaise is quite simply that of the sleeper who awakens. . . . Beauty is a value that can never be applied to anything but the imaginary and that involves the reduction of the world to nothingness in its essential structure. . . . To claim that one has an aesthetic attitude toward life is constantly to confuse the real and the imaginary." This, as Chateaubriand puts it in *René*, means projecting oneself into a consoling, compensatory life. It means plunging back into the credulous, irresponsible, astonished life of one's childhood: "Arise, you desired tempests, that have to carry René off into the spaces of another life!" It means, as Rimbaud was to state, rediscovering eternity, that *"mer* ('sea,' but homonymous with *mère*, 'mother') gone with the sun."

I know the lightning-shredded skies, the waterspouts
And undertows and currents; I know dusk,
The Dawn exalted as a flock of doves,
And I have seen things that man thinks he has seen.

Thus sang Rimbaud in *Le Bateau ivre*.

While painting this wild beast "surprised" by a storm in the primeval forest, the Douanier was actually terrified by the outbreak. He had to race over to the window and open it to remind himself that he was living in Paris. But, disappointed at being caught *in flagrante delicti*—i.e., escaping his obsession—he promptly returned to his canvas, so that he could wallow in the delights of this hallucination.

Picasso once gave a banquet for Rousseau in his Montmartre studio. Under a lantern that dripped wax on his head, the guest of honor ground away at his violin, singing in a tremulous voice: "Bang! Bang! Open up!" Meanwhile, Guillaume Apollinaire improvised a poem at the end of the table, which was crowded with bottles. When the Douanier finished his anguishing cantilena about the return of a dead man to his incredulous household, the author of *Alcohols*, slightly the worse for drink, solemnly declaimed his lines, with a glass in his hand.

> Do you recall, Rousseau, the Aztec landscape,
> The forests of mango and pineapple trees,
> Monkeys spilling the blood of watermelons
> And the blond emperor who was shot down there?
> The paintings you do—you saw them in Mexico,
> A red sun decorated the banana bushes. . . .

Actually, it was not Mexico that the painter recalled (as many of his biographers have thought), for he never visited this country, even though he may have blushingly let others believe he had been there. No, all he had to do was think of it: he never forgot the phantoms of his early readings, the ghosts that haunted his blocked memory, which rejected conventional knowledge and hovered in the new twists of history, the flight of time.

It was not time that passed. *He* was the one who fled. He changed the locations!

The Seeing Ear

The spell of exoticism is no recent thing in France. Long before Chateaubriand, it captured the hearts of rovers, captains, sailors, sending them across the ocean in vessels themselves drunk with faraway explorations.

In the year before the French Revolution, Bernardin de Saint-Pierre, influenced by Defoe's *Robinson Crusoe*, penned the fourth volume of his *Studies of Nature*, a novel imbued with the philosophy of Jean-Jacques Rousseau. This novel was entitled *Paul and Virginie*.

"I planned," Saint-Pierre announces in his preface, "great things in this little work. I tried to depict a soil and plant life different from those in Europe. Our poets have let enough of their lovers stretch out on the banks of streams, in meadows, and under beeches. I wanted to have them sit in the shade of coconut palms, banana bushes, and blossoming citrus trees."

Three years after the extraordinary success of the love of Paul and Virginie in Isle de Bourbon (later Réunion), Bernardin de Saint-Pierre took up Jean-Jacques Rousseau's theme of man's regeneration through total return to nature; this new work was called *Indian Hut.* And in 1792, the author was appointed director of the Jardin des Plantes in Paris, which he also filled with live animals, to the great joy of the Parisians.

No book had a more seductive impact on young Henri Rousseau than the poignant tale of the adventures of Paul and Virginie, which made so many children dream and weep late at night in huts deep in the remote countryside of France.

"The monkeys," Henri read, "play in the dark branches of these forests; they are visible because of their gray and greenish hair and their pitch-black faces. Some of them hang from the branches by their tails as they swing in the air. . . . One hears only shrieks of joy, and the unknown warbling and twittering of southern birds, who, far away, repeat the echoes of these forests."

If "the eye listens," one may also say that the ear sees and sees again. In the medieval tower of Laval, Rousseau's father ran a hardware store, where Henri was born on May 21, 1844, in the middle of the night, and where he spent his entire infancy. Here the little boy listened to his great-aunt Nono, who told him stories about wolves and children lost in the forest. He was all the more alive to these tales because he knew that the Beucheresse tower got its name from the fact that woodcutters passed through here on the way to the woods:

Listen, woodcutter, lower your arm!
Those aren't woods that you chop to the ground.
Don't you see the blood that gushes out,
The blood of nymphs who lived beneath the harsh bark?

This elegy by Ronsard, *Against the Woodcutters of the Forest of Gastine,* which the little boy had to study at school, was doubly distressing to him. Leaning over the crenels of the towers in his ancient town, watching the Mayenne flow toward the sea, he often imagined he was Tom Thumb fleeing the boredom of the nearby school. At the end of the 1859–60 school year, he was still in a low grade—at the age of fifteen—and managed to get halfway decent marks only in singing and drawing. At least these subjects offered him consolation for his scholastic failures, which he repressed by pretending to be Robinson Crusoe, René, or Paul, by dreaming of overseas voyages (as did, later on, Alain Gerbault, the great French navigator, who was also born in Laval).

"In the trees painted by the Douanier Rousseau," says Père Couturier in *Dieu et l'art dans une vie,* "the thing that touches us is that he was himself, that he revealed the liberty of his inner world. The liberty of his dreams, which open up whole realms to us. The liberties that he takes with reality, and that reveal our own inner realm, that make us cross our frontiers, that liberate us."

Isn't this the essential secret of Rousseau's art? His inner freedom, certainly, his refusal to submit to formal education, his ever new, childlike view of the world; but also his extreme rigor in translating the forms and colors reflected by the fairy-tale mirrors of his unconscious. "It's not me that's painting, it's my hand!" he said, just as Picasso stated, "I don't seek, I find." He only sought to render well what he found within himself and what his brush imposed upon him.

"Henri Rousseau, an old innocent, a true primitive, a Giotto with no trade or education, a customs inspector, to be sure, and probably as incapable of performing this job as that of an academician, but haunted by tropical landscapes, so dense, so pure, so fresh, so brilliant and candid, so far from us, so close to imaginary paradises and miraculous gardens that everything pales before their humility," writes Elie Faure in his *Histoire de l'art moderne.*

I

The Colonial Conquest

n 1845 a lovely book about the Jardin des Plantes came out. It was written by a Monsieur Boitard (the same surname as that of Clémence Boitard, who later became Rousseau's first wife). Reading the lyrical introduction, one instantly enters the state of mind that reigned in Rousseau's exotic creations:

"There is a place, at the very edge of Paris, which is surely the loveliest spot for refreshment and relaxation that one may encounter in this vast, dark, and tumultuous universe of Paris. There we find an admirable medley of calm, freshness, shade, burgeoning flowers, all the sweet joys of nature, all the admirable and haphazard features of the country, all latitudes, the birds of the sky, the ferocious beasts of the desert, the lion and the Bengali, the elephant and the hummingbird, the royal tiger and the Tibetan goat. Lend an ear! What amorous birdsong, what dreadful howling! Here the monkey families, obsessive, in love, and full of lovable whims. Farther on . . . What a story to tell, the tale of this charming little piece of earth, this miraculous garden, on the banks of the Seine. . . ."

How could Rousseau help being convinced that people would be interested in the depiction of this story, given the growing preoccupation of the Parisian public with the descriptions of African, Asian, and South American landscapes during the "colonial conquest"?

While leafing through the many French periodicals, with their words and pictures of far-away places, he found marvelous engravings by Riou, Gustave Doré, Benett, Bayard, Méaulle, and others, which revived the chimeras of his boyhood dreams. Such realistic engravings showing cruel scenes of animal life and the customs of the "savages," the strange natives, were initially based on summary sketches brought back by the explorers. From 1880 on, these engravings were generally based on photographs, as is often indicated in the captions of these journalistic drawings, these pictographic reportages.

How reassuring this was for a self-taught painter—so awkward at first with a pencil—who was making such a sincere effort to be even more naturalistic than the academic painters. There is only a short leap from the photo to the drawing, only an enlargement from the drawing to the painting, only a coloring from the engraving to the canvas! Rousseau perused these illustrations, for he concluded that an artist must be truthful, factual, in order to succeed with the public. Yet despite such artifices, the Douanier remained a master of visionary art. For it was the essence of this poet to re-create nature through its spellbinding effect on him. Since he was immune to reality, his sensory perception of the visible had a refracting impact: it radiated through the paradisal prism of his paranoic sensibility. Henri Rousseau imitated only the better to recall what he had imagined and what he was less afraid to project on the white canvas or the prepared wood—and the better to be ravished. Ultimately, he was not unfaithful to his instinctive rebellion "against the rules of art": perspective, correct proportions, verisimilitude, anatomy, relief, chiaroscuro, and real shadows. However, he clung to the subject he had taken on, the scene that had fascinated him, the ambience that had enchanted him—he clung to them with the same meticulous and religious craftsmanship as the cave artists, as primitive artists. He couldn't abstract himself, and so, once again, despite his realistic intentions, he became a Surrealist. "Of derisory interest from the Realist point of view, his works are quite simply Surrealistic way ahead of his time," André Breton said about Rousseau.

During the exhibition at the 1907 Salon d'Automne, in which the Douanier showed several exotic landscapes, he was angry at seeing certain paintings included in the Cézanne retrospective, canvases that Rousseau felt were unfinished. "You know," he exclaimed, "I could finish all these paintings." He understood nothing about the art of the innovators in his time. Baroness Hélène d'Oettingen (Roch Grey) was to help Guillaume Apollinaire gather memories of Rousseau in *Les Soirées de Paris,* January 15, 1914. She reports the conversations on art that she and her brother, Serge Férat, had with Rousseau.

"Whenever we asked what he thought about any kind of painters, he would always reply in a cold and confident voice, 'I don't hate him.' He hated no one except Matisse, who infuriated him: 'If it were at least funny! But it's sad, *mon cher*, it's horribly ugly! Look, I like this much better!' And he glanced at a perfume ad of a lovely, beaming face."

The Fame of the Orientalists

After 1885, after the conference that worked out the rules for the occupation of African territories by European nations, the explorations (like that by Savorgnan de Brazza, who had just founded Brazzaville) increasingly became military expeditions. The Marchand column met the Kitchener column in Fashoda in 1898; the Gentil, Foureau, Lamy, and Joulland "missions" came to the Chari in 1900. The French took root in North Africa and Indochina. The columns of illustrated periodicals exploited this appropriation by the army, then by colonialists, adventurers, and businessmen, of these new tropical and equatorial areas. The nationalistic pride of mainland readers and their insatiable curiosity about these strange universes—feelings already aroused by the grand exhibition of 1889—were flattered by these developments. It was the heyday of exotic illustrations; the renaissance of numerous vocations for Orientalist artists followed hard upon the travelers. In his drab neighborhood, Plaisance, along the railroad tracks of Montparnasse Station, the Douanier envied these voyagers. (One of them was named Henri-Emilien Rousseau.)

Exoticism in art is not the monopoly of the late nineteenth century. Lavish hunts for tigers, leopards, elephants, crocodiles had been painted in earlier centuries by Rubens, Lancret, Van Loo, Boucher, Stubbs, and others. In 1884, the Douanier Rousseau had obtained a card as a copyist, which admitted him to the Louvre, and to the Luxembourg, Versailles, and Saint-Germain museums. Passing through these galleries, he must have been struck by the realism of, say, François Boucher's *Lion Hunt*, just as he was impressed by the expressive wealth of the Gobelins, the tapestries representing trees and foliage, and the tapestries in Angers and in the Cluny Museum, especially the marvelous *Lady with the Unicorn*.

"I think I could be helped by a voyage that tore me away from the sight of everything that surrounds me and that inevitably prolongs my sorrow. . . . The novelties that pass before your eyes as countries change in front of you fill your imagination so effectively that griefs have no chance to resurge," wrote Rubens. And Delacroix keenly appreciated "the movement and variety" in Rubens's *Hippopotamus Hunt*.

Like Boucher or Rubens, Rousseau fled into his painting, exploring the flora of his interior world and tracking the fauna of his instincts and his repressed hostility. He found support in more recent painters, Géricault, Delacroix, Barye, and Gérôme, as he encountered their skittish wild beasts. But he never succeeded in capturing their science of movement, their technique of space and relief; nor did he manage to depict the glowing colors and the opulence of the Orientalist painters, whose reputation he envied and whose lavishness he craved. Even with the aid of a pantograph or decals, Rousseau's imitations of Delacroix, Rudolph Ernst, Charles Verlat, Gérôme, Alphonse de Neuville, and Devéria owe these artists only what a dream owes yesterday's experiences. By breaking free of his vigilance, his application, his preoccupations, his creation came to belong only to himself; and that was why his contemporaries had such a hard time recognizing themselves in his works. Only poets and a few great artists loved him right away. With his highly personal style of mastery of the universe, he was purely his own disciple. He couldn't launch a school; he was utterly betrayed by falsifiers. Such integrity cannot be imitated. Rousseau was a loner.

The Value of Photos

The huge Parisian department store Galeries Lafayette published a collection of Meisenbach Riffarth's photos of animals in zoos and in the Jardin des Plantes. Rousseau was drawn by the title: *Wild Beasts: Approximately 200 Amusing Illustrations Drawn from the Life of Animals, with an Instructive Text.* Leafing through it, Rousseau read about flamingos: "Their varied and picturesque postures have frequently induced painters to use them in order to lend an exotic air to certain landscapes." Rousseau bought the book and sneaked it into his studio. After his death, his daughter found it there. Its pages are smudged with green and black fingerprints (green and black were his favorite colors). The feverish fingers, smeared with the pigments that he hastily applied to the animals—he had often combed through these photographs, looking for the immutable animals to tenant his jungles, the visions suggested by the descriptions of their "natural habitats" and their behavior. Aside from helping him to draw his subjects, the photographs had the value of being eternal. Don't they capture forever some moment of natural history? Don't they arrest evolution, accidents, ephemeral life, disappearances?

"Actually," affirmed Delacroix in his journal on May 21, 1853, "let a man of genius use the daguerreotype the way it should be used, and he will rise to a height that we are unfamiliar with." He will contemplate the everlastingness of the world.

Before the Douanier, Courbet, whom Rousseau venerated, Delacroix, who was friends with Nadar and belonged to the Heliographic Society, Charles Nègre, Millet, and Degas (just to list the most important ones) had economized on studies and models by using photographs when they painted. It even seems that Manet employed photographic portraits to reconstruct the execution of Emperor Maximilian. And Gauguin himself, who had, after all, gone to the Polynesian source of his tropical inspiration, based his 1893 painting *Pape mae, Mysterious Water* on a photo: a Tahitian in a grass skirt leaning over to drink from a small waterfall among the ferns. Gauguin did not boast about using this method. On the contrary! He returned to Paris the following year, and, in his studio at 6 Rue Vercingétorix (not far from the studio soon to be occupied by the Douanier Rousseau), Gauguin told people that he had gotten the idea for his painting during a walk through the jungle. He said he had come upon a young wahine drinking from a spring. "She fled," he claimed, "like a frightened doe."

It's easy to lie when you come from far away!

Rousseau, incidentally, was once taken in by a practical joke that Gauguin played on him. Gauguin managed to persuade him that the president of France had asked him, Gauguin, to invite Rousseau to a grand reception at the Palais de l'Elysée. The Douanier's genius was finally to be recognized! Rousseau went to the palace. The joke was on him, but he tried to make a joke out of it. Coming home empty-handed, he claimed that the president had received him at the gate only to tell him, "I'm sorry, Rousseau, but you're not dressed up. You see, everyone's wearing a suit and tie. I can't let you in. Come back another time!"

Rousseau never entered the president's palace. But in 1961, his paintings were gloriously exhibited across the street in the Galerie Charpentier and photographed in all the periodicals, which couldn't praise him enough.

An Interior Exploration

The Douanier Rousseau went further than Gauguin, but the path he explored and then retraced was within himself. In 1891, Paul Gauguin had painted *The Loss of Virginity.* A young maiden lies naked on the ground and caresses a lubricious fox that grazes her head ("the fox is an Indian symbol of perversity," said Gauguin), while, in the distance, a Breton wedding party crosses the harvest landscape of Pouldu. Rousseau, who saw the great retrospective of Gauguin's works at the fourth Salon d'Automne (1906), took up the theme of that painting in **Beauty and the Beast.** The maiden is now a prostitute armed with a mirror (like that of the *Apocalypse* at Angers); she makes love with a wolf, who grunts with pleasure, but whose hindquarters are those of a donkey—inspired by a pornographic engraving by Devéria.

"The greatest explorer on this earth never takes voyages as long as those of the man who descends to the depth of his heart," Julien Green noted in his journal.

What erotic fantasies did the Douanier Rousseau pour into his exotic painting? Who knows? Didn't he unconsciously allow his wild beasts to play roles that he denied himself? Didn't he project his desires onto them—desires he was ashamed to admit, sexual repressions, secret obsessions, and inexpressible violence? Did he become a voyeur of animals in order to release his true feelings, to relax and unwind? Didn't he unwittingly depict himself in his creatures, who are so free in their jungle? Might not these belated obsessions express a return to Rousseau's Oedipal inhibitions, a relapse into childhood, a revival of his anxieties about competing with his father to seduce his mother, who hadn't known how to develop the natural intuition that was in him and that they had pushed back in the same way the Laval woodcutters hacked down the trees?

Abandoned by his parents, then by his wives and children, this little Tom Thumb, upon growing old, instinctively returned to his old forests, among his brethren, the untamed animals, whom he lovingly caressed with his egotistical brush. It was the brush of a sorcerer's apprentice, a brush that guided him just as the hazel wand guided the sorcerer's apprentice toward the underground water of his regrets.

Roch Grey eloquently evoked this poignant quest for a past resurrected amid disguises and uprootings. On many Sundays, instead of heading for a distant suburb, Henri Rousseau, old and tired, took a stroll to the Jardin des Plantes or the zoo. Accustomed to the poverty of his studio, whose only note of splendor was the sofa covered with the faded purple of Utrecht velvet, Rousseau paused in sheer admiration at the entrances of hothouses. Here were exhibited marvelous plants, cunningly arranged: umbellates, stripes, fan shapes, rockets, cascades like those of a torrent plunging from the highest mountain peak to the deepest chasm. Flowers with immaculate cups, with unimaginable corollas. And others like indefinable constructs, bursting in the green, opening and blossoming in an atmosphere where the artifice of heat under the iridescent glass vault made their exaltation even more intense than in their own climes. Next door, the lions were roaring, the tigers scenting the death of animals they wanted to pounce on. Huge serpents stretched out sadly under their covers, which were hand-me-downs from hospitals. Red-blue-and-yellow parrots shrieked insults over the heads of geese, who suspected nothing; and idle monkeys quietly pined away.

"Extreme ardor, almost terrifying dreams invaded the heart of this old genius, whose sheer presence contradicted the categories of convention. He did not tremble under the action of time; instead, embalming himself with tropical emanations, he sprang into life, taking on a new and unexpected audacity, a profound astonishment that guided his imagination. . . .

"Late at night, he went out, hugging the fences of hermetically sealed parks. Their clumps of trees and bushes, immeasurably magnified by some mysterious light, were wrapped in black, fantastic shadows. Their strange underbrush, isolated by his imperious gaze from its surroundings, became savannas, virgin forests, where the shrieks of rutting cats replaced the roars of lions and tigers. . . .

"These moments of extreme intoxication, equivalent to a supreme happiness, gave birth to his exotic paintings, whose value, excessive to the point of eccentricity, has never been sufficiently investigated, never evaluated in terms of its true importance."

The Douanier Rousseau, as he admitted, sauntered about in a semiconscious state as he passed through the hothouses of the Jardin des Plantes. "When I enter these hothouses and see these strange plants from exotic countries, I feel as if I have stepped into a dream," he revealed to Arsène Alexandre. He left these places with the irresistible desire to put this dream on a canvas, so that he might embrace it forever.

In 1844–45, around the time of Henri Rousseau's birth, the French writer George Sand discovered the tapestries of The Lady with the Unicorn in the depths of a château in Creuse, France. These tapestries were displayed at the Cluny Museum forty years later.

M. Boitard published a very lovely book on the Paris Jardin des Plantes, the new hothouses of which were described in Le Magasin Pittoresque: "When the trees of the two grand pavilions reach their glass roof, we will feel as if we have been whisked away to a forest in the New World." These images show where Rousseau found the inspiration and techniques for his exotic painting, which may be compared to those of the Gobelin artists doing their tapestries on The Ancient Indies. These hangings were based on the paintings that the Dutch artist van der Eckhout brought back from his voyage to South America with the prince of Nassau; they were also inspired by the animals in the Versailles menagerie of Louis XIV.

The Lady with the Unicorn. *Tapestry, fifteenth century. Cluny Museum. The lion (detail from Sight) and the leopard (detail from Touch).*

The Ancient Indies. *Gobelin tapestry, 1690. The French National Furniture Collection (Mobilier National).*

Le Jardin des Plantes *by M. Boitard. Illustrated work published in 1845 by J.-J. Dubochet.*

The Hothouses of the Jardin des Plantes, Paris. *Drawing by Freeman, in Le Magasin Pittoresque, vol. XIII (March 1845).*

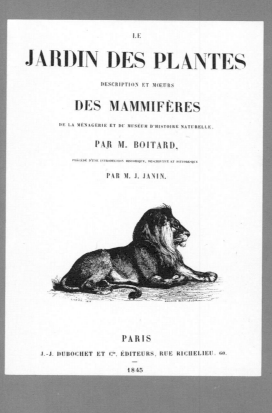

143

Delacroix: A Tiger. Pastel, reproduced on p. 11 of Eugène Delacroix à l'Ecole des Beaux-Arts *(March-April 1885), published by Ludovic Baschet.*

Rousseau's first big exotic painting was **Surprised!** *shown at the 1891 Salon of the Independents. It owes its tiger to Delacroix. The Douanier accentuates the tiger's leap with the slanting of the tree branches and plants and with the stripes of lightning and rain. The idea for these effects was supplied by the engraving in Le Tour du Monde. Rousseau also tries to intensify the terrifying impact by means of vivid colors, running from yellow to red, with added brilliance provided by the glazing. Deviating from most of the other critics, who were highly ironic, Félix Vallotton lauded this work as "the alpha and omega of painting." Rousseau, in order to succeed in expressing the movements of wild beasts, had practiced by copying those of Eugène Delacroix.*

Eugène Delacroix: Encounter Between a Lion and a Tiger.

Henri Rousseau: **Surprised!**

Henri Rousseau: **Copy of Encounter Between a Lion and a Tiger by Delacroix.**

*Cover of the album
Wild Beasts, special
publication of Les
Grands Magasins
"Aux Galeries
Lafayette," which was
founded in 1895 and
built in 1906 on
Boulevard Haussmann
in Paris.*

BÊTES
SAUVAGES

ENVIRON 200 ILLUSTRATIONS
AMUSANTES DE LA VIE DES
ANIMAUX
AVEC TEXTE INSTRUCTIF

Editions Spéciales des
GRANDS MAGASINS "AUX GALERIES LAFAYETTE"
Rue Lafayette, Boulevard Haussmann, Chaussée d'Antin (Opéra)
PARIS

*H*aving become like
Daudet's Tartarin
de Tarascon *in
exotic painting in the eyes of
his contemporaries, Rousseau
wondered how he could hurl a
Siberian tiger, locked in his
cage, on top of an Indian
buffalo. Rousseau's album
taught him that the buffalo,
"disdainful of fighting, . . . is
content to lower his powerful
head and receive the shock." It
was very simple: the artist
went back to a Pirodon
etching, which he enlarged
with the aid of a pantograph.
Next he added lush vegetation
bending under the weight of
fruits and flowers, as well as
the two animals. After
managing to sell his "hunting
picture" to Ambroise Vollard
in December 1909, he painted
a smaller replica, which
ultimately became part of the
Stchukin collection, so that
Russia regained this voracious
tiger, who came from the cold.
The first painting, on the other
hand, was eventually taken to
the United States. Rousseau's
work on this first painting was
interrupted by his stay in the
Santé Prison. In his cell,
Rousseau felt wretched because
he had lost the key to depicting
the fields and had not really
restored his unfinished
creatures to nature.*

*The Siberian Tiger and
The Carabao. In Bêtes
sauvages (Wild Beasts),
Galeries Lafayette, pp. 49
and 50.*

146

Henri Rousseau: **Fight Between Tiger and Buffalo**, 1908.

Eugène Pirodon: Royal Tiger
Attacking a Buffalo.
Etching, after Charles Verlat.
L'Art (1906), p. 120. The
engraving was reversed by the
photographer.

"The Jaguar's Dream." Poem
by Leconte de Lisle, published
in L'Illustre Soleil du
Dimanche (February 19,
1899).

LE RÊVE DU JAGUAR

Sous les noirs acajous, les lianes en fleur,
Dans l'air lourd, immobile et saturé de mouches,
Pendent, et, s'enroulant en bas parmi les souches,
Bercent le perroquet splendide et querelleur,
L'araignée au dos jaune et les singes farouches.
C'est là que le tueur de bœufs et de chevaux,
Le long des vieux troncs morts à l'écorce moussue,
Sinistre et fatigué, revient à pas égaux,
Il va, frottant ses reins musculeux qu'il bossue ;
Et du mufle béant par la soif alourdi,
Un souffle rauque et bref, d'une brusque secousse,
Trouble les grands lézards, chauds des feux de midi,
Dont la fuite étincelle à travers l'herbe rousse,
En un creux du bois sombre interdit au soleil
Il s'affaisse, allongé sur quelque roche plate ;
D'un large coup de langue il se lustre la patte ;
Il cligne ses yeux d'or hébétés de sommeil ;
Et, dans l'illusion de ses forces inertes,
Faisant mouvoir sa queue et frissonner ses flancs,
Il rêve qu'au milieu des plantations vertes,
Il enfonce d'un bond ses ongles ruisselants
Dans la chair des taureaux effarés et beuglants.

LECONTE DE LISLE.

Henri Rousseau: **Scouts Attacked by a Tiger.**

Delacroix: Fight Between Arabs and Lions. *Reproduced in* Eugène Delacroix
à l'Ecole des Beaux-Arts (*March–April 1885*), *published by Ludovic Baschet.*

In 1904, Rousseau made another hit at the
Salon of the Independents with his **Scouts
Attacked by a Tiger.** *He scrupulously pasted
this press clipping (February 27) into his notebook:
''What great pains went into this composition, where,
on top of huge plants whose outlines confusingly
resemble the giant pear trees of Aubervilliers, a horrible
drama is unrolling. . . . Ah! The green, fierce eyes of
this wild beast—the painter has devoted all his ability
to depicting them. And we are confused by so much
conscientious work, so much naïveté, so much concern*

Henri Rousseau: **Fight Between a Jaguar and a Horse.**

for truth, all thwarted, alas, by inexperience." Bringing back the tiger of **Surprised!,** *though this time coming from the right, Rousseau had found his subject in the reproduction of a Delacroix painting, just as he competed with Géricault in 1910 by having his white horse attacked by a jaguar. Failing to render the nervous and sumptuous vitality of the Romantic painters and hiding his inexperience with three-dimensional space in a tangle of palms and dark branches against the background of a dark sky, Rousseau manages, strangely, to make time stand still—by forgetting it!*

Théodore Géricault: Lion Attacking a White Horse. After a painting by George Stubbs.

Henri Rousseau: **Lion's Head.**

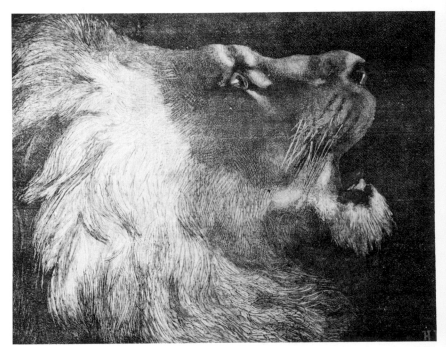

The Lion Hunter. An Atlas Lion. *Engraving in* Le Journal des Voyages (*November 16, 1879*).

Rousseau's depictions of lions come from different sources: the Cain statue in the Luxembourg Gardens, Delacroix studies, engravings in newspapers and books about the conquest of Africa, photographs of the Abyssinian lions presented to French President Carnot by Emperor Menelik. In each depiction, however, the Douanier tried to impose his own personality, to affirm his identity. He passed from puerile realism to heraldic stylization, from timidity to audacity, from awkwardness to accurate renderings of the king of the beasts, with whom he identified. "No other creature," he read in Wild Beasts, "combines such a high degree of strength, agility, beauty, and courage." Rousseau's ambition was to stand up against all his detractors by displaying equal imperturbability. He was indifferent to the perfidiousness of the serpent and the ambushes of hunters; he knew that he was the greatest painter of his time. "Ego nominor leo": My name is Rousseau! And I sign my name with a fine flourish.

Livingstone Struck Down by a Lion. *Engraving in* Les Grand Voyageurs de notre siècle, *Hachette, 1889, p. 239. (The engraving is reversed in the photograph.)*

2098. – PARIS – Jardin du Luxembourg

The Convalescent Lion. *In* Bêtes sauvages (Wild Beasts), *Galeries Lafayette, p. 72.*

Henri Rousseau: **The Lion Hunter.**

Eugène Delacroix: Lion Keeping a Serpent, 1846. Watercolor, reproduced in Eugène Delacroix à l'Ecole des Beaux-Arts (March-April 1885), published by Ludovic Baschet.

Henri Rousseau: **Lion Reclining.**

LE SALON D'AUTOMNE

On nous a dit : « Pourquoi L'Illustration, qui consacre chaque année aux traditionnels Salons du printemps tout un numéro, affecte-t-elle d'ignorer le jeune Salon d'automne? Vos lecteurs de province et de l'étranger, exilés loin du Grand Palais, seraient heureux d'avoir au moins une idée de ces œuvres de maîtres peu connus, que les journaux les plus sérieux (le Temps lui-même) leur ont si chaleureusement vantées.

— Nous rendant à ces raisons, nous consacrons ici deux pages à reproduire de notre mieux une douzaine de toiles marquantes du Salon d'automne. Il y manque malheureusement la couleur ; mais on pourra du moins juger le dessin et la composition. Si quelques lecteurs s'étonnent de certains de nos choix, qu'ils veuillent bien lire les lignes imprimées sous chaque tableau : ce sont les appréciations des écrivains d'art les plus notables, et nous nous retranchons derrière leur autorité. Nous remarquerons seulement que, si la critique, autrefois, réservait tout son encens aux gloires consacrées et tous ses sarcasmes aux débutants et aux chercheurs, les choses ont vraiment bien changé aujourd'hui.

CHARLES GUERIN. — Baigneuses.

Dans le clan des jeunes, Guérin est un des premiers qui se soient frayé une voie neuve... Les transcriptions de la forme féminine qui constituent son envoi principal ont ceci de très particulier qu'elles sont à fois familières, extrêmement réalistes, et pourtant sans vulgarité. Elles se relèvent d'une ingénuité de sentiment qui, dans une très forte mesure, les stylise...
THIÉBAULT-SISSON, le Temps.

PAUL CÉZANNE. — Les Baigneurs.

Paul Cézanne donne une sensation d'harmonie, de gravité. La nature est, chez Cézanne, solennelle et éternelle... Je ne puis m'empêcher de voir, en ce singulier et si simple artiste, une des plus belles incarnations de l'art de peindre... J'ai, devant ces œuvres si pures, la sensation de me trouver devant des aspects à jamais fixés... Je crois que cette peinture traversera les temps. Sa beauté est profonde et sereine...
GUSTAVE GEFFROY, le Journal.

Cézanne : le public va-t-il comprendre enfin ce langage rude et haut qu'on ne parle guère à ses oreilles ?... Il est temps de s'imposer l'âpre grandeur de cette œuvre inégale, mais toujours émouvante... Les Baigneurs michelangesques sous un ciel obscur d'été orageux.
LOUIS VAUXCELLES, Gil Blas.

HENRI ROUSSEAU. — Le lion, ayant faim, se jette sur l'antilope.

Ancien douanier en retraite, M. Henri Rousseau, auquel les Salons des Indépendants firent autrefois pour sa naïveté miraculeuse et sa gaucherie non apprise, a été accueilli avec un pieux respect au Salon d'automne, où la toile reproduite ici occupe une place d'honneur.
C'est une miniature persane agrandie, transformée en un énorme décor, non dépourvu d'ailleurs de mérite.
THIÉBAULT-SISSON, le Temps.

M. Rousseau a la mentalité rigide des mosaïstes byzantins, des tapissiers de Bayeux ; il est dommage que sa technique ne soit pas égale à sa candeur. Sa fresque n'est pas du tout indifférente ; je concède que l'antilope du premier plan s'adorne à tort d'un museau de brochet ; mais le soleil rouge et l'oiseau apparu parmi les feuillages témoignent d'une rare ingéniosité décorative.
LOUIS VAUXCELLES, Gil Blas.

J.-E. VUILLARD. — Panneau décoratif.

Un des plus beaux peintres que ces dernières années nous aient révélés ; une harmonie sourde et une perpétuelle fête pour le regard.
ARSÈNE ALEXANDRE, le Figaro.

ALCIDE LE BEAU. — Le long du lac (Bois de Boulogne).

Il est tout un groupe qui continue le mouvement impressionniste avec talent, mais sans assez changer à forme générale et l'aspect particulier des choses déjà vus par des peintres tels que Monet et Sisley. Ainsi MM. Manha... Alcide Le Beau (qui, lui, même, cette fois, avec Van Gogh). Ils sont peintres et ils exposent de belles toiles : on ne peut leur demander de découvrir la nature pour leur compte.
GUSTAVE GEFFROY, le Journal.

"Le Salon d'Automne." Article in L'Illustration *(November 4, 1905).*

I

n 1904, Rousseau's daughter Julia exhibited a decorative tapestry (no. 2435) at the office Salon of 1904. The father felt a bit jealous, so he conceived this painting as a high-warp tapestry. Measuring two meters by three, the largest painting he ever did, it was the attraction of the 1905 Salon d'Automne, where Fauvism was born. Rousseau's painting was even reproduced in L'Illustration, next to works by Matisse, Manguin, Derain, Rouault, Cézanne, etc. Incidentally, it was because of Rousseau's fauves (wild animals) that critics began speaking of the cage aux fauves, cage of wild animals, even though the Douanier had nothing to do with the Fauvists' quest for violent color and expressive stroke. His wild animals came from the periodical Musée des Familles or a book on the Jardin des Plantes. And his flora was so entrancing that it eventually influenced the Surrealist painter Max Ernst.

Max Ernst: Joie de Vivre, 1936–37.

Henri Rousseau: **The Hungry Lion Leaps upon the Antelope, Devours it, the Panther Anxiously Awaits the Moment When She Too Can Have Her Share. Birds of Prey Have Each Torn Out a Piece of Flesh from the Poor Creature Emitting a Cry! Sunset.**

Leloir: The Black Panther. *Engraving, in* Musée des Familles *(August 1842).*

The Jaguar. Cats of America. *Engraving, in* L'Histoire naturelle. Le Jardin des Plantes, *by Boitard, p. 185.*

Riou: Sandis and Lycopods (Horsetails). Drawing, in Le Tour du Monde, *no. 2 (1865), p. 170.*

Yuccas. *Drawing after nature by Freeman, engraved by Sargent, in* Le Magasin Pittoresque *(1856), p. 37.*

Eugène Delacroix: Fight Between a Lion and a Tiger. Pen-and-ink drawing, in Eugène Delacroix à l'Ecole des Beaux-Arts *(March-April 1885), published by Ludovic Baschet.*

A twofold subject frozen at the center of the canvas; scattered masses of largely stylized vegetation to give the impression of a foreground; a dark-green and black curtain of stalks and leaves rising toward the clarity of the sky, which is punctuated by the

Henri Rousseau: **The Lion's Meal.**

sun or the moon, interlaced to conceal the absence of a third dimension; flowers and fruits in bold, frank colors to make up for the artist's inability to depict this lighting naturally; undulations of sansevierias and high grasses to create the illusion of movement and life. These are the chief pictorial features of Rousseau's exotic compositions, whose dominant theme is the hunger of wild animals. Hunger and thirst also tormented the artist personally! In order to paint **The Lion's Meal,** the Douanier referred to Delacroix, Freeman, and Riou, freely digesting and disposing of their drawings, which turned into anamorphoses.

Young Jaguar.
In Bêtes sauvages
(Wild Beasts),
Galeries Lafayette, p. 152.

JEUNE JAGUAR. Le Jaguar, nommé improprement Tigre par les colons d'Amérique, ne doit pas être tout à fait inconnu de nos lecteurs, qui ont dû souvent l'étudier à travers les barreaux des cages du Muséum. Son pelage ressemble à celui de la Panthère, avec cette différence que les rosaces sont plus larges et ont généralement un point noir au milieu, c'est-à-dire constituent ce genre de taches que l'on a, d'un mot si juste, appelées « taches en œil ». L'animal est plus grand, plus trapu et plus fort que la Panthère, égalant presque la lionne sous ce rapport. Il habite l'Amérique, depuis le Rio-Bravo, qui sépare le Mexique des États-Unis, jusqu'à la chaîne de Tandil et Patagonie, par 40e de latitude sud. Il ne se trouve pas aux Antilles. C'est un carnivore très redoutable qui décime les animaux domestiques et ne craint pas de s'attaquer à l'homme lui-même. Il est surtout commun dans les vallées boisées du Brésil, dont il traverse aisément les cours d'eau à la nage. On lui fait, d'ailleurs, une chasse très active, parce que sa fourrure est très recherchée et constitue une branche importante de commerce entre l'Amérique et l'Europe. Dans certaines régions du nouveau monde, presque régulièrement au lever et au coucher du soleil on entend le cri du jaguar retentir à une très grande distance. Il consiste en un son flûté, avec une très forte aspiration pectorale, ou bien, quand l'animal est irrité, en un râlement profond qui se termine par un éclat de voix terrible. L'animal ne quitte sa retraite que la nuit, s'embusque dans les buissons, attend sa proie, se lance avec son dos en poussant un grand cri, lui pose une patte sur la tête, de l'autre lui relève le menton, et lui brise ainsi le crâne sans avoir besoin d'y mettre la dent. Quoique de grande taille, il grimpe sur les arbres avec autant d'agilité que le Chat sauvage, et fait aux singes une guerre cruelle. La nuit, rien n'égale son audace, et sur six hommes dévorés par les Jaguars, à la connaissance de M. d'Azara, deux furent enlevés devant un grand feu de bivac. Il va sans dire que le jeune Jaguar ci-dessus est loin d'être aussi terrible.

The New Rotunda for Wild
Animals in the Jardin des
Plantes. *In* Le Petit Journal
(March 31, 1895). *Above right:*
The Sapote Canal. *Drawing by
Riou, engraved by Sargent, in* Le
Tour du Monde, *no. 2 (1865).*

Jumah Fighting with Leopard.
*Drawing by Riou, engraved by
Barbant, in* Le Tour du Monde,
no. 1 (1888).

Criticizing the menagerie of the Jardin des
Plantes, the reporter for Le Petit Journal
wrote: "The wretched creatures trudge in
circles, dazed and ill, in a narrow box where they
bump into all the corners. Do not be astonished if
our painters usually depict lions falsely, either sitting
or reclining. What else can they do, how else can
they get them to pose?" To restore these wild beasts

Henri Rousseau: **Negro Attacked by a Jaguar.**

to freedom and reinvent their natural surroundings, the Douanier consulted travel periodicals as well as his album, in which he found a young jaguar playing with his keeper. "In certain regions of the New World, one can hear the jaguar's shriek from very far away almost regularly at sunrise and sunset. . . . This creature leaves his den only at night to hide in the bushes and lie in wait for his prey; leaping upon the victim's back with a loud shriek, the jaguar thrusts one paw on the victim's head, while the other paw pulls up the chin; he thus breaks the skull without having to use his teeth. . . . Needless to say, the young jaguar shown above is far from being that dreadful." And yet, when Rousseau reproduced him, he felt scared. "He was so upset by the strength of his own visions," reports Uhde, "that, feeling oppressed and fearful, he had to open the window to draw his breath."

157

Henri Rousseau: **The Port of Algiers.**

Rouargue: Algiers
(General View). *Engraving.*

Bombled: The Veiled Warriors. *Engraving in*
Le Journal des Voyages (*March 18, 1894*), *p. 168.*

Henri Rousseau: **The Tiger Hunt.**

Triumphal Evening. *Engraving based on a painting by Rudolph Ernst (1895), published in* Le Monde Illustré *with this caption: "Intrepid hunters have just killed a tiger, who is expiring at their feet; their proud, bold posture truly justifies the title that the painter has given to this composition."*

Rousseau's maternal grandfather, Captain Jean-Baptiste Guyard, took part in the conquest of Algeria and died at Bône in 1832. Was it in memory of his forebear that the Douanier painted this peaceful bay in Algiers? He could see it only in his Paris studio, where he studied old engravings in order to reconstruct the bay as he had imagined it when his mother praised her father's derring-do. Rousseau always traveled into himself. "It seems," wrote Michelangelo in a madrigal, "that I always use my own image when I think I am doing his. . . ." In his own way, the Douanier was no less introverted.

Two tiger hunts by Rudolph Ernst had attracted the Douanier: Triumphal Evening at the 1895 salon, and The Royal Tiger Vanquished at the 1897 salon. The engraving in Le Monde Illustré triggered a cathartic process of pictorial reimagining in Rousseau. Thus the precise relief of the engraver's drawing gives way to synthetic forms, which Rousseau's inward gaze retained. He carries us from the empirical reality to the esoteric imagery of the death of this, the cruelest of animals; and the Arab hunters seem to mourn the tiger, as though grieving for its virile aggressivity.

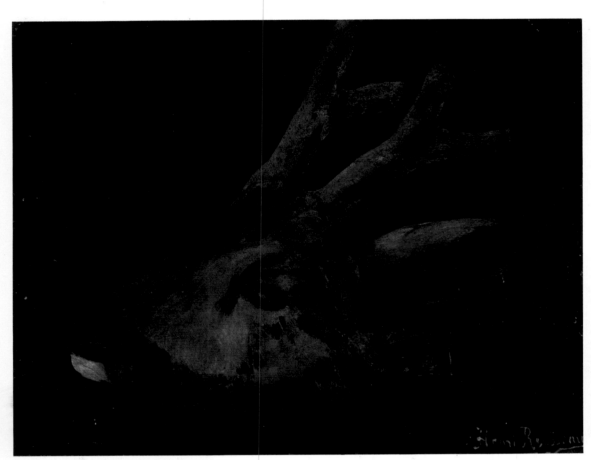

The Virginia Deer of the Savannas. *In* Bêtes sauvages (Wild Beasts), *Galeries Lafayette, p. 91.*

Henri Rousseau: **Head of Virginia Deer.**

Géricault: Piece of Game

Henri Rousseau: **The Owl.**

Reading at Night. *In* Musée des Familles *(July 1842).*

Touched by the expressive tenderness of the Virginia deer of the savannas ("originally from the tropical region of America"), Henri Rousseau painted the most poignant of his still lifes on the dark background of two awkwardly joined wooden panels. A lovely harmony of yellows, fawn colors, and blacks; under the glaucous eyes, a red dot: the impact of death; under the nicely rounded muzzle, the tongue drawn out by a final thirst. Had Rousseau seen Géricault's Piece of Game, to which this painting is germane? Was Rousseau's mysterious owl, which he took from the Musée des Familles, done in memory of his friend Jarry, who loved this nocturnal bird?

Henri Rousseau: **The Waterfall,** 1910.

Under an immense paulownia, each leaf of which is autonomous, a compressed waterfall climbs toward the light-brown rocks, from which it ought to be plunging, and conceals the feet of a black woman with bare breasts. Below, it conceals the hoofs of a dazed stag and a bashful antelope. At the center of the canvas, five grass huts scratch the pale sky with their crests, surmounted by crossed flowers. To the right, spurting from a small curtain of luminescent plants, a second paulownia, a younger one, holds up three unexpected pink flowers like hands. This scene is as beautiful as a botanical garden reflected in the eyes of an intimidated child!

Stag *and Antelope. In* Bêtes sauvages (Wild Beasts), *Galeries Lafayette, pp. 20 and 14.*

Monkeys Playing in an American Forest. *Illustration in* Cent récits d'histoire naturelle. *Hachette, 1884.*

"The Monkey Palace at the Jardin des Plantes." Postcard.

The Little Monkey *and* Coconuts, *illustrations for* Swiss Family Robinson, *"the tale of a father shipwrecked on a desert island with his wife and children," 1837.*

Henri Rousseau: **Exotic Landscape,** 1910.

A Funny Divinity.
In Bêtes sauvages
(Wild Beasts),
Galeries Lafayette, p. 131.

Aside from what we have said about the Hindu worship of this animal, we must add that . . . the langurs or leaf monkeys are so accustomed to following their whims . . . that they truly seem to command like masters.'' This caption in Rousseau's album (from which he took and modified a monkey, letting it eat an orange) may have reminded the painter of a passage in Jules Verne's The Mysterious Island: "Gideon Spilett asked whether these agile quadrumanes might not regard him and his companions as degenerate brothers!" These quadrumanes' resemblance to human beings, emphasized in the books Rousseau read as a boy, and pranks at the Jardin des Plantes made the painter laugh. "He was brimming with love for creatures and things, and there was so much peace, so much sunlight that no sadness could grab hold of him," said Uhde. The Douanier seldom lost his typical Angers gaiety and his youthful humor.

Henri Rousseau: **Zizi.**

Butikofer's White-Nosed Cercopithecus.
In Bêtes sauvages (Wild Beasts),
Galeries Lafayette, p. 186.

The Monkey. *Detail from* Smell,
tapestry of The Lady with the Unicorn.

At the Cluny Museum, before the monkeys of The Lady with the Unicorn, *and in the Louvre, where Rousseau observed Chardin's* Painter Monkey, *the Douanier's idea was confirmed: the monkey imitates man! Thus he shows a langur fishing and a macaque playing with a shovel. Rousseau freed the macaque from its cage, but without giving it any space. He respected the colors in his album, but found it easier to use the name Zizi for Butikofer's white-nosed cercopithecus. This delightful monkey, whose eyes are as brilliant as those of the live animal, offers a broad, beaming grin to its zealous portraitist. "I like to make my paintings smile," Rousseau confided.*

Henri Rousseau: **Tropical Forest with Monkeys**, 1910.

LE MACAQUE. Vous est-il déjà arrivé d'entendre dire de quelqu'un de très laid : « Oh! le vilain macaque »? A-t-on eu à raison, jugez-en vous-mêmes par le portrait ci-dessous, ce genre de singes ne peut pas pour disputer à l'Apollon du Belvédère le prix de la beauté. C'est peut-être pour cela que l'animal ci-dessus, son habitat à voir les photographes se dessiner pour lui, louera. En Europe, il y en a une colonie sur les rochers de Gibraltar; et les officiers anglais défendent sévèrement à leurs hommes de lui faire la chasse. En Asie, les macaques remontent jusqu'au plateau du Thibet, dont le climat serait mortel pour presque tous les autres singes. Par contre, ils se s'étendent pas en Afrique, au sud du Sahara. Les espèces de leur séjour sont certaines

The Semnopithecus *and* The Macaque. *In* Bêtes sauvages (Wild Beasts), *Galeries Lafayette, pp. 19 and 50.*

The Kinkajou.
In Bêtes sauvages
(Wild Beasts),
Galeries Lafayette, p. 178.

Henri Rousseau: **The Gibbon Apes.**

The Gibbon Apes. *In* Bêtes sauvages
(Wild Beasts), *Galeries Lafayette, p. 130.*

Henri Rousseau: **Joyous Jokesters.**

Henri Rousseau: **Monkeys in the Virgin Forest.**

Amused by the precise data his album supplied about Gibbon apes ("incomparably superior to acrobats who soar from one trapeze to another, Gibbon apes traverse enormous distances through the empty space between two widely separated trees"), the painter awkwardly stuck them in a rapid sketch; the distances in it are no greater than that of the veterinary's arm span. In his painting **Joyous Jokesters,** Rousseau depicted monkeys scratching themselves and knocking over a bottle of milk; he also gave them anthropomorphic faces. However, in the forest of orange trees above, he tried to be as naturalistic as possible. The kinkajou at the left is as faithfully reproduced on its branch as the two Himalayan monkeys at the center. But we wonder how they can hold on to orange trees without their hands (while enhancing the decorative effect of these trees). Human hands are difficult enough to draw, and how much more so monkey hands! But it really doesn't matter. Perhaps these lucunae and these awkward features are the least original part of Rousseau's genius.

The Himalayan Semnopithecus. *In* Bêtes sauvages (Wild Beasts), *Galeries Lafayette, p. 37.*

Henri Rousseau: **Wader.**

The Numidian Crane. *In* Bêtes sauvages
(Wild Beasts), *Galeries Lafayette, p. 134.*

.E FLAMANT (Phoenicopterus roseus Pall.).

The Flamingo. *In* Bêtes sauvages
(Wild Beasts), *Galeries Lafayette, p. 171.*

Egyptian Lotus. *In* Le Magasin Pittoresque
(1834), p. 281.

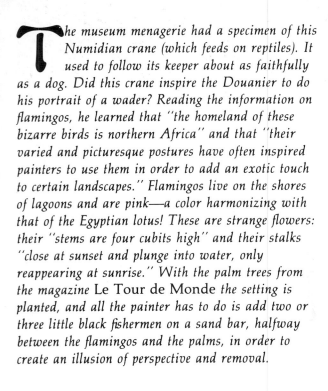

The museum menagerie had a specimen of this Numidian crane (which feeds on reptiles). It used to follow its keeper about as faithfully as a dog. Did this crane inspire the Douanier to do his portrait of a wader? Reading the information on flamingos, he learned that "the homeland of these bizarre birds is northern Africa" and that "their varied and picturesque postures have often inspired painters to use them in order to add an exotic touch to certain landscapes." Flamingos live on the shores of lagoons and are pink—a color harmonizing with that of the Egyptian lotus! These are strange flowers: their "stems are four cubits high" and their stalks "close at sunset and plunge into water, only reappearing at sunrise." With the palm trees from the magazine Le Tour de Monde the setting is planted, and all the painter has to do is add two or three little black fishermen on a sand bar, halfway between the flamingos and the palms, in order to create an illusion of perspective and removal.

Henri Rousseau: **The Flamingos.**

Palm Trees in Ucayali, Amazon.
In Le Tour du Monde,
no. 2 (1865), p. 190.

Henri Rousseau: **The Banana Harvest.**

General View of the Village of
Bahele. *Detail of drawing by Taylor
based on a sketch by Lieutenant
Berttoloty. In* Le Tour du Monde, *no.
2 (1866).*

A Village in Condé. *Drawing by Riou
based on sketches and photographs by the
ensign of the* Victor Giraud. *In* Le
Tour du Monde, *no. 2 (1886).*

The Banana Harvest *most likely had, at best, a second-degree
model: reminiscences of engravings depicting the conquest of Africa.
Rousseau painted this picture more freely, using a limited range of
greens and yellows; his heavier strokes added a certain thickness, a tropical
weight to his banana bushes, and a highly coherent mystery to his rather
spontaneous composition. On the other hand, during this final year of his
life he outdid himself, singing a swan song in his painting of an Indian
being attacked by a gorilla. He perfected the linear purification of his
plants, the stunning freshness of his coloring, its harmonious balance. Uhde
said that Rousseau knew how to blend the terror and beauty of these
primeval forests, which children dream about. The terror is no more
terrifying than the terror an advertising vignette showing a bison hunt
seeks to arouse.*

Henri Rousseau: **Exotic Landscape**, 1910.

*Advertising vignette
by Liebig showing
a bison hunt
by Indians.*

Henri Rousseau: **Beauty and the Beast.**

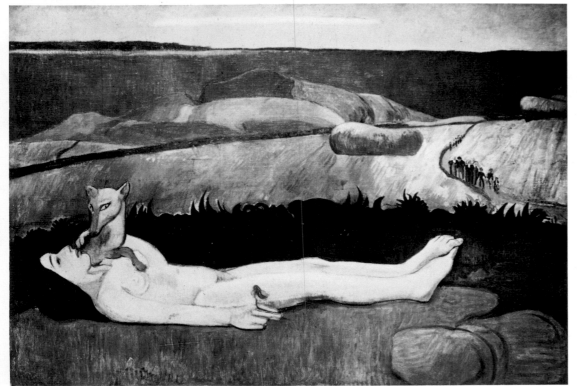

*Lithograph by Devéria for Gamiani,
the novel attributed to George Sand and Alfred de Musset.*

Paul Gauguin: Spring Awakening,
or The Loss of Virginity.

Léonard Foujita: The Lion Tamer and the Lion.

Alphonse de Neuville: A Surprise.
Drawing, reproduced in Le Tour du Monde.

(The Barnes Foundation, Merion, Pennsylvania.)

Henri Rousseau: **Unpleasant Surprise.**

I t's curious,' Renoir once said to me," according to the art dealer Ambroise Vollard, " 'how repulsed people are when they find painterly qualities in a painting. One painter who must make their flesh creep more than any other is the Douanier Rousseau! That scene from prehistoric times, and, right in the middle, a hunter in a department-store suit, carrying a rifle . . . But can't we enjoy a painting only in terms of harmonious colors? Do we have to understand the subject? And what a lovely tone in this Rousseau painting! Do you recall a nude woman facing the hunter? I'm certain that even Ingres wouldn't have disliked that!' " Is this so certain?

Rousseau's **Unpleasant Surprise** astonished and exasperated the visitors to the 1901 Salon of the Independents. The Douanier pasted this review from La Plume in his scrapbook: "If one feels the dismal necessity, one must also delight in the view of the naïve figures drawn and painted by Monsieur Henri Rousseau. This artist may be the only one to deserve the fine title of an Independent. . . . Ingenuously, he goes along as best he can; poor, spontaneous means serve him more or less; he approaches in his own terms the form he wishes to depict. . . ." His devices are simple, to be sure, but their metamorphosis is his alone! If he borrows the Eve from Lévy-Dhurmer's triptych Eden in order to situate his nude female, and a bear and a hunter from Alphonse de Neuville, Rousseau still manages to assimilate them in his own terms. Likewise, he brings together Gauguin and Devéria to make **Beauty and the Beast** come together in secret.

173

*"Isn't it true that
we need an explanation for paintings?"*
HENRI ROUSSEAU
to a *Comoedia* reporter

6 Allegories and Dreams

The Douanier Rousseau's most celebrated works, the ones that most draw our attention and our intrigued complicity, are his dreams and allegories. They are also the most unusual, the most sibylline—and the most deceptive if, in trying to understand their astonishing seductiveness and their amazing resonance within us, we rely purely on the simplistic expression of their theme (generally in verse) by their painter, who insisted on offering precise definitions of the subjects of his canvases.

"Isn't it true that we need an explanation for paintings? People don't always understand what they see," Rousseau told a *Comoedia* journalist, who objected that the Douanier's allegorical paintings were very clear. "That's true, but it always helps to have a few lines of poetry," replied the painter.

What power do his paintings exert over us? How do they catch us off guard? Why are we impressed by their mysteriousness?

Dreams or Puzzles

A dream is a picture puzzle," Freud explained. "Our forerunners made the mistake of trying to interpret it as a drawing. That is why dreams struck them as absurd and unimportant." Likewise, the Douanier's thematic lucubrations and chromatic aberrations struck his contemporaries as ridiculous; almost all of them considered him silly. What were his sources? How are we to decipher these puzzles?

Roger Shattuck was one of the latest of many authors to study Rousseau's work since the death of the painter and the birth of his legend. This critic knew how to approach Rousseau from the angle of reading his paintings without being taken in by their deceptive aspects. In *The Banquet Years*, Shattuck observes: "The atmosphere of these works participates in some rite or magic ceremony. The nature of the emotion they transmit is like the hieratic emotion aroused by Egyptian art. Yet, our fear, like Oedipus' fear in front of the Sphinx, is mixed with a feeling of irreverence and defiance. For the indifferent spectator, the religious rite can easily assume the aspect of a formal absurdity, and one must recognize the existence of an art that can both disturb and divert." Establishing numerous parallels between Rousseau, Satie, Jarry, and Apollinaire,

Shattuck then quotes Huizinga: "The enigma, to pinpoint one of the cultural contexts often neglected in regard to art, was originally a religious diversion, and any distinction between seriousness and playfulness is made impossible here." Shattuck concludes, "Rousseau's most fascinating compositions are enigmas in the profound meaning of the term: truly grotesque, they provoke a timid laugh followed by a long astonishment. Once you have seen them, you never forget them."

Doesn't this also hold true for certain haunting dreams that pursue us and hold us, maintaining the immanence of our emotions and tying us to the past?

According to Shattuck, Rousseau's creativity is characterized by a "magic realism," of which he correctly says that "Chirico and Dali, sensitive to his influence, carried this technique to its perfection." All well and good. But is it enough to speak of magic to explain the magnetism of this technique? We have to find out where it comes from, we have to learn the solutions to the enigmas of this inspired and instinctive illusionist, this magician of the palette.

We can certainly cite Toulouse-Lautrec and question the interest in a more assiduous interrogation, a more determined investigation of the origins of such allegories or the gestation of such euphoric and nightmarish dreams. We can go along with Toulouse-Lautrec's crass judgment that "painting is like shit; it smells, you don't explain it." Similarly, in more poetic terms, we can share Picasso's annoyance: "Why does everyone have to understand my painting? Do people try to understand the singing of birds?" Did the Douanier himself try to analyze what he happened to paint? He simply painted—*voilà!* He had a gift, he was gifted! Let's not complicate his life, damn it!

Delacroix once stated, "The primary merit of a painting is to be a feast for the eye." In this respect, we may say that Rousseau's visions, commemorations, and celebrations are quite delightful. On the other hand, we cannot forget that, as Leonardo da Vinci remarked, "painting is a mental thing." The portraitist of the *Mona Lisa* affirmed that "one can neither love nor hate something without first getting to know it." And, incidentally, didn't Olivier Messiaen try to study the singing of birds with an ornithologist's patience? Don't we appreciate a Bach partita more when we know the score? The graphism of hieroglyphs is beautiful: Champollion convinced us of this by deciphering them! And how can we neglect the research of anthropologists and archeologists on the meaning of rites and myths in oral and gestural traditions, the customs and fashions of social life today and in the vestiges of forgotten cultures? Couldn't we learn a lot from paleontology about the origins of art?

Once revealed, the "mysteries of art" repeat the sensory adherence that is enriched by the pleasures of the mind. One pleasure in art is to read between the lines and under the brush strokes. Thus, understanding is joined to perception, as fragrance is joined to a flower, or its song is joined to a bird. These are the answers one might have offered the two great painters of the "*demoiselles*" of Montmartre and Avignon, painters who, no less than Delacroix, thought about their painting techniques and their motivations, their deliberate and underlying intentions, their discoveries and their labors.

Let me make myself clear: this study aims at demystifying the Douanier only in order to enter his world more effectively and to discover his ideographic revelations more accurately, to grasp their sense and nonsense. Knowledge helps to see, to see again, to savor fully.

The Myth of the Cave

No indeed, not everything has been said throughout the years that some men have been painting and others have failed to understand why they admire them and how they are reflected in them. For fear of clarity, people are content with silhouettes created by light. They ignore the invitation offered by Socrates through his myth of the cave: namely, to leave their obscurantist habits. This myth, reported by Plato in his *Republic,* applies so accurately to Rousseau's way of seeing that we are surprised to rediscover in his work the full analytical and symbolic pertinence of the myth.

"Imagine the condition of our own natures under the influence of education or lack of education," Socrates tells Glaucon. "Picture men who live in an underground home with an entrance wide open on the daylight side. Inside the cave, they have been chained since their childhood in such a way that they remain in the same place, seeing only what is in front of them. The light comes from a fire that burns behind them, high and remote. Now, between this fire and the prisoners, imagine a small road rising, and across it, we have to imagine a small wall blocking it, the way puppet masters put up a wall to maneuver all sorts of man-made objects, statues, animals of stone or wood. . . ."

Socrates then explains to Glaucon that these prisoners are like us: they regard as true absolutely nothing but the shadows projected on the cave wall facing them. And if they were forced to turn their eyes toward the light, their eyes would hurt and they would turn them back to the shadows, to which they would continue attributing a more certain reality than the true objects from which these shadows emanate.

Alfred Jarry disappeared; so did, unfortunately, his portrait by the Douanier Rousseau. All we have left are a few newspaper descriptions—for instance, this one by the *Gaulois* critic (April 11, 1895): "If you haven't seen the unspeakable exhibition of Monsieur Henri Rousseau, who certainly didn't use his hands to paint, if you haven't seen his portrait of a man, with tawny owls and other owls, on a window ledge in broad daylight, if you haven't seen this zinc man with a dirty face, against the background of a yellow drapery daubed with all sorts of people and animals, then you haven't seen anything."

And what was written under this painting? A quatrain that Jarry might very well have helped the painter to write; for once, the verses are purely symbolic:

Muses whose dreamy foreheads are lapidary triangles,
Decorate his eyes with your image so that he may always please
Readers seeking in all sincerity
To agreeably savor whatever gives light.

From what marionettes and under what light did the Douanier draw his Ubuesque and Platonic forms, his emblematic figures? How did his "Muses" inspire him?

Where was **The Sleeping Gypsy** before she came into this lunar desert? Where did the spectral lion (with his mane brushed the wrong way) come from to sniff her here? Rousseau may have gotten the overall theme and subjects from Louis Matout's painting *Boghari Woman Killed by a Lioness,* which the Douanier had seen ten years earlier at the Luxembourg Museum. But how did he translate, transport, betray the inspiration by transfiguring it? Jean Cocteau answers this question in his preface to the catalogue of the John Quinn auction, on October 27, 1926.

"We are in the desert. A dream carries off the Gypsy lying in the middle ground, or else a dream has brought her from far away, the way a mirage brings the river to the fourth level and a lion to the third level, a lion that sniffs her without being able to reach her. Perhaps the lion and the river are dreamed by the sleeper. What peace! Mystery believes it is all alone and it strips itself naked. . . . The Gypsy sleeps, her eyes are shut. . . . Could I depict this immobile flowing figure, this river of oblivion? I think of Egypt, which knew how to keep its eyes open in death, like divers in the sea. . . . Where does something like this drop from? The moon . . . Also, there may be a good reason why the painter, who never forgets any detail, puts no print in the sand around the sleeping feet. The Gypsy didn't come here. She *is* here. She isn't here. She is in no human place. . . ."

The dreamlike atmosphere of **The Sleeping Gypsy** is Surrealist ahead of its time, before the Dadaist vogue, before its *nouvelle vague.* Rousseau wrote to the mayor of Laval, offering to sell him **The Sleeping Gypsy** because he would have been happy if "the town of Laval had a souvenir of one of its children." In his letter, the Douanier tried to describe the painting in a realistic, an Orientalistic manner. Here is his description: "A wandering Negress, playing the mandolin, with a jar at her side (a vase containing drinking water), sleeps profoundly, exhausted. A lion happens to come by, sniffs her, but doesn't devour her. The moonlight is very poetic. The scene takes place in a completely arid desert. The Gypsy wears Oriental garb."

Incidentally, isn't it surprising that she can at the same time wander, play the mandolin, and sleep profoundly? And if the desert is completely arid, why do we see a river flowing by? The explanation is given: "moonlight." Cocteau is not wrong. The painter is the victim—or the beneficiary—of a twilight mirage.

In his original French text, Rousseau misspells *jarre* (a large, glazed earthenware jar) as *jars* (gander). Still more surprisingly, he adds the word *vase.* What is the male goose doing here? Might he be an involuntary association with Leda's swan, who would no more dare to abuse the Gypsy than would this chance lion, though he is petrified with the desire to devour her? "The feline, although ferocious, hesitates to leap upon its victim, who, worn out with fatigue, has probably fallen asleep," said the painter in the caption he suggested for the Salon of the Independents in 1897.

W The Forbidden and the Possible

What probabilities and what curious chances! Who can calculate the reflective and repercussive force of an incident in a dreamer's life?" asks Baudelaire in *The Artificial Paradises* ("An Opium Eater"). "Who can think, without trembling, of the infinite widening of circles in the spiritual waves caused by a chance stone?"

Actually, "chance" is merely a modest word to cover our fears of taking a chance with our latent desires and unspeakable anxieties: our desires for love, to keep from dying:

The precipice is under ice;
Such is the light surface of your pleasures.
Slide, mortals, never lean upon it.

This was the advice to which Pierre-Charles Roy was inspired by Lancret's painting *Skating*.

With Rousseau's incredible juxtaposition of horizontal and moonlit flat tints, the rainbow streaks of the mummified sleeper near her almost funereal impedimenta (the stick, the lute, and the jar), with the unevenness of the levels (desert, river, mountains, and sky) of his vision, both syncretic and disruptive, the painter manages, despite his associations, to dissociate himself from the drama. He has congealed the elements and actors of this drama so intensely as to prohibit their fateful encounter and executory denouement. The artist keeps us in an incantatory silence on this side of angst. We almost feel as if we were looking at one of the Egyptian frescoes of Anubis, the god of death, with his jackal's head, leaning over a mummy before carrying off the soul. (We have seen these pictures in our schoolbooks on the civilization of the pharaohs.) Thus, we are watching "the struggle beween Eros and death, between the instinct for life and the instinct for destruction, such as takes place in the human species. . . . A strange struggle, indeed; because on the one hand, civilization kills us in order to make us live by using the sense of guilt for its own benefit and against us; and on the other hand, we have to loosen its hold in order to live and have pleasure." (Freud, *Beyond the Pleasure Principle*.)

Here is the magical essence of this painting: it situates us in an ambiguous no man's land, where our sexual appetite dares to approach the limit of the forbidden and the possible. Sneaking up to the half-slumbering Gypsy, her eyes half shut, her body rigid though abandoned, one might hear these lines from Valéry's *Charms*:

If with your advanced lips
You prepare the nourishment
Of a kiss in order to appease
The inhabitant of my thoughts,
Do not hasten this tender act,
A sweetness of being and nonbeing,
For I lived to wait for you
And my heart was only your footsteps.

The sacralized expectation of this priestess of the night puts the lion on the defensive, and he suddenly distrusts her less than the violence of his immemorial instinct.

"If one could only arouse all these echoes of the memory simultaneously," said Baudelaire, "they would form an agreeable or painful concert, but it would be logical and without dissonance." It was in order to rediscover the resonances of his emotional memory that the Douanier Rousseau looked at photos and images, like the Greeks, who enter death backward in order to keep their past before them, and like the Egyptians, who had painters depict their environments and life stories in their future tombs. After all, Rousseau told the mayor of his native town that he would like Laval to keep "a souvenir of one of its children." And what did he recall when painting this masterpiece? Will we ever know? Did he ever find out himself, some day, some night?

The Cathartic Effect of Photos

"One photographs things in order to drive them out of the mind," said Kafka. "My stories are a way of closing my eyes." Noting this comment by the author of *Metamorphosis*, Roland Barthes writes (in *Camera Lucida*), "Photography must be silent. . . . Absolute subjectivity is achieved only in a state, an effort of silence. . . . Say nothing, close the eyes, let the detail alone rise to the affective consciousness."

With regard to the role of photography in Rousseau's dreamlike and allegorical painting, I must quote what Gide said in his *Journals* on January 29, 1943: "Photography was able to liberate painting by a sort of catharsis." This word, "catharsis," which Aristotle used to suggest the purification experienced by spectators during a dramatic performance, is employed by modern-day psychoanalysts to designate phenomena of abreaction, "a discharge of emotion attached to a previously suppressed experience"—a discharge that finally allows the patient to enter into direct contact with his unconscious and to grasp the full meaning of its symbolic manifestations. Psychoanalysts also use the term "insight," corresponding to "intuition" (from latin *in* and *tueri*, observe, see). The cathartic effect that certain photos and certain reproductions of paintings had on the Douanier is absolutely astonishing. With their help, he freed himself from his adventitious apprehensions and his secondary defenses so that he might make a direct connection with his fleeting fantasies, his suppressed obsessions, and suddenly *see* them in himself, with his resistance gone, see them "unadorned, in the simple array of a beauty that one has just torn from sleep," as Racine's Nero says.

Let us take **The Dream** (1910) and its description:

Yadurgha in a love dream,
Having gently fallen asleep,
Hearing the sounds of a musette
Of a well-meaning charmer,
While the moon reflects,
On the flowers, the greening trees
The wild serpents lend an ear
To the gay tunes of the instrument.

Who is Yadurgha? According to the painter, she was a young Polish woman he was smitten with, Yadwigha. (The different spelling of this first name is based on a misprint in the catalogue of the Salon of the Independents.)

Like children who make up stories based on a word whose consonance entrances them, the Douanier once again invented fables in order to make this dream more credible. Now, Yadwigha is actually nothing but a postcard reproducing the *Nude Woman Reclining* on a lion's paws, exhibited by Louis Béroud at the Salon of 1906. This woman was lascivious and appealing; she closed her eyes with pleasure under the breath of a purring lion. She was a model of sensuality, which the academic painter used to titillate us. Rousseau's woman, on the other hand, is so stylized and ethereal that she becomes unreal, like those purely imaginary giant lotuses surrounding her. She stretches her arms toward the lions and the snake charmer (to attract them or keep them away?); but they are dumbfounded by this apparition, as afraid to approach it as the serpent is. Besides, we are told that the snake charmer is "well-meaning." He would never give in to bad thoughts; this is a "lovely dream"!

And the Louis-Philippe couch? Where does it come from? Quite simply, from the Douanier's studio. André Dupont, an art critic, was astonished at the unexpected presence of this couch in the jungle. Rousseau prosaically told him, "I am answering your letter promptly in order to explain the reason for the couch in question. The woman asleep on this couch dreams that she has been brought into the forest upon hearing the sounds of the charmer's instrument. This is the reason why the couch is in this painting. Let me thank you for your fine appreciation; and if I have preserved my naïveté, it is because Monsieur Gérôme, who was professor at the School of Fine Arts, as well as Monsieur Clément, director of the School of Fine Arts of Lyon, have always told me to preserve it. You will no longer find this astonishing in the future. And I have also been told that I am not of our century. . . ." His dreams are age-old. Those gentlemen were right in advising him to preserve his naïveté, just as his mother advised him to act sensibly. He made up his mind to it, and thus he remained.

Besides, would he have been able to act otherwise if he had happened to feel like being an Impressionist, even a Hyperrealist? Could he have accepted his sexual impulses, robbing the Negro of his horizontal-striped loincloth across his lower abdomen? Could he have lowered the elephant's trunk and the arm of the enraptured monkey? Could he have allowed the serpent to reach its objective or the lions to leap upon their prey?

Yadwigha's eyes are open. She has the satisfied air of a desired but inaccessible deity. She is naked but clad in moonlight on the purple of her couch altar. She offers herself to our eyes only, like the goddess of reason, who didn't have to know the reasons of the heart or the senses.

In a March 5 letter to Ambroise Vollard, announcing that **"The Dream** is done," Rousseau complained, "I have to prove to obstinate people, who only want to hear evil and who only want to harm me, that I am not what they think. My heart has suffered greatly. . . ."

The Hypnagogical Power of Images

No, he couldn't get Léonie to love him or her aged father to give him her hand, despite the assurances of his honorability and talent that he requested from Vollard, Apollinaire, and Uhde in order to convert the girl and her father. "He collected these testimonials to present them to the lady's father and thus give him written proof that he was as sensible a man as anyone else," Udhe reports.

After the opening of the salon, Rousseau regained confidence. Numerous newspapers mentioned his **Dream.** Their articles were "all generally good, this will encourage me," he wrote on March 20, adding, "Ah, if only I were younger! I would be very happy; why didn't my parents thrust me into the path of art?" (In other words: Why did my father, like Léonie's, despise me or fear my profession of artistic painter?) In the same letter, Rousseau promised, "I will try to do even better." This can mean both that he would be wiser than an image and that he would try even harder to be faithful to the images he could "leaf through" on Place Hardy in Laval. Images fixing him at the edges of protected gardens and carefully arranged hothouses in Laval and Angers, where the decent citizens did their best to grow the exotic plants and trees—coleus, sansevieria, phoenix, screw pines, oranges, and paulownias—that he drew. He helped himself along by making attentive visits to the hothouses of the Jardin des Plantes as well as the Palmarium in the Zoological Garden. He also soaked up the colonial ambience of the salons of 1900 and the illustrations in travel journals.

Discussing some 1830 book engravings that were redone as watercolors, Leon Werth, who discovered them in a secondhand bookshop, wrote about **The Dream** (in La Phalange, April 20): "I do not know whether Monsieur Rousseau was gazing at similar images when he did his painting. Besides, these engravings are far superior to his painting. But he must have looked at them at some time, he must have been moved by them. And perhaps they have been in his memory for years now, ever since his childhood. . . ." This, at last, is a truly lucid insight by an art critic contemporary with Rousseau! By observing these engravings, the Douanier learned how to give order to his compositions. The freshness and decorative qualities of his works (features to which his mistakes in drawing make us more sensitive) are not unrelated to those engravings. "His art had purity; in the female figures, in the construction of trees, in the harmonious song of different tones of the same color, Rousseau has a style belonging solely to French painters," said Apollinaire in *Les Soirées de Paris.*

Rousseau had certainly seen prints of women lying on couches (for instance, Titian, Velázquez, Greuze, David, Goya, Cabanel). But it was Béroud's nude, probably because of the lion, that provoked the resurrection of Rousseau's fantasies, which were given fresh life by the wine he had begun to drink (he ordered it directly from warehouses on the Quai de Bercy). Engravings and photographs then acted on his memory, which was sluggish and hence liberated from its customary and monotonous surroundings, its dismal and disappointing environment. These photos and engravings were an exhilarating catalyst—like the sip of tea mixed with madeleine crumbs that revived the happiness of Proust's buried childhood among the flowers in the garden of Combray, those in Monsieur Swann's park, the water lilies of Vivonne, "and the good people of the village and their little homes and all Combray and its surroundings, all this, taking form and solidity, emerged, both the town and the garden, from my cup of tea." (Marcel Proust, *Remembrance of Things Past.*)

The Douanier Rousseau made reference to images only in order to redo the images that haunted him, and of which his visual memory was exacerbated by his rejection of reality such that he had to make this whole imaginary field materialize. His illuminations thus exert a strange hypnagogical power on us. They make us lose our foothold and, as long as we gaze at his paintings, our contingency. They give us a sense of immanence with his creation, which captures us, the way the cave shadows fascinated Socrates' troglodytes. And all the more so in that this re-creation, through its marvelous harmony, gives us a spellbinding impression of balance, of stiff, stark peace, Dantesque silence. In short, something otherworldly, a cosmos preceding the Biblical tale of our sin. Hence, we are not ashamed to be naked: Eve has not yet tasted the forbidden fruit from the tree of the knowledge of good and evil; she has not yet given in to the serpent's charm; Adam has not yet slid into his misdeed, his sin of pride.

The Charmer by Alexandre-Jacques Chantron (who had studied with Bouguereau and whose "flesh colors" Rousseau admired) is provocative. It is she who seduces the serpent: she has already tasted of the forbidden fruit and hidden her nakedness under a blouse that is scarcely held in place by her loose belt. All she has left of the earthly paradise is a palm which is negligently held in her left hand, and which she seems to lift like a tail; her breast swells with the desire to be bitten as she awaits a venomous kiss from the serpent coiled in her right hand. This canvas was both disturbing and academic, and the Douanier amended its eroticism in order to restore the woman to her original Genesis. He turned her into an **Eve in Paradise,** shown at Bernheim in the posthumous exhibit of 1912. Rousseau depicts Eve in an environment of palms and snakeplants (sansevierias); she is totally unclad, unhesitatingly ready to receive the apple that is denounced by God but still innocent. Her stiff hair, the awkwardness of the nude, the ludicrousness of the pink-and-blue serpent, are striking evidence that she is no more of an expert than the painter himself. Several moments from now, when the reddening sun has vanished, the world will rock under the wrath of Yahwe, who will drive this poor Yadwigha from Eden. Alone before her temptation, simple and silly in her untamed nudity, this Eve manages to amuse us while moving us. She arouses our compassion for her obvious lack of experience in the face of such a great risk. Whereas Chantron's woman makes us want to embody, to identify with, the serpent hissing around her head, to give in to the prickling of the flesh. But how sad one is after animal coitus!

The Creation of the World

Night has fallen upon the earth. The moon has risen over the waters. This is the hour when the shadows of the forest are transformed into ritual apparitions under the eyes of children who have been visited by the sandman, and in the superstitious spirit of the naïve, unobscured by agnosticism or scientific arrogance. "Modesty is to merit as shadows are to figures in a painting; modesty gives merit strength and relief," observed Jean de la Bruyère. Rousseau's **Snake Charmer** is merely the negative shadow of Eve, translucent and iridescent like opal, in Lévy-Dhurmer's *Eden*. But what a somber apparition this cat-eyed Indian is! A mega-counterpart of the photographic reproduction of the Lévy-Dhurmer painting (he collected it in the Panorama-Salon of 1889), which massively infringes upon the light of the full moon and its curling, parallel reflections in the lagoon. Everything unites to reinforce the impenetrable mystery: The Mephistophelian pupils—holes in the black rectangle of the head, emphasized by the flute of Pan. (Who can tell whether they shine with fury or terror at being surprised by the painter?) The fantastic and jagged plant above her. The heavy undulations of the boa constrictors, suggested by the cover of Rousseau's *Wild Beasts* album; the high grasses and large branches that mimic their disorderly movements. The thick bunches of heart-shaped paulownia leaves, punctuated by three yellow beaks of parrots who seem embarrassed about coming from the pages of the Larousse. The vertical rod of a plant stem: too slender to support such a fan of leaves. And, contrasting with the massive background of vegetation (so hermetic that we wonder what can be swarming on the other side of the water), a young spoonbill, flushed with pleasure at having flown from the pages of Rousseau's album ("wooded marshes are their usual habitat"): beyond the ever-present sansevierias, gold blazes reaching toward two high royal-blue campanulas, the spoonbill sights round hortensia shrubs as pink as its own wings and artificial crest. Finally, right in the foreground, an edging of fine herbs, like tapestry borders, among which the artist has embroidered his full name (first, middle, and last), thus signing and dating this antediluvian fresco, of which he was quite proud.

Rousseau had good reason to be proud. And Madame Delaunay (the mother of the young painter), who had commissioned this painting after telling Rousseau about her voyage to the Indies, was delighted with the results—even if she didn't recognize the sacred banks of the Ganges.

Shakespeare said that nature lacks the power to equal the strange creations of the imagination. Nature preceded man, and the stars preceded the animals. That was how God created the universe; and at every phase of Genesis, "He saw that it was good." Consider the story of Creation that Henri Rousseau learned at elementary school in Laval. (The school was founded and directed by the Abbé Jules Dours, and at the opening of every school year a mass for the Holy Ghost was conducted. In 1851, Rousseau received his first reward—there would be few others—a certificate of merit in religious instruction.)

In the beginning, everything was "without form and void": the Spirit hovered over the face of the waters. "Let there be light": the separation of light from darkness, then the separation of the firament from the waters. "Let the earth put forth vegetation": the appearance of grasses and fruit trees. "Let there be lights in the firmament of the heavens": "the greater light to rule the day, and the lesser light to rule the night; he made the stars also." Then came the snakes and birds, then the beasts big and small. Finally, God said, "Let us make man in our image, after our likeness; and let him have dominion over the fish of the sea, and over the birds of the air, and over the cattle, and over all the earth, and over every creeping thing that creeps upon the earth."

Well, Rousseau had only to emulate Him, because He taught us how to create! And it was in this order of creation that the Douanier, who could have no better reference than God Himself, composed his paintings, reserving for man or his helpmeet the final phase, the place of honor.

"You are delightful in every way, my little Joséphine, my beloved, you are intelligent, and I would like to develop your intelligence, which is as useful in a woman as in a man. On the one hand, even more so in a woman, because she has to be his companion, charming him with her grace, her beauty, her knowledge, and on many occasions, she even has to help him. God gave women the same gifts as men, but they are not developed. . . ." Thus Rousseau wrote to his second wife to be.

There is a photograph of the Douanier, almost as dignified as God the Father, holding his palette in front of the unfinished painting **The Poet and His Muse.** In this photograph, one can see on the canvas the barely visible silhouettes of Guillaume Apollinaire and his mistress, Marie Laurencin, with trees flourishing all around. Man and woman appeared only after the plants!

So, Rousseau stands before the formless void of the virgin canvas or white page, his head swarming with his creative project and its central theme. Next, having divided the earth and the heavens, he grants his favors to plant life, but not without foreseeing a place reserved for the principal subject, human or animal. He uses photos or engravings to outline his subject, using a pantograph or tracing from a counterdrawing. Then he fills in his flora, doing all the same tones in the painting at the same time. As Soffici wrote in *La Voce,* "He spreads his tones over the canvas one by one; first, for instance, all the greens, then all the reds, then all the blues, etc." The light of the "lights"—sunset or full moon—has no influence on these previously established colors. And the "animals" will sometimes have trouble camouflaging themselves here!

There is a strange quality to his paintings because of these chromatic juxtapositions, which owe nothing to the subtle investigations of the Impressionists or Pointillists; they might be related to the techniques of decorative simplification employed in cloisonné enamels.

"One bit of advice: don't paint too much after nature. Art is an abstraction, take it from nature by dreaming in front of nature and think more about the resulting creation; this is the only way to ascend toward God, by doing as our Divine Master does: create," wrote Gauguin to Schuffenecker on August 14, 1888. The Douanier unconsciously gave himself this advice as he constituted the expression of his visions and confirmed his own affirmation, in order to safeguard his independence despite the temptation of ubiquitarianism in the visible and supernatural worlds. "I am a bit of a spiritist," he enjoyed saying, half jokingly, so that he might appear as if he didn't really believe in it—though he willingly took part in spiritualist seances.

"Those who knew Rousseau," said Apollinaire, "recall his taste for ghosts. He had run into ghosts everywhere, and one of them had tormented him for more than a year when he was a customs inspector. Whenever our good Rousseau was on duty, his familiar ghost stood ten paces away from him, annoying him, poking fun at him, letting out smelly farts, which nauseated Rousseau. Over and over again, Rousseau tried to shoot the ghost; but a phantom cannot die again. Whenever Rousseau tried to grab him, the ghost vanished into the ground and reappeared somewhere else. . . . Rousseau also stated that Catulle Mendès had been a great necromancer. 'He dropped by my studio one day,' said Rousseau, 'and took me to a house on Rue Saint-Jacques; on the third floor, there was a dying man whose soul floated about the room in the shape of a transparent and luminous worm.' "

Illusory Allusions

Allegories, for Rousseau, even more than dreams, were the art of saying something different from what he seemed to be saying. This, incidentally, is the very principle of the allegory, a word derived from Greek: *allos* (other) and *agorein* (speak in the public square). When Pythagoras, for instance, asked that the fire not be poked with the sword, what he meant was that one should not give weapons to inflamed people! And why did he use this allegory to convince his listeners? Quite simply because the metaphorical image speaks more effectively to the common folk than the verbal, orthographic image of abstract words. The inventor of the multiplication table and the square of the hypotenuse thus doubled his idea: he made fire blaze instead of anger.

The Douanier Rousseau reversed this procedure. He displayed general concepts in order to avoid revealing all too objectively a real and personal sentiment that moved him. The nobility and generosity of the themes of his allegories mask an inexorable yet inexpressible desire—inexpressible because it might have seemed presumptuous—ambition. The lowly customs man—lowly in physical stature, lowly in position—was very eager to be known by the whole world and recognized by the big people in this world. He didn't want to be "lowly"!

What does he give us to see in theory?

The Republic in person; **Liberty Inviting Artists to Take Part in the Twenty-second Exhibition of Independent Artists** (he placed himself in the top rank of these artists); **The Centennial of Independence** and **The Carmagnole,** where one celebrates one's Liberty tree; **The Representatives of Foreign Powers Coming to Salute the Republic as a Sign of Peace,** which Rousseau also called **The Union of Peoples.**

What does he actually let us divine? The fact that people come to salute and acclaim him. "For him, glory is something necessary and quite natural," observed Uhde.

Let us listen to the Douanier Rousseau himself. In 1910, at the end of his career, he finally admitted, quite naïvely, the true meaning of his allegories by offering the second term of his comparisons.

"When I learned about the founding of [the Salon of] the Independents, I set off to find the president, who at the time was Gendarmerie Captain Dubois-Pillet. He explained this institution to me, and since I liked the idea, I joined [this salon] and renounced the official salon. All in all, it's the finest society and the most legitimate, because every member has the same rights."

"And is that where you had most of your successes?" the sly journalist asked him.

"Damn it, yes! I can say that I had my successes. Look. The year I painted my allegory of **The Centennial of Independence,** I depicted our ancestors in short pants, dancing to celebrate the arrival of liberty, and in a corner of my composition, I wrote out the opening lines of an old French song: '*Auprès de ma blonde, qu'il fait bon, fait bon, fait bon . . .*' Well, my dear friend, when I arrived at the opening, everybody was dancing in front of my painting and singing '*Auprès de ma blonde*'! Everybody was happy. And later on, when I painted **The Union of Peoples,** where you see the representatives of foreign powers coming to salute the Republic as a sign of peace, truly, I couldn't leave the exhibition because there were so many people coming to shake my hand, surrounding me, congratulating me. And do you know why? It was because this was the exact time of the Hague Conference, and I hadn't even thought of it; it was a nice coincidence. Ah! How many letters I received from all countries! I got letters from Belgium, Germany, Russia, everywhere, you know!"

In sum, people were honoring not the Republic, but him! The reality, however, was quite different. To begin with, he was not admitted to the official salon. And the showing of his allegories was a resounding flop, humiliating and appalling. Wilhelm Uhde is precise about it: "At no comedy, in no circus, have I heard people laugh the way they laughed at Rousseau's painting **The Sovereigns.**" (This was Uhde's name for **The Representatives of Foreign Powers.**)

Rousseau's hope and conviction that the French government would buy this work collapsed under the mirth and banter of the public. "Anyone claiming to find qualities [in this painting] would have been dragged off to Charenton [insane asylum]," adds Uhde, who elsewhere describes the Douanier as "above it all and indifferent." Rousseau had mentally cast himself in the part of the lion, "superb and generous"; but he was nothing more than an old, grotesque lion. And even the donkey was kicking him.

A symbol of courage, strength, and pride, the lion frequently also symbolizes the masculine ego. A man identifies with the lion in order to express his great need for individuation, as shown by Marie-Louise von Franz in Jung's book *Man and His Symbols.* However, Rousseau's lions are different. They seek refuge at the feet of a matriarchal Marianne in **The Republic** (whose incarnation he borrowed from a simple advertising vignette in the newspaper *La République Française*) and in **The Representatives of Foreign Powers,** or under the protection of the female angel in **Liberty Inviting Artists.** These allegorical lions seem more terrified than terrifying, more tame than wild. They do not so much resemble the powerful lions of Cain and Barye, creatures rampant in the Luxembourg Gardens and the Tuileries; or those in Bartholdi's *The Lion of Belfort* or Dalou's *Triumph of the Republic* on Place de la Nation; or those in the group on Place de la République. Or even the wild animals in bronze or stone that guard the fountains (like the one on Place Daumesnil), porticoes, and proud monuments of Paris. Rousseau's lions are more like those sleepy watchdogs with droopy ears and pendulous jowls that you find in lower-class neighborhoods—dogs that don't even know whom to bark at.

Metaphorical Currents

The pacifistic and democratic ideals of the Douanier Rousseau are the same ideals (and equally nationalistic) as those of the Third Republic, which was founded just before he began painting. The allegories representing and vulgarizing those ideals were in vogue at the time. These allegories dispensed numerous symbolic rewards to the official artists, but revenues in name only. Stimulated by his lofty notion of his own genius and by the modesty of his financial resources, Rousseau tried to make himself a "modern painter." He was carried away by the metaphorical current, which, in 1878, bore him to the World's Fair. The fair was dominated by the construction of the Trocadéro palace, which sent Mercié's *Renown* out into the world. This angel with a trumpet was to turn up again in the sky of Rousseau's **Liberty Inviting Artists.**

During his visit to the 1878 fair, the Douanier could delight in the colossal head of Frédéric Auguste Bartholdi's *Liberty Enlightening the World.* Standing on the Champ-de-Mars, the *Statue of Liberty* was dedicated to French-American unity. (I might note, in passing, that for Rousseau, all foreigners were Americans, inhabitants of the New World!) And in his views of the Grenelle bridge and the Passy footbridge, he included the replica of the *Statue of Liberty.*

Liberty is synonymous with independence. So when Paris announced its centennial celebration of the birth of the First Republic, Rousseau decided to paint his **Centennial of Independence.** The magnificent festival was to take place on September 22, 1892. Immense parades of Parisians would follow allegorical chariots, and the populace would finish the day at dances organized by the municipal councils. When Rousseau heard about these preparations, how many earlier celebrations was he reminded of?

Did he, for instance, recall the folklore celebration of September 6, 1857, on Place de Hercé in Laval, to commemorate the arrival of Charles VIII in that "good town"? The inhabitants, disguised in period costumes, had crowded around the floats, the most beautiful of which was that of the weaving industry (one of the principal resources of the *département*, Mayenne). Did Rousseau also remember the great industrial and agricultural fair of 1852, and the lovely galleries that were built for this occasion on Place de Gast? These galleries were subsequently used to distribute the awards of his *lycée:* the pupils walked toward the galleries, led by the band.

Singing, dancing, celebrating, having a good time—a fine way to overcome the boredom that serious people impose upon life, upon official art.

Rousseau's **Centennial of Independence** (1892) reproduced the popular joy of a farandole (a popular Southern French dance) engraved by Angevin Méaulle for the illustrated supplement to *Le Petit Journal.* Rousseau's **Liberty** was invoked a bit opportunistically: "O Liberty, always remain the guide of those who, with their work, wish to aid the glory and grandeur of France." But little attention was paid to these two works. To make up for this lack, the Douanier hoped he would win the competition to decorate the town hall of Bagnolet.

For this reason, in his second version of the **Centennial of Independence,** he left out a decorative panel entitled **The Carmagnole.** Its lovely round lanterns had elicited an unpleasant response from a journalist: "A customs inspector exhibiting compositions that a man at a shooting gallery would regard as attractive targets." Rousseau was confident. Alas: on November 10, 1893, the Bagnolet jury, made up primarily of the three painters Puvis de Chavannes, Merson, and Roll, far preferred the projects of Rachou, Vauthier, and Béroud. The Douanier was right back where he had started from! To say he was hurt by this rejection is an understatement. Mortally wounded, he got even the following year by sending **War** to the Salon of the Independents. It was an apocalyptic war, which, in its artist's own words, "passes, terrifying, leaving despair, tears, and ruin everywhere."

Roll, one of the Bagnolet jurors, had painted a *July 14, 1880,* a joyous scene taking place on Place de la République. Rousseau did not forget it. But the main influence on **The Representatives of Foreign Powers** came from a reproduction of Gervex's *The Distribution of Rewards at the Palace of Industry.* This shows the line of foreign delegations filing past French President Carnot, who is up on a dais, surrounded by his ministers under a canopy (at the exposition of 1889).

Bloch, in *The Reception of Italian Sovereigns at City Hall on October 18, 1902,* shows (on the left) a canopy raised in front of the Paris Hôtel de Ville against one of the large statues and (in the background, to the right) the Cathedral of Notre-Dame. The Douanier similarly divided his painting in two: on the one side, the solemn canopy; on the other, the statue of Etienne Dolet on Place Maubert. Why Etienne Dolet and Place Maubert? Because in 1546, at this popular intersection, the authorities burned several heretics at the stake. One victim, the printer Etienne Dolet, "one of the glories of typography," was "martyr to his bold and aggressive opinions," as Rousseau learned from the Larousse. The Douanier, who resisted the academists and had become their scapegoat, was thus, indirectly, paying homage to himself. Besides, he liked the song to which he made the little children dance around the statue:

> I wonder what they're thinking of
> When they extend Rue Monge.
> What's the good of parks,
> What's the good of statues
> If they demolish our streets
> At Place Maubert?

This square is very important in the history of Paris. According to Auguste Vitu's *Paris*, it used to be the "meeting place of students, boatmen, out-of-town merchants and goodwives, as well as the center of the academy of the suburban parlance. Didn't Parisians use to refer to a man of gross speech as having learned 'his compliments on Place Maubert'? And this was, in fact, the title of the first catechism of Parisian billingsgate."

Rousseau's painting, a veritable jigsaw of postcards of the statue, the square, the dancing children, the austere heads of the personalities, forms an assemblage both bizarre and scandalous, as amusing as it is shocking. It challenges the Cartesian notions of space and pictorial time—like most of the paintings by the Douanier, who was unconcerned about such matters, indifferent to the flow of time and the distance of places.

Juxtaposition and Simultaneity

In the preface to Rousseau's farce *A Visit to the World's Fair of 1889*, the Dadaist writer Tristan Tzara discovered in the Douanier's writings an astonishing juxtaposition of scenes in no logical sequence. He offers an interesting thought about this irrational succession of snapshots characterizing Rousseau's visionary spirit:

"The principle of juxtaposition and simultaneity that rules his painting, in which the commonplaces are sublimated and exceed their conventional limit, was instinctively discovered by Rousseau on the level of a temporal awareness which happened to be that of the painters of the Quattrocento. Rousseau wandered into our civilization, where he was confronted with the spectacle of perpetual discovery; it was by formally adapting his mentality to the material conditions of his time that he produced the mythical strangeness and empiricism of his conception of the world. Those who talk about Rousseau's ingenuousness may believe that this single word can resolve a problem that, in human terms, is infinitely more complex. A certain form of maturity of vision, strengthened by his concordance with historical experience, which Rousseau believed was life experience, may have a certain effect on people who I do not say are simple, but who are disposed to call a spade a spade and are content with evoking things. Such people may be induced to scarify themselves, to envelop themselves in a shell that is impervious to outside influences. Faced with the complexity of life, such people take refuge in a position of utmost simplification, denying the problem simply by refusing to confront it. The complexity itself, failing to disappear, thus becomes a multitude of details. The rational mind can deal with it more easily by arranging these details in a primary concatenation and classifying their individual importance according to a scale of attributes, which common sense both judges and shares. This closed system involves a more intense development of a personal mythology—and even of an interior life—than in people having constant relations of exchange with exterior life.

"This lack of communication with a world that was not strictly his caused Rousseau to develop a personality sufficiently marked to give birth to a style which is not only painterly or theatrical, but also a life style. Granted, at its base one recognizes the characteristics found in people whom the so-called important people have gotten into the bad habit of calling 'the little people': the most notable of these characteristics are natural generosity, credulity, and good humor. However, Rousseau's mysterious and triumphant faculty for giving the world an Edenic interpretation is reserved to those for whom childhood has expanded without abandoning its primordial purity."

This is the true secret of Rousseau's work and life, which are one and the same.

The National Holiday in Paris, Place de la République. *Color engraving published by Coyen.*

"O *glorious painter of the Spiritual Republic.*" These were the laudatory words that Apollinaire used when toasting Rousseau at the famous banquet given by Picasso. The Douanier would have loved glory and fame. Inspired by the advertising vignette at the right (itself inspired by the statue on Place de la République), he conceived this imposing Marianne. His prepainted natural setting, which included the laurel branches (symbol of immortality) from the original, prevents Rousseau's Republic from raising her olive branch. He had to lower her right arm and separate her from the flora by the flag, which plays the same role here as the newspaper in the vignette. The displaced arms are awkward, but the lion is as debonair as ever. The Douanier, as he often does when taking his subject from an iconographic source, has reversed the image in order to mislead his viewers.

Colored advertising vignette in the newspaper La République Française.

"*Paris, Place de la République.*" Postcard depicting the statue of the Republic by Léopold Morice.

Allegorical engraving illustrating the March 1882 law that made primary-school education obligatory.

192

Henri Rousseau:
The French Republic.

193

Henri Rousseau: **The Carmagnole.** Decorative panel.

Patriotic refrains: "Si vous aimez la danse," "Dansons la carmagnole," "Ah! ça ira." Popular color engraving.

Rousseau ardently wished to be accepted as one of the official painters of the Third Republic. He tried his luck by taking advantage of the coming Paris celebration of the centennial of the Republic of 1792. The Douanier rather faithfully reproduced a Méaulle engraving of "free-hearted men" dancing the farandole in front of the Palais des Vallées. "Happy little people of Andorra," commented Le Petit Journal, "how we envy you and how greatly we would prefer a farandole on our Place de la Concorde." Rousseau used more vivid, more distinct colors than in the engraving, but he retained the gaudy colors in the woman's fichu in the foreground, transformed the mountain-dwellers' caps into Phrygian hats, omitted the laces of the canvas shoes, and added two dancers at the center of the round holding French and Parisian flags that are crossed. To the right, indirectly influenced by Revolutionary engravings, he placed some sans-culottes with bare calves; to the left, a small male choir and some children. Behind the round of dancers, the Liberty tree mingles its star-shaped leaves with oriflammes and lanterns, which Rousseau left out of a replica he entered in a contest after a journalist compared them to a shooting gallery. Yet he was very proud of them! "Puvis de Chavannes told me: 'Monsieur Rousseau, I don't generally like the gaudy colors you see among the Independents, but I very much like your colors because they're accurate.' He was talking about my **Centennial of Independence.** There were sixty-two different tones in the lanterns," Rousseau reported.

"In their enthusiasm for the liberty that they felt they had won for themselves, the French thought of planting trees to perpetuate its memory. Trees were planted everywhere with pomp and circumstance. The National Guard accompanied the mayor and a brilliant band made this festive occasion interesting." Popular color engraving.

194

Henri Rousseau: **One Centennial of Independence. The People Dance Around Two Republics, That of 1792 and That of 1892, Holding Hands and Singing: "Auprès de ma blonde, qu'il fait bon, fait bon dormir,"** 1892.

The Festivals in Andorra (The Farandole). *Engraving by Fortuné Méaulle.*
In illustrated supplement to Le Petit Journal (*April 11, 1891*).

This **Liberty,** inviting artists from all over the world to rally to the exhibition of independent artists, is none other than Mercié's Renown. It flew from the Trocadéro and pointed its little finger at the old hothouses of the World's Fair of 1900, on Cours la Reine, where the salon took place. Stiff and proud, the flags of Paris (blue and red), the flags of France, the United States, and Great Britain, as well as other imaginary flags, celebrate the international independence of art. Lining up in serried ranks, wearing black hats, countless painters, including two women, bring their canvases under their arms, in horse-drawn carrioles, or on flat carts like those that line the sidewalk outside the Foinet shop. An Abyssinian lion, trying to hold itself as beautifully as the lion of Belfort, rests its front paws on the names of the most estimable painters; the last name is not the least: Henri Rousseau! Is that Rousseau in the foreground, shaking hands with the founder of the Salon of the Independents, or at the left, leading a little girl along? Courteline bought this painting for his Museum of Horrors.

Mercié's Renown, on top of the Palace of the Trocadéro at the Exposition of 1878. Engraving published in L'Histoire des Expositions et des Beaux-Arts *(1884).*

Henri Rousseau: **The Lion of Belfort.** Sketch.

The Abyssinian Lion. *In* Bêtes sauvages *(Wild Beasts), Galeries Lafayette, p. 5.*

"Paris. Lion of Belfort." Postcard.

Photograph of the Foinet-Lefèbvre family in front of their art-supply store, 54 Rue Notre-Dame-des-Champs, Paris.

Henri Rousseau: **Liberty Inviting Artists to Take Part in the Twenty-second Exhibition of Independent Artists.**
"The Valtons, Signacs, Carrières, Willettes, Luces, Seurats, Ortizes, Pissarros, Jaudins, Henri Rousseaus, etc., etc., are your emulators."

Henri Rousseau: **The Representatives of Foreign Powers Coming to Salute the Republic as a Sign of Peace,** 1907.
"Union of Nations. Peace. Work. Liberty. Fraternity."

Henri Rousseau
1907

The Heads of State Throughout the World. *In L'Almanach Hachette, p. 248.*

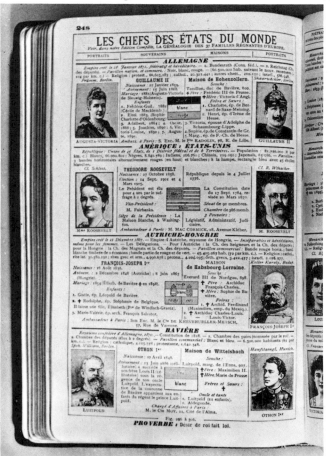

The canopy overhead is dominated by the flags of
Great Britain, France, the United States, and
Paris. Lined up underneath, as stiff as figures
in a shooting gallery, the Douanier's heads of state and
monarchs owe their features to postcards and almanacs.
One can make out from left to right: King Edward VII
next to a kilted Scotsman, President Fallières under
Marianne's arm, President Theodore Roosevelt, Tsar
Nicholas II, Emperor Franz Josef, Kaiser Wilhelm II,
King Victor-Emmanuel III, King Leopold II, Sultan
Abdul-Hamid, the young King Alfonso XIII, Emperor
Menelik II, etc. They all hold olive branches that come
from urns dedicated to peace, work, liberty, and
fraternity. This is a lovely program of universal peace!

199

Henri Rousseau:
The Representatives of Foreign Powers . . .

"Paris. The Statue of Etienne Dolet." Postcard.

oping that his allegory, which glorified
Fallières, would touch the French president, the
Douanier tried to imitate the solemn academic
compositions of Gervex or Roll. Rousseau set the scene
on Place Maubert, decking out all the windows with
flags. Around the statue of Etienne Dolet, children
wearing boaters are dancing in a circle; they have all
come from the Botanical Garden of Angers. Lying at
the feet of the Republic, the tired lion grumbles like an
old dog. This lion supposedly amused the son of
Picasso, who showed him this canvas whenever the little
boy cried. According to Hélène Parmelin, Picasso looked
at Rousseau with attentive admiration. "On the one
hand, he seemed to be amused at and enjoy the
Douanier's prowess. And he watched the Douanier
himself sitting under his canopy at Bateau-Lavoir the
day of the famous grand party" that Picasso organized
in Rousseau's honor. Ambroise Vollard sold Picasso the
painting, which Brassaï photographed in Picasso's
apartment on Rue La Boétie.

32. Angers. — Jardin des Plantes. - Le Lac et la Cascade

"Angers. Botanical Garden. The Lake and the Waterfall." Postcard.

H. Gervex: The Distribution of Awards at the Palace of Industry (*World's Fair of 1889*).
Painting, reproduced in Panorama-Salon 1897, published by Ludovic Baschet.

*Photograph by Brassaï taken in a room of Picasso's apartment
and reproduced in Brassaï's* Picasso and Company, Doubleday and Company, 1966.

Henri Rousseau: **Eve.**

o one could have done as good a job as Monsieur
Chantron in pushing the model as far as possible and
showing youth in bloom and the living suppleness of
flesh," said the catalogue. What did the Douanier get from this
Snake Charmer? He subjugated her to mental schemas, to his
notion of a stunned Eve hypnotized by her tempter, the Biblical
serpent. It was not without difficulty that he undressed her
completely and thrust her against this background of palm trees.
She faces a palm whose fruits resemble oranges rather than
apples. There she is, rigid with fear and the desire to commit
the fatal sin, the temptation for which is even stronger because
the serpent is garbed in seductive colors.

Jean-Léon Gérôme: The Snake Charmer.

The Meeting at 2 bis Rue Perrel.
Victor Brauner: The Charmer Conglomeros,
1946.

Henri Rousseau: **The Snake Charmer,** 1907.

Agitation. *Left-hand painting in* Eden *triptych by*
Lévy-Dhurmer, reproduced in Panorama-Salon 1899,

Young Spoonbills. *In* Bêtes sauvages (Wild Beasts),
Galeries Lafayette, p. 100.

I t was the mother of my friend Robert Delaunay who introduced me to Rousseau, while he was working on **The Snake Charmer,** which is in the Louvre. From my very first visit and during the following visits, I saw with what heroic discipline in terms of abstraction and intensification Rousseau succeeded in mastering the crushing vision offered so superabundantly." This vision, evoked here by Wilhelm Uhde, arose from an association of images: Gérôme's Snake Charmer, Lévy-Dhurmer's Eve, the snakes and spoonbills in Wild Beasts, plus the hothouse plants in the Paris Museum of Natural History. Alfred Jarry nicknamed Henri Rousseau "le Visité," the Visited Man. His visitor is the unconscious, which invaded him so profoundly that the Surrealists (like Victor Brauner, who took up Rousseau's painting and added one of his Conglomeros) made him their master.

Henri Rousseau: **The Sleeping Gypsy**, 1897.
"The feline, although ferocious, is reluctant to pounce on its victim, who, worn out, has fallen into a deep sleep."

Henri Rousseau: **The Sleeping Gypsy.**

Mademoiselle Jeanne Bernard-Rousseau leafing through her grandfather's scrapbook. In the background, the mandolin that he had turned into a lute in his Gypsy painting.

Jean-Léon Gérôme: The Two Majesties. *Reproduction published by Boussod, Valadon et Cie.*

Jean-Léon Gérôme: The Lion on the Watch. *Salon of 1891. Reproduction published by Boussod, Valadon et Cie.*

Matout's chaotic desert, raging lion, swooning Algerian woman, and broken jug are recovered by the Douanier, who rejects the highly realistic cruelty of this scene and adds a lute. Transcending it by transgressing the rules of academic Orientalism, Rousseau outdoes himself, while projecting upon the canvas a "dream screen," his own guilt, which is inscribed in the lion's stupor. The artist's sublimation might have been tinged by the poetic views that Gérôme had studied in the Egyptian desert. It is imbued with the religious mystery of certain funerary frescoes of the pharaohs, of which the Douanier had several reproductions. The strongly dreamlike atmosphere of **The Sleeping Gypsy** influenced many Surrealist painters, such as de Chirico.

Louis Matout: Boghari Woman Killed by a Lioness. *Painting acquired by the French state, entered the Luxembourg Museum on March 1, 1856, and transferred to the Louvre on December 3, 1889.*

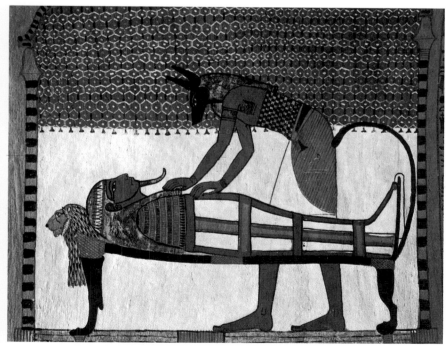

Anubis and the Mummy. *Egyptian tomb of the XXth dynasty.*

Giorgio de Chirico: Lion and Gladiators, *1927.*

Henri Rousseau:
The Dream, 1910.

Yadurgha in a
   lovely dream,
Having gently
   fallen asleep,
Hearing the sounds
   of a musette
Of a well-meaning
   charmer,
While the moon
   reflects,
On the flowers,
   the greening trees
The wild serpents
   lend an ear
To the gay tunes
   of the instrument.

Henri Rousseau:
Detail from **The Dream,** bird of paradise.

Bird of Paradise. *Illustration in*
Cent récits d'histoire naturelle. *Hachette, 1884.*

Henri Rousseau:
Detail from **The Dream,** the elephant.

A Young Elephant. *In* Bêtes sauvages
(Wild Beasts), *Galeries Lafayette, p. 116.*

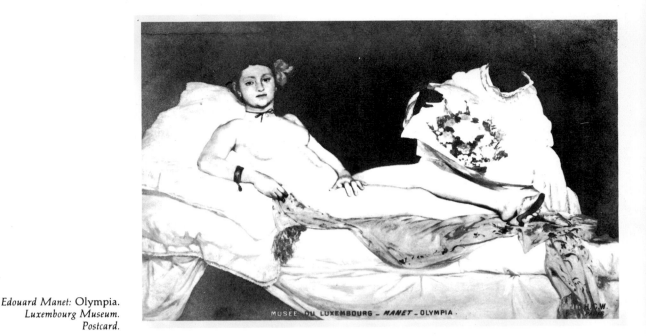

Edouard Manet: Olympia.
Luxembourg Museum.
Postcard.

Louis Béroud:
Female Nude Reclining.
Salon of 1906.
Postcard.

The Dream *was Rousseau's one and only offering to the Salon of the Independents. As the etymology of the word indicates,* **The Dream** *is a mental vagabondage, a delirium. The title had a twofold inspiration. First was* The Dream, *a novel by Zola, a friend of Manet and Cézanne. In the Rougon-Macquart series, the novelist tells the story of the chaste and unhappy love of Angélique, an embroideress, and Félicien, a young painter. The other influence on Rousseau's painting was Edouard Detaille's painting from 1888,* The Dream *(exhibited at the Luxembourg Museum). It showed a throng of ghosts of the Republic and the Empire over soldiers sleeping on the battlefield. At that time, the Douanier was afflicted with an unrequited passion for Léonie and with frustrated dreams of glory. His creative imagination produced a wonderful assemblage of images, of the nudes of Louis Béroud, Manet, and Cabanel, and these nudes attracted the animals from his album. How wonderfully he mastered his dream, filtering its hallucinatory coloring! The evocative strength of his painting comes both from the harmonious density of this amalgam and from the intensity of his libidinal investment. He thus opened the royal road to Surrealism, which painters like Dali and Delvaux did not hesitate to travel.*

Alexandre Cabanel: Albaydé. *Presented at the Salon of 1900.*

Henri Rousseau: Detail from **The Dream,** Yadurgha.

Salvador Dali: Nude in the Plain of Roses, *1942.*

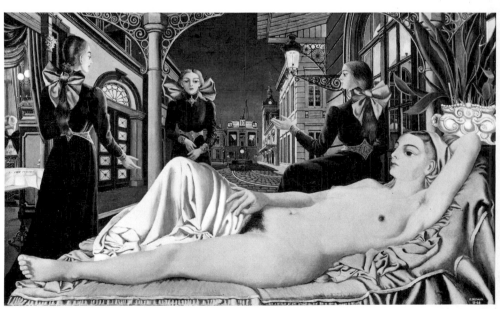

Paul Delvaux: The Public Voice, *1948.*

211

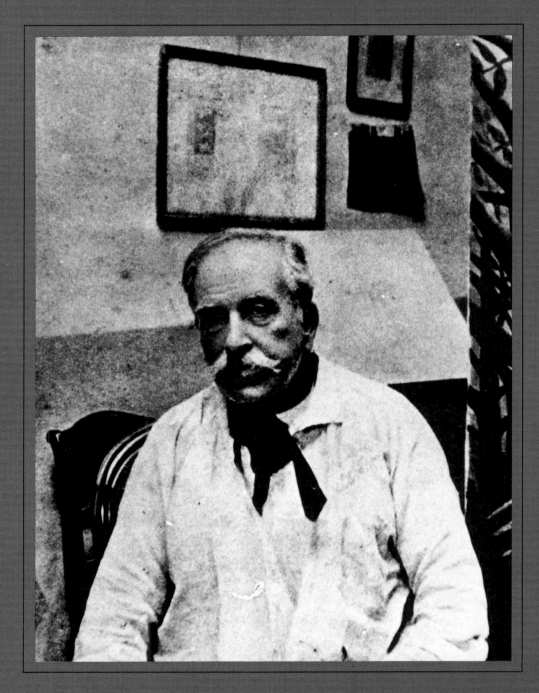

*"When a king wants to wage war,
a mother must go to him
and order him not to do it."*
HENRI ROUSSEAU
to Wilhelm Uhde

7 The Myth of War and Death

From April 7 to May 27, 1894, at the tenth Salon of the Independents, on the Champ-de-Mars, Henri Rousseau presented his **War,** a huge painting (1.14 by 1.95 meters). The painter added the following comment: "It passes, terrifying, leaving despair, tears, and ruin everywhere."

Where did this allegory come from? In what despair, tears, ruins was it born? Through what memories, images, visions did the fear of war and the anguish of death rise from his subconscious to emerge in this funereal fresco, where, tradition has it, the painter painted himself lying in the foreground, his eyes still open—eyes that are fixed on us?

When he painted **War,** Rousseau was undeniably shaken by the assassinations and bombings performed for the past two years by the anarchists in Paris (despite the execution of Ravachol). The painter was struck by the bloody actions of these resolute enemies of authority and the bourgeoisie, and he strongly disapproved of their violence. But didn't Rousseau have his own ax to grind? The unconscious is a worker without a boss!

Rousseau had just lost out in the official contest for decorating the town hall of Bagnolet. He had already lost all hope of having the French government buy his **Centennial of Independence** and his **Liberty,** which had been exhibited at the two preceding salons. He suffered from being unknown, ridiculed by the public, derided by the press. He realized that he was a great innovator; in fact, he was the most modern, the most important until the discovery of Picasso. Eventually he was to tell the master of *The Women of Avignon,* whose hieratic and archaic expressionism evoked the Egyptian archetype for him, "We are the two greatest painters of our time, you in the Egyptian mode and I in the modern mode." He also told Robert Delaunay, "I wonder if I'm not a little anarchistic."

Would this "ride of discord" finally whip the imagination of the visitors at the Salon, confront the art critics' nastiness, and draw a cry of admiration from the directors of the School of Fine Arts? No, on the contrary: the painting was a failure. However, as Rousseau stood guard at his painting, attentive to the least sign of approval, he managed to meet someone who turned out to be very important for his career. The meeting was inevitable and the part played by chance was not astonishing!

A Conjunction of Circumstances

A young poet, free and easy, was going through the exhibit when he halted in front of **War.** Alfred Jarry had just presented his *Ubu Roi* to the readers of *Le*

Mercure de France, in which he had bought several shares. Three years earlier, they had published Arthur Rimbaud's *Le Bal des pendus*:

> The raven somersaults over these cracked heads,
> A piece of flesh trembles on their skinny chins. . . .
> Ah. Right in the midst of the danse macabre
> A huge, mad skeleton leaps into the red sky,
> Carried by the impetus like a rearing horse. . . .

Perhaps Jarry also recalled one of the poems he had written at fifteen, "The Second Life or Macaber."

> For moments a lightning bolt shredded the dark sky
> And the birds of night uttered shrieks of dread. . . .
> Oh, what a heavy burden!
> I never stop
> And my scythe is always ready
> And always sheds blood!

A native of Laval like Rousseau, Jarry discovered that his father had been a schoolmate of the painter at their *lycée*. Highly enthusiastic, Jarry handed him his calling card and decided to publicize this "primitive visionary," this astonishing customs man, who had just retired from the Paris Customs Office. It was Jarry who nicknamed him the Douanier Rousseau. Having "recognized" each other, as it were, they got to know each other. Their minds sparked each other's. The Douanier told Jarry that his tours of duty at the gates of Paris and on the banks of the Seine were more of an ordeal at night because insolent ghosts came to harass him with their stinking farts. The pranks, gumption, and deliriums of the future author of *Doctor Faustroll* were not unappealing to Rousseau ("so much himself, so independent of everything, even nature, and showing a **War** that he rightly calls 'terrifying': we may even say 'dreadful,' " as *La Plume* wrote). A friendship was born.

In June, the Douanier began his portrait of Jarry. The poet sits, dressed in black, surrounded by his attributes, a chameleon and the famous owl he lived with on Boulevard de Port-Royal. (Jarry says the painter used his brush to measure the size of the model's nose, mouth, and ears, so that he could honor their proportions on canvas, and he held the tubes of paint very close to the sitter's face in order to find the right flesh tone.)

For his part, Jarry wrote about **War** in *L'Art Littéraire*, then in the "Essais d'art libre" series: "Of H. Rousseau, especially **War**. On its splint bones, the horse stretches its dancer's head in the frightened extension of its neck; the black leaves inhabit the mauve clouds, and the debris runs like pine cones among the corpses on the translucent edges of jagged axolotls of ravens with bright beaks."

October brought the first issue of *L'Ymagier*, an illustrated journal founded by Alfred Jarry and Rémy de Gourmont. Their aim was to suggest a deeper and correlative reading of old popular images, both religious and legendary, and to draw attention to unpublished drawings by

Gauguin, Emile Bernard, Seguin, Maurice Denis, and Filiger that Jarry had just discovered in Pont-Aven, while in Gauguin's company. (Gauguin appreciated the quality of Rousseau's black tones, which he called "inimitable." Alluding to them, Henry Certigny wonders, in *The Truth About the Douanier Rousseau*, "whether this painter's predilection for this tone was not unconsciously triggered by a painful past filled with men wearing hearse cloth. After all, he had seen the bailiffs seize his home; then he got to know the robes of magistrates; then he saw the undertaker's mutes carry off his children; then he wore mourning for Clémence. . . .")

For *L'Ymagier*, Jarry convinced Rousseau that he ought to do an original lithograph on the theme of his **War.** This lithograph was published on red Japanese vellum in the second issue of the magazine (January 2, 1895), which also proposed the sale of the painting, along with **Centennial** and various landscapes by Rousseau. The pen-and-ink drawing of **War** is even closer than the painting to the iconographic source that directly influenced the artist: a crude illustration that Rousseau had discovered in *Le Courrier Français* (October 27, 1889). It served as an advertisement for P. Andrev's novel *The Tsar*, which was being serialized in a socially progressive newspaper, *L'Egalité*. The illustration was accompanied by a caption: "Wherever the mysterious black horse passed, a misfortune came down, a crime was committed."

R

An Age-Old Language

ousseau was all the more attentive to such things because, after the military convention of August 17, 1892, following the Franco-Russian pact, the artist, like any good Frenchman, was passionately concerned that there be friendship between these two nations. Their friendship had just been confirmed when some naval officers and sailors of Tsar Alexander III came to visit Paris. Rousseau saw this visit as the harbinger of universal peace, the necessity of which France was preaching. The artist saluted the visitors by decorating his studio with Russian flags. In the sentimental play that he wrote five years later, *The Vengeance of a Russian Orphan*, he demonstrated his solidarity by having a valiant French general adopt a Russian orphan girl. The general tries to raise her morale with this edifying speech:

"Now, Sophie, I beg you never to utter the word 'fear' and to adopt the principle of never trembling ahead of time. Had I been like that, by thunder, my hair would not have turned white on the battlefield in the glow of the cannon flames and the smell of powder. This little red ribbon that I wear in my buttonhole is something that I truly earned, risking my life over and over again for my country, France, the first nation in the world. . . . O France! Dear France!"

The Douanier was carried away. Inspired by such a mediocre drawing in *L'Egalité*, he borrowed just about the entire theme of his **War,** but transposed it. The Slavic horseman becomes a furious Amazon. Armed with a smoking torch and a short sword, she gallops through a mountainous area scattered with stripped and broken trees. The head and neck of her mount are like those of a thirsty black anteater, the mane and tail as wild as the Amazon's unbridled hair. The ground, with its tiny oval stones, bristles with naked corpses being gnawed by ravens. The bearded corpse on the right is supposedly the husband of Joséphine Le Tensorer, née Nourry, who would become Rousseau's second wife in 1899. One raven perched on this corpse's huge stomach has a special taste for it. . . .

It is interesting to note here that around the time he painted **War,** Rousseau had occasion to meditate on death when he posed for Alfred Lenoir's bas-relief on the high altar in the Church of Saint Francis Xavier on Boulevard des Invalides. The Jesuit saint, shown dying in the arms of angels, holding a crucifix in his hands, bears the features of the Douanier Rousseau. The altar was dedicated on May 23, 1894, during the Exhibition of the Independents. Did the coachman Le Tensorer genuflect on that day, before the effigy of his rival, who was to have the good fortune to learn about the coachman's death—this time, his *real* death—at the end of the year 1895?

"The Douanier Rousseau," writes Malraux in *The Voices of Silence,* "goes beyond his Sunday drawing and joins the most remote popular domain. . . . He is less a naïf than the translator of an age-old language. . . . The horse in **War** is that of Magdalenian painting. The greater paintings of Rousseau are tied to a past without history."

A Synthesis of Images

Malraux suggested the notion of the Imaginary Museum, which, as he said to Picasso (recalled in *La Tête d'obsidienne*), is primarily a "mental place." Before Malraux, Arthur Rimbaud (in *A Season in Hell*) defined *his* mental museum, which could also have been Rousseau's:

"For a long time, I boasted of possessing all possible landscapes, and I found the fame of modern painting and poetry derisory. I loved idiotic paintings, decors, circus-performer canvases, signs, popular illuminations; old-fashioned literature, Church Latin, erotic books full of misspelled words, old operas, silly refrains, naïve rhythms. I dreamed about crusades, unreported voyages of discovery, suppressed religious wars, revolutions in customs, displacements of nations and continents: I believed in all the enchantments. . . ."

Rousseau was so ambitious in his drawing that he was afraid of doing it awkwardly. If his imagination needed the iconographic aid of the *Tsar* illustration, it also drew on fecund sources in other childhood visions that still inhabited his mental universe, especially those in the *Tapestries of the Apocalypse* in Angers, which date from the fourteenth century. Young Rousseau could have seen them in the vast nave of the cathedral on days of solemn ceremonies. Three of these tapestries, which had some effect on his painting, describe three passages from the Book of Revelation:

The second seal, the red horse and war. "And when he [the Lamb] opened the second seal, I heard the second living creature say, 'Come!' And out came another horse, bright red; its rider was permitted to take peace from the earth, so that men should slay one another; and he was given a great sword. . . ."

The fourth seal, the pale horse and death: "When he [the Lamb] opened the fourth seal, I heard the voice of the fourth living creature say, 'Come!' And I saw, and behold, a pale horse, and its rider's name was Death, and Hades followed him; and they were given power over a fourth of the earth, to kill with sword and with famine and with pestilence and by wild beasts of the earth."

The birds devour the impious. "Then I saw an angel standing in the sun, and, with a loud voice he called to all the birds that fly in mid-heaven, 'Come, gather for the great supper of God, to eat the flesh of kings, the flesh of captains, the flesh of mighty men, the flesh of horses and their riders, and the flesh of all men, both free and slave, both small and great.' "

A mysterious synthesis took place in Rousseau's mind, which also eagerly absorbed the tales of his ancestors' military feats—and he heard a lot of these in his family! His maternal grandfather died at Bône early in the conquest of Algeria. And his great-grandfather, whom he had known, took part in Napoleon's Spanish campaign as commander of an infantry regiment, becoming its major on April 15, 1811.

The Douanier's horror of war was comparable to that of Goya, and he appreciated the Spanish artist's engravings exposing the massacres committed by Napoleon's soldiers: *The Disasters of War*. Consider these words by the German art critic Uhde: "The Fourteenth of July—the last one in his life—I saw him early in his room. . . . He was dressed in his Sunday best and receiving visitors. He was pouring wine into glasses. 'Do you like peace?' he asked me. And when I said yes, we all drank to peace. Then he took my hand, led me over to the window, and, amid many small flags, he showed me the flag of my country. . . .

"It was in his old age that I got to know Rousseau. He came to see me in the old convent on Boulevard des Invalides; the high windows were wide open and the evening air wafted across the park, passed over the terrace, and entered the room. It was dark, I could barely make him out, I could only hear his fine voice, which has something solemn about it. He spoke to me about Mexico, old forests, fierce beasts. Then war, which he hates. He grew angry: 'When a king wants to wage war, a mother must go to him and order him not to do it.' "

Can a painter have more success than a mother in stopping war? Rousseau believed he could. In any case, it was as sole support of a widow that Henri Rousseau was exempted from the army in the Franco-Prussian War of 1870. His good-conduct certificate notes that his left ear was cut off. But the reason for this was quite simple: when he and his wife moved into an apartment at 135 Rue de Sèvres, he opened the outside shutters—and was hit by a Communard's stray bullet. Or at least that was what Rousseau told people.

Remorse and Nostalgia

Why did Rousseau boast about his alleged heroism during the Franco-Prussian War? Why did he claim he had taken part in the Mexican campaign with the Angers 51st Line Infantry Regiment to save the Emperor Maximilian? And why did he begin painting **The Battle of Champigny** after the great panorama by Alphonse de Neuville and Edouard Detaille on the same theme? And **The Battle of Reichshoffen** after the painting by Aimé Morot?

Because his life lacked glory, and he believed he could win it by showing he was as worthy as the greatest epic painters of his time. This would also exorcise his own inferiority complex, brought on by his family's scorn for his artistic vocation.

He had no choice but to join the 51st Infantry Regiment, on December 1, 1863, so that he could be pardoned for the petty thefts he had committed when employed in an Angers law firm. Actually, he had been quite reluctant to sign up for seven years' military duty in order to escape dishonor. His army career was far from brilliant, but he wanted to edify his parents, who piously preserved Colonel Guyard's decorations (the colonel had been decorated by the Legion of Honor and made a knight of Saint-Louis in 1815). So the Douanier Rousseau confabulated.

And his tales were believed by Guillaume Apollinaire, who reported in *Les Soirées de Paris* in 1914: "Rousseau did indeed visit America, when he did his military service during the Mexican war. When asked about that period of his life, he appeared to remember only the fruits he had seen there and he recalled that the soldiers were not allowed to eat them. However, his eyes retained other memories: the tropical forests, the monkeys, and the bizarre flowers. . . . Wars had an important place in the Douanier's life. In 1870, the presence of mind shown by Sergeant Rousseau [actually only a private second-class] spared the town of Dreux the horrors of civil war. He liked to give a detailed account of this lofty feat, and his old voice took on singularly proud inflections when he spoke about the people and the army acclaiming him with the words: 'Long live Sergeant Rousseau!' "

In 1893, one year before **War,** he had exhibited a now vanished painting, **The Last of the 51st,** at the Salon of the Independents. The painting bore an edifying caption: "After long struggles, the regiment was completely decimated: only this poor mutilated soldier survived to save the standard under which our forebears won so much glory." This was Rousseau's way of participating in the campaign in Mexico, where he had never set foot (except in his mind's eye), and in the war of 1870, about which he could dream when he viewed Alphonse de Neuville's highly successful paintings. (Rousseau particularly liked the most famous, *The Last Cartridges.*) The Douanier waited in vain for such successes as he tried to do similar military and patriotic scenes. His fame was posthumous.

If one looks at his painting **The Artillerists (Fourth Battery, Third Piece),** which he based on a photograph, one can't help being struck by the calm of these soldiers resting around their cannon, near their rifles and their piles of sabers, in a deeply peaceful rustic landscape. There is nothing martial about this 105 cannon, which appeared in the army around the 1880s, or about the soldiers mounted on it. They are frozen for all eternity in a framework whose mellow autumn colors add to the serenity of the pose—which was fixed by the photographer and then recaptured by the painter.

And what peace emanates from Rousseau's small canvas **Winter Landscape with War Scene** (dated January 1, 1877)! The houses clustering around the church in the snowy village and the soldiers resembling tin soldiers could have been painted by a well-behaved child fascinated by tales of patriotic battle.

Another snowbound landscape contains a soldier, standing at attention on the fortifications of Paris, and a passerby, as solemn and somber as an undertaker's assistant. The painting might have been designed to illustrate *Consolations*, the poem that Malherbe wrote to console Du Périer:

> The rigors of death are like no other.
> It's no use praying to death
> Cruel as it is, it stops up its ears
> And lets us cry.
> The poor man covered with hemp in his shack
> Is subject to death's laws,
> And the guard at the barriers of the Louvre
> Does not keep death away from our kings.

His Spiritual Children

Yes, death was cruel to the Douanier Rousseau. Having lost six children, he also had to suffer the death of his first wife, Clémence Boitard, in 1888. She had been consumptive since 1876. He adored her, as he later confirmed in his prison letter to the examining magistrate. "I was alone. The great emptiness; especially the two eyes, which I missed so much in my life. Ah! It would have been better if I, too, had left with her."

On December 24, 1890, he lost his mother, Eléonore Rousseau. In 1897, his only son, Henri-Anatole, an engraver—barely eighteen years old. In 1903, his second wife, Joséphine, whom he buried in the Bagneux graveyard.

> Misery pounced upon your offspring:
> You lost your children and then your wives
> And so you got married again, to painting,
> To paint your pictures, your spiritual children.

These lines are by Guillaume Apollinaire, from a poem he improvised in 1908. His works are his revenge against death and indifference.

An artist who wanted to be complete and who did his best to be known, to be recognized as a master, the Douanier Rousseau was not content with painting. He composed and published a waltz dedicated to Clémence's memory. He wrote comedies and even began a sculpture on a theme that haunted him. . . .

In his comedy *A Visit to the World's Fair of 1889*, Henri Rousseau depicts a decent Breton family visiting the Museum of the Invalides during the World's Fair of 1889. Here are some important passages:

Madame Lebozeck: Yes, let's go in and start by looking at all these cannon here to the right and the left, and then the statues and the garden, which seems very lovely.

Monsieur Lebozeck: Let's hurry up and look. Ah! These are museums over here. Look, another statue, General Daumesny; he's only got one leg and he's still fighting. Ah, there were some tough customers in those days. If I'd had generals like that in 1870, we wouldn't have lost Alsace and Lorraine, and the Prussians wouldn't have come into France to commandeer and make us pay five billion francs. That's a nice bundle of dough we gave 'em, plus two rich provinces, Alsace and Lorraine. War is so sad and ugly. Why make those poor guys kill one another like that; how awful, how awful!

On May 26, 1873, a statue of General Daumesnil, paid for by a national subscription, was solemnly inaugurated on the town-hall square of Vincennes. When Rousseau went strolling in the woods and painted Lake Daumesnil, he had several chances to admire the valiant posture of this national hero. General Daumesnil is pointing at his wooden leg and seems to be repeating what he told the Russian officers who ordered him to surrender on March 31, 1814: "Give me back my leg and I'll give you the fort of Vincennes!"

This Rochet statue was reproduced by the Douanier Rousseau. It is forty centimeters high, and, oddly enough, the head of this awkward but touchingly naïve statue resembles the Douanier's head so closely that he must have identified with him profoundly: *"Le général Daumesnil, c'est moi!"*

The Imaginary Museum

A surprising coincidence: the Douanier Rousseau died of gangrene in his leg, the result of a phlegmon, on September 2, 1910, at Necker Hospital. In his delirium, "he said he saw the eternal Father, the seraphim, the angels and archangels, and he believed he heard celestial music." He also wondered why his young friend, the painter Robert Delaunay, who was painting dislocated Eiffel Towers, had broken the Eiffel Tower. He was desolated at leaving unfinished his last work and those of his pupils.

Having hurried to Angers, his daughter found in front of the studio a poor old man sobbing at Rousseau's final canvas: a painting of monkeys who hadn't finished playing in the virgin forest.

In 1913, the sculptor Brancusi, helped by Ortiz de Zarate, carved this beautiful epitaph by Guillaume Apollinaire on Rousseau's tomb:

Gentle Rousseau, you hear us
We greet you
Delaunay his wife Monsieur Queval and I
Let our baggage pass free through heaven's gate
We'll bring you brushes, paints, and canvases
So that you can devote your sacred leisures
In the Real light to painting, as you did my portrait,
Painting the face of the stars.

He did continue painting, in a sense, through others: the artists who could receive his message and take it up in their own way.

A strange superimposition of images and a mysterious meeting of influences. Picasso borrowed the inspiration for his *Guernica* from both the Douanier Rousseau and Goya. Take a close look at that terrified horse sticking out its tongue, the disheveled woman with the kerosene lamp, the carnage on the ground, the hand clutching a broken sword: Rousseau's allegorical theme has been picked up and shaken up, fractured and marked by Cubism. More than anything else, however, *Guernica* is, in its way, a homage to the Douanier: among the Rousseau paintings that Picasso collected, he particularly loved **Self-Portrait with a Kerosene Lamp.** On the right side of *Guernica*, a woman collapses in the flames of a house destroyed in the bombardment. We find her again in Goya's series *The Disasters of War:* the engraving titled *Estragos de la Guerra* (*Horrors of War*) shows women upside down in a house razed by the Napoleonic army's cannon fire.

As for the bull in *Guernica*, we may remember that for one of his paintings, Rousseau (like Picasso) referred to a lithograph in Goya's *Tauromachia.*

If we reread Malraux's conversations with Picasso, we find a confirmation of the elective affinities between Picasso and Rousseau: "Because of the Spanish Civil War, Picasso talked to me about Goya. More than any other painter, Goya knew with certainty that he gained from his colors and engraving things that no one else had ever gained before him; and first of all, his supernatural. What would Goya say if he saw *Guernica?* I wonder. I think he would be satisfied."

Speaking about the Douanier Rousseau, Picasso added: "Father Rousseau was not a naïf who was better than the others, but a genius of a colorist who was a naïf. It's not because Goya was brilliant that the painting of his time was good, right?"

In 1955, in a painting shown at the Drouant David Gallery, *Horrors of War*, Bernard Buffet, like Rousseau and Picasso before him, took up this mythical theme, thus illustrating Malraux's insight in *The Imaginary Museum:* "All paintings form a single empire, but [there are] many small kingdoms, and life unites in survival without being confused with survival."

For works of art bring human beings together across space and time.

The Tsar. *Illustration from the serialized novel* Le Tsar, *in* L'Egalité (*October 6, 1889*).
Published as an advertisement in Le Courrier Français (*October 27, 1889*).

The War. *Original pen-and-ink lithograph by Henri Rousseau
for* L'Ymagier, *January 1895, no. 2, p. 102.*

The socialist newspaper offered a vulgar engraving to illustrate The Tsar, *a
serialized novel describing the criminal exploits of a young Russian wife
who commits her misdeeds incognito with the help of a chestnut horse dyed
black. The illustration was transformed into a vast mythical fresco under the
painter's vengeful brush. Rousseau also found his anguishing inspiration in the*
Apocalypse *hangings that he had observed in his childhood. These tapestries in
Angers describe the lines from the Book of Revelation: "By these three plagues, a
third of mankind was killed, by the fire and smoke and sulphur issuing from their
[the horses'] mouths. For the power of the horses is in their mouths and in their
tails; their tails are like serpents. . . ." The ebony charger becomes a monstrous
anteater sticking out its tongue. The Slavic horseman changes into a harpy, whose
torch fills the falling night with smoke. With her spear, she castrates the naked,
twisted limbs of the bare trees and of the men entangled among the testicular stones.
The ravens are already picking at them. "The angel cried with a loud voice to all
the birds: 'Go . . . eat all their flesh.'"*

Nicolas Bataille and Hennequin de Bruges: Apocalypse.
Late fourteenth century tapestry, Angers.

The Myriads of Lions.

222

Henri Rousseau: **War. It Passes, Terrifying, Leaving Despair, Tears, and Ruin Everywhere.**

The Fourth Horseman of the Apocalypse.

The Birds Devouring the Impious.

Henri Rousseau: Detail from **War.**

Francisco Goya: So Much and More, *1810. From* The Disasters of War.

Francisco Goya: The Horrors of War.

*I*t was under the twofold influence of Goya's lithographs (showing the artist's disgust at Napoleon's war in Spain) and Rousseau's lithographs (ordered for L'Ymagier by Alfred Jarry, author of Ubu Roi) that Picasso expressed and organized his iconoclastic and Cubist wrath against the bombing of Guernica. And the Miserabilist painter Bernard Buffet depicted the death camps, which the Douanier Rousseau had "fore-seen" in 1894.

Pablo Picasso: Guernica, 1937.

Bernard Buffet: Horrors of War, 1955.

Henri Rousseau: **The Artillerists (Fourth Battery, Third Piece).**

Eugène Chaperon: The Barracks Photographer, *1889.*
In Le Panorama-Salon 1899, *published by Ludovic Baschet.*

We must point out that for several years now, our military painters have been more intent on focusing our interest on the peacetime life of soldiers," notes the commentator in Le Panorama-Salon. Chaperon painted a photographer immortalizing the soldiers of the glass of '95 in the third squadron of the 1st Regiment of Cuirassiers. Why shouldn't Rousseau consult a photograph (probably like the picture postcard of the fort of Vincennes) to find the peaceful subjects for his artillerists resting around their third cannon?

AU FORT DE VINCENNES

"At the Fort of Vincennes." Postcard.

Henri Rousseau: **The Battle of Reichshoffen.**

To the Glory of the French Cuirassiers (1803–1906), Reichshoffen, August 6, 1870. *Based on the painting by Aimé Morot at the Museum of Versailles. In* Le Petit Journal, *illustrated supplement (December 23, 1906).*

Henri Rousseau: **The Battle of Champigny.**

Alphonse de Neuville and Edouard Detaille: The Battle of Champigny, November 30, 1870.
Panorama, in supplement to Le Monde Illustré (*November 4, 1882*). *Engraving by F. Méaulle.*

Using photographs of Aimé Morot's painting in the castle of Versailles, the illustrator for Le Petit Journal *made a sort of comic strip. The Douanier Rousseau must have used this kind of image when he reproduced the famous Battle of Reichshoffen. "At a time when people are talking about getting rid of the big cavalry, whose role is naturally reduced by the demands of modern war, we found it opportune to pay a just tribute to the regiments of cuirassiers and to recall the annals of their heroism," said the daily gazette.*

Rousseau merely traces part of plate four of F. Méaulle's engraving of Panorama of the Battle of Champigny *by Alphonse de Neuville and Edouard Detaille, which appeared as a foldout in* Le Monde Illustré (*November 4, 1882*). *However, Rousseau reinterpreted it, shifting the bell tower from left to center and having a shell explode in the shape of a cross (it looks like an airplane). Likewise, Rousseau added an exploding howitzer shell and a horse whose rider has been unseated, to the center of the charge of the cuirassiers of Reichshoffen.*

Henri Rousseau: **The Mexican Picador.**

Francisco Goya: Bullfighting. *Engraving, published in 1876 by Loizelet, 12 Rue des Beaux-Arts, Paris.*

Bull Branding in Arles. *In* Le Petit Journal, *illustrated supplement (June 26, 1898). Engraving by F. Méaulle.*

In the spirit of Goya's bullfighting pictures, but inspired more directly by a Méaulle engraving in the illustrated supplement to Le Petit Journal, the Douanier Rousseau traveled to a purely imaginary Mexico. A wooden barrier and palm trees function as an exotic background. But the white horse nevertheless looks like the small wooden horses of the manèges in the Luxembourg Gardens.

228

Henri Rousseau: **Baron Daumesnil.**

"Statue of General Daumesnil in Vincennes."
Postcard.

On his way to the forest of Vincennes, the Douanier liked to stop at Louis Rochet's statue of General Daumesnil. The work was dedicated in 1873 in front of the town hall of Vincennes. Rousseau admired the courage and humor shown by the governor of the fort of Vincennes: he refused to surrender to the Russians unless they restored his real leg. Rousseau also referred to this statue in his comedy A Visit to the World's Fair of 1889. His own version of the statue, awkwardly reproduced in wood and only forty centimeters high, bears the traits of the Douanier's face. "In such a case," said André Breton, "it's always a self-portrait."

J. Striberni: *"General Daumesnil in Vincennes."* Drawing on postcard.

"Don't forget, we always have to study nature!"
HENRI ROUSSEAU
to the American painter Max Weber

8 The Soul of Still Lifes, the Language of Flowers

In the Larousse dictionary, which Rousseau owned and consulted, a dried chrysanthemum can be found on the page where men named Rousseau appear. The Douanier did not yet have his appointed place among them. In regard to Jean-Jacques Rousseau, the Larousse says that the principle of his philosophical system is "the invincible faith in the excellence of nature." Like this philosopher, the Douanier stated that he had "no other master but nature." He felt that one should always refer to nature. He did not miss the dedication of the statue of "the immortal author of *The Social Contract*" on Place du Panthéon. And in one of his notebooks, he pasted the long account of the ceremony, published in *Mot d'Ordre* on February 5, 1889.

Like Jean-Jacques Rousseau, the Douanier loved solitary promenades in parks, public gardens, and forest interiors, and along rivers and ponds. He would return from his walks with bouquets of flowers, leaves, and branches. Inspired by numerous engravings of the famous cherry picking in Jean-Jacques Rousseau's *Confessions,* the Douanier did a painting that has been lost since he exhibited it in 1907: **The Little Cherry Pickers.** With its stiff upright tail, the cherry was a fruit that the Douanier loved to depict in his still lifes.

The Douanier was similar in many ways to the author of *Reveries of a Solitary Stroller*, Jean-Jacques Rousseau. They shared an Oedipal sentimentality about women, and they were both incapable of taking care of their own children. Both men had paranoiac projections in dreams and artistic creation, and they also took refuge in music, nature, birds and flowers, watery stretches. . . .

Jean-Jacques Rousseau devoted himself to botany in order to find relief from his obsessions, and he composed herbariums to forget his troubles, "the persecutions by men, their outrages and all the ills with which they have rewarded my tender and sincere attachment to them." In his "Seventh Promenade," he wrote: "Botany recalls to my imagination all the things that flatter it more: meadows, waters, forests, solitude, above all peace."

For the Douanier, too, the bouquets he recomposed in the misery and solitude of his wretched studios were microcosms of nature. Doesn't *bouquet* come from the French word *bosquet,* a grove? A nature was here, inviting him and loving him. His compositions were often accompanied by a sprig of ivy symbolizing love and faithfulness: "I die if I don't attach myself." The Douanier chose most of his flowers for the symbolic meanings that were traditionally attached to them or that he attributed to them. For instance, to thank his lawyer for his fine handling of a case, Rousseau offered to do his portrait, and they set up an appointment. "That day," recalls Guilhermet, the lawyer, "Rousseau made his preparations. When I arrived, I saw a small vase on the table; it contained a columbine. 'You're going to hold it in your portrait,' he told me, 'for this is the flower of eloquence.' " The Douanier was wrong. With the five little fools' caps it wears as a corolla on its stem, the columbine is the flower of fools. It is the emblem of "joyous folly": the folly of the painter who wished to paint his lawyer entirely in the nude, a wish the lawyer wouldn't go along with.

Likewise, to do **The Poet and His Muse,** his portrait of Guillaume Apollinaire and "his lady," Marie Laurencin, Rousseau absolutely insisted on real "poet's narcissus," which he symbolically planted in the foreground, partly in order to conceal his subjects' ugly feet.

To You, My Thoughts

The painter was also fascinated by pansies, whose petals resemble carnival wolves, mischievous figures; and he added a few pansies to most of his bouquets, to animate them.

However, the flower he cherished most was the forget-me-not. According to a German legend, this is the flower of remembrance. A girl was walking with her betrothed along the Danube, and its waves agitated the stalks of forget-me-nots in bloom. The girl wanted to pick some, and the boy, anticipating her desire, bent over the water. He lost his balance, fell in, and was swept away by the current. Before disappearing forever, he managed to toss the bouquet of forget-me-nots to his beloved, begging her never to forget him.

So, before Rousseau's young friend the American painter Max Weber returned to New York, the Douanier gave him a ceramic vase with a circle of swallows, those harbingers of spring that are faithful to their nests; and these swallows were surrounded with tender wreaths of forget-me-nots. Then, on March 20, 1909, Rousseau wrote Weber a long letter reminding him of their time together and advising him "to work hard in seeking beauty, reality."

He was anxiously looking forward to spring. "I don't know if you have nice weather in your hot America, here we have snow, rain, the sun rarely comes out and it doesn't allow us to go and do outdoor studies in the country. . . . I think that you can do lots of fine studies in the beautiful exotic nature of your country. . . . I would be happy to get a long letter from you as soon as possible, full of good news." The good news he hoped for was to see his paintings conquer that "hot America." Rousseau had even written on the back of the still life he had given Weber: "Union of America and France, the two Republics."

Weber, who organized the first posthumous exhibit of Rousseau's works (two months after the Douanier's death), reported the following two anecdotes.

One day when Weber was watching him paint, he noticed a tiny nosegay in Rousseau's hand, the flowers getting crushed against the palette. Weber asked him the reason for the bouquet. "Don't forget, Weber, we always have to study nature."

On the platform in the Gare Saint-Lazare in Paris, where Rousseau was seeing Weber off, the Douanier, with tears in his eyes, shouted to Weber as the train rattled away, "Don't forget nature, Weber!"

Rousseau also fancied daisies, those pearls of the floral world. People even pluck off the petals of a daisy to find out whether they are loved: a little, a lot, passionately, madly, or not at all.

Nor is the marigold, a flower that "follows the sun," absent from Rousseau's still lifes. According to the ancients, the sorrow of Venus presided at its birth.

Bereft of her lover, Cytherea mingled
Her tears with her dear Adonis' blood,
The blood, they say, bore the purple anemone,
The tears gave birth to the marigolds.

A bashful lover, rejected and humiliated by a matron whose father didn't want her to marry him—that poor hack painter—Henri Rousseau, after drawing a pansy on a letter, wrote her a final love letter on August 19, 1910. (Note that the French word *pensée* means both "thought" and "pansy.")

"To you all my thoughts, my beloved Léonie. Before going to bed, I have to say a few words to you about what you told me in Vincennes when we were on the bench, waiting for the trolley car. You said that if I were useless to you, you could at least use me as a buffoon. Whose fault is it if I'm of no use to you in regard to living together? . . . We could have spent a nice Sunday together tomorrow, happy, very happy, but no, instead of joy in our hearts, there'll be sadness, instead of strolling, inhaling the pure country air, the two of us together, we'll be separated, far away from one another and you find this good. . . ."

Like the begging letters he sent her, the language he spoke to his flowers was not heard by "the sinister Léonie," as Rousseau's friends called her.

To get his mind off his frustrations, the painter plunged back into his friendships with his students. Proud of having been a professor of "drawing, watercolors, faïence and porcelain painting, and pastels" at the Philotechnical Association of the City of Paris, he assigned still lifes to the "little old men" and the young people surrounding him. Sprigs of flowers, pots of geraniums, laurel branches, compositions with oranges, which he carefully touched up, admonishing his pupils to be faithful. This was his "Academy, a Living Model"!

For Rousseau, the most beautiful symbol of love was the rose; and the garden rose was the most sincere. On August 15, 1892, inspired by greeting cards, he depicted a hand holding two branches of stylized roses among pines; the picture bore the dedication "Happy Holiday." It was the festival of the Virgin; also the birthday of Marie Biche, who had just lost her husband, Frumence. The Douanier hoped to win her heart. . . .

Secret Loves

Mademoiselle Bernard-Rousseau has preserved the postcards that the Douanier sent her in Angers. "My grandchild," he writes on one of them, "I'm sending you this card with little children like you presenting flowers to their parents for New Year's. Your grandfather kisses you."

When he came to visit her, they were both beside themselves with joy. "Giving him my hand," she recalls, "I learned to have an air of merriment, which avoids a lot of unpleasantness. We started out from Place Saint-Maurice, where we lived. No sooner had we arrived at Rue Plantagenet than he began to hum *'Auprès de ma blonde, qu'il fait bon dormir,'* and he gave my hand a little squeeze to make me jump. Knowing that you're supposed to walk properly in the street, I was stupefied. But little by little, I went along with his lively mood. We were walking toward the old part of Angers to see old friends of his from Laval, painters and sculptors of the moment. And then there was that lady, whom I thought very old, though she may not have been all that old; she looked at Grandfather with very soft eyes, which I didn't like at all. And I was even more furious when he kissed her and said, 'Here are some flowers, Marie!' Later on, I found out that they had had a romance in their youth. My grandfather had a loyal heart! As soon as we got back home, I asked him not to tell my parents that we had skipped and sung in the street. He promised not to tell them, in exchange for my silence about that kiss."

Such childhood secrets have been kept. How many more are hidden in the bouquets that Rousseau painted with so much sincerity, timidity, or modesty, offering them to friends, neighbors, and the wives of shopkeepers whose bills he couldn't pay?

If these still lifes resemble his secret loves, they also candidly express his longing for the time of cherries, his nostalgia for family life around the rustic table with the porridge spoon, the jugs of orangeade and lemonade, the bottle of liquor for the father, the fragrant coffee maker, the kerosene lamps or tallow candles burning at night to banish the anguishing shadows and the solitude. And, the better to retain the intimate, comforting memory, Rousseau wrapped them in heavy napkins and warm curtains.

He Wanted Them Immortal

An unusual harmony of these usual objects, evocative of his oral fixation: a precarious equilibrium of these fruits arranged in odd numbers, these bouquets awkwardly maintained by simple branches of privet, laurel, or acacia, and sending out tender touches of gay and simple mimosas, borage, pimpernels, and forget-me-nots. What the Douanier Rousseau offers us in his *natures mortes* is his ingenuous soul. He wanted them immortal, just as he wanted everlasting life for the flowers of Corpus Christi, a holiday proudly celebrated by his parents, who were intent on having the most beautiful wayside altar, outside the Beucheresse Gate (very close to the cathedral).

Like Lamartine in *Milly, or Native Soil*, Rousseau wondered, "Inanimate objects, do you have souls that attach themselves to our souls and do you have the power to love?" And Rousseau's brush replied yes.

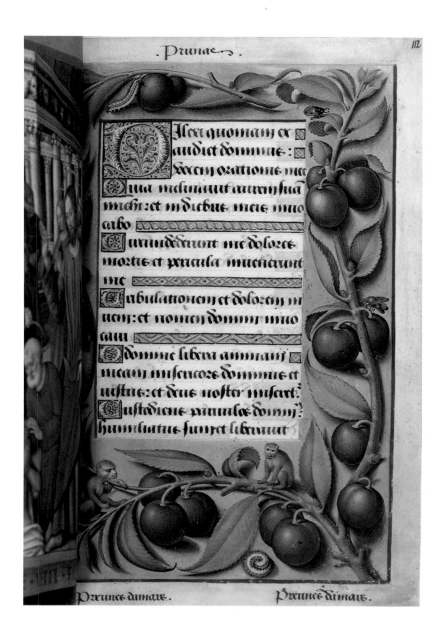

Viola. Violette de Mars. Bouquets.
Illuminations in The Book of Hours of Anne of Brittany.

Illuminations
by Jehan Bourdichon and Jehan Poyet
from The Book of Hours of Anne of Brittany, *1508.*

S o naïve and simple, so conscientiously painted,
Rousseau's fruits and flowers reflect his candor and
that of the illuminations in The Book of Hours of
Anne of Brittany. *The spirit of this book, which Napoleon III*
helped to make known, is defined in the Latin text surrounded
by plums and monkeys: "The Lord watches over the humble: I
was humiliated and he delivered me."

Stiff, aligned, and superimposed, like those illustrated in
his dictionary, Rousseau's flowers, observed or gathered in
public parks or in the gardens of the Parisian suburbs, speak a
symbolic language. Hence the pansy [pensée = "thought" and
"pansy"]: "My thoughts are for you!"

Postcard addressed to Louise Guyard.

Lovers of Flowers. Readings for All.
"Monsieur Opoix, head gardener of the Luxembourg,
looking at a precious plant."

Flowers. *Color plate in Rousseau's* Larousse pour tous.

Medallion portrait of the Douanier Rousseau and the bouquet composed by his granddaughter.

Paule Dedeban: Bouquet inspired by the Douanier Rousseau.

Henri Rousseau: **Bouquet of Flowers,** 1910.

Pensée (pansy). Illustration on p. 407 of the Douanier Rousseau's Larousse pour tous.

Henri Rousseau: Ceramic vase painted and signed on the base, "Henri-Julien Rousseau 1908." The painter's gift to Max Weber.

Simplifying in order to amplify, the Douanier spreads his draperies, inventing planes and pleats; he liberates flowers to make them more autonomous and singular. As shown by this reconstruction, he plays tricks with his flowers, turning their expressive corollas toward himself and making his michievous pansies smile among the rose leaves. In order to lighten his round rustic pots, he uses sprigs of mimosa and forget-me-nots, the latter borrowing their stylized leaves from the mimosa. These stylized leaves eventually surrounded the swallows on the vase that Rousseau gave to Max Weber. It was this young American painter who got Rousseau to paint on ceramic.

Henri Rousseau: **Bouquet of Flowers.**

Tapestry at the Cluny Museum.

Henri Rousseau: **Bouquet of Wild Flowers.**

Henri Rousseau: **Poet's Flowers.**

Whether they've escaped from the fields, a "priest's garden," an ancient tapestry, the Larousse dictionary, or quite simply from his imagination, the Douanier's flowers insist on their independence. They don't much like meddling with others: each flower seeks its own place. Just as marigolds look up at the sun, these flowers show their faces to the painter, the better to give him their messages. The forget-me-nots: "Remember me." The scarlet pimpernels: "Come, I'm waiting for you." The poppy: "Let's love one another as soon as possible." The daisy: "Pluck my leaves." The heliotrope: "All I want is your friendship." And so on. Crowding them a bit in the bouquet on the right, he draws out the vase and the wallpaper designs. As for the poet's flowers, he gives them some sky on the left and on the vase.

Henri Rousseau: **Bouquet of Flowers.**

Henri Rousseau: **Bouquet of Flowers.**

Henri Rousseau: **Lotus Flowers.**

Henri Rousseau: **The Oak Branch.** Pen-and-ink drawing.

One of the Douanier's few
pen-and-ink drawings still extant
is this oak branch. He did his
best to reproduce the lobate leaves and the
jutting acorns. He loved this symbol of
glorious robustness, just as he loved ivy,
with which he often signed his bouquets:
"I die if I am not attached, I am
faithful!" However, Rousseau wasn't
faithful in depicting his lotus blossoms,
which are as imaginary as the flowers in
his exotic paintings.

Henri Rousseau: **Still Life with Exotic Fruits.**

Fruits. *Plate in the Douanier Rousseau's* Larousse pour tous.

I f this still life is by the Douanier alone (*something not so improbable as has sometimes been claimed*), it would be a very careful *exercise de style. The display—most likely borrowed from some illustration of tropical fruits, drawn with no other shadow than a dark background, isolated and stacked up like the fruits in his dictionary—could have been composed to make the fable of his Mexican sojourn more credible. "When he was asked about that period of his life, he seemed to recall only the fruits he had seen there, which the soldiers were not allowed to eat," says Apollinaire. "Henri Rousseau delights in the luxurious abundance of greenery, and fruits and flowers," Soffici stated after visiting the Douanier's studio.*

241

Henri Rousseau: **The Forget-Me-Nots.**

H. Lemonnier: Plums. Painting on wood, dedicated "to my friend H. Rousseau," 1908.

Henri Rousseau: **Still Life.** "Presented to my friend [Max] Weber, August 20, 1908. Union of America and France. The 2 Republics."

Henri Rousseau: **The Pink Candle.**

B y isolating his objects and focusing intensely on their sheer presence, trying to enhance their value with contrasting colors that stress their volumes and angular planes that accent their spatial situations, the Douanier Rousseau, already in contact with Picasso, announced the first beginnings of Cubism, though without realizing it or intending to do so. To see this, one need merely compare his **Pink Candle** to Picasso's still life. Picasso had not yet entered the analytical phase of this great pictorial revolution. Later on, Picasso was to say, "Rousseau represents the perfection of a certain kind of thought."

Pablo Picasso: Still Life with a Carafe and a Candlestick, *1909.*

243

On March 29, 1910, Ardengo Soffici visited the Douanier to buy his Breton landscape (inspired by Bernier), which Soffici had so greatly admired in 1907.

"I already sold it to a Russian gentleman," said Rousseau.

"I know, but I'd be content with a replica."

"It's a fine painting. But I have to deliver it right away. . . . For the time being, I could paint a still life for you, fruits, a vase of flowers."

"Near us," Soffici goes on to relate, "there was a small table with a kerosene lamp and a white enamel coffee pot."

" 'I could paint that,' said my host, 'with a red cloth underneath.' "

He finished his nature morte by April 7, and his old pupils found it to be so beautiful that he offered to sell it to Soffici "for thirty francs, since they were friends." A few months later, he died in the hospital, desolate at abandoning the works of his dear disciples, while one of them wept at the closed door of Rousseau's studio.

Henri Rousseau: **Still Life with Coffeepot.**

Still lifes by two old pupils of the Douanier Rousseau, done with his help.

The house Rousseau was born in at Laval: the Beucheresse Gate at the time of his childhood. (Mouilleron. Lithograph)

Biography

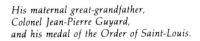

His maternal great-grandfather,
Colonel Jean-Pierre Guyard,
and his medal of the Order of Saint-Louis.

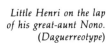

Little Henri on the lap
of his great-aunt Nono.
(Daguerreotype)

1767   January 3
Birth of Henri Rousseau's maternal great-grandfather, Jean-Pierre Guyard, to Jean Guyard, weaver, and Renée Renard, in Méral, a small township in Anjou.

1774   June 20
Baptism of Henri Rousseau's paternal grandfather, Julien-Gervais-Protais Rousseau, born to Georges Rousseau, merchant, and Charlotte Labaste, in Cossé-Le-Vivien, a township bordering on Méral.

1808   May 5
Birth of Henri Rousseau's father, Julien Rousseau, to Julien-Gervais-Protais Rousseau, ironmonger, Rue des Serruriers in Laval, and Renée-Magdelaine-Julienne Fouillée, born in Gennes, Ille-et-Vilaine, on January 30, 1774; the couple were married in 1806 at Gennes, where Augustin Fouillée (Renée's uncle) was a justice of the peace.

1811   April 15
Jean-Pierre Guyard appointed major second-class of the Marching Regiment of Napoleon's Army in Spain.

1818   December 10
Marriage in Mans of Henri Rousseau's maternal grandfather, Jean-Baptiste Guyard (born in Laval on October 1?. 1791, to Jean-Pierre Guyard and Catherine Valmont), to his first cousin Michelle Guyard, born in Laval on May 23, 1796, with whom he has already had a daughter, Henriette. Jean-Baptiste Guyard is captain in the Third Battalion of his department's legion on the Gold Coast. (The Douanier Rousseau's close relatives saw this intermarriage as the reason for Rousseau's bohemian, artistic temperament and his "originality.")

1819   August 15
Birth in Laval of Henri Rousseau's mother, Eléonore Guyard.

1833   August 21
Death of Captain Jean-Baptiste Guyard at the Bône military hospital in Algeria. Henriette and Eléonore Guyard, having already lost their mother (who died in Dieppe on June 7, 1821), are taken in by their grandfather Colonel Guyard. Eléonore had a strict upbringing in the boarding school of the Legion of Honor; she was deeply religious.

1837   May 5
Marriage in Laval of Henri Rousseau's parents, Julien Rousseau and Eléonore Guyard.

1838   August 18
Birth of Marie-Eléonore, older sister of Henri Rousseau.

1839   November 22
Birth of Eléonore-Louise-Renée Rousseau, who dies on January 14, 1840.

1841   September 2
Birth of Henriette-Anatolie Rousseau.

1844   May 21
Birth at 1:00 A.M. of the future painter,

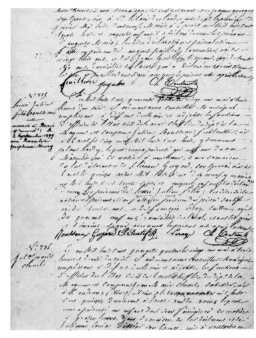

Rousseau's birth certificate.

Place Hardy, Laval, during the Second Empire.

Henri-Julien-Félix Rousseau, to Julien Rousseau, ironmonger, and Eléonore Guyard, in the family house of Beucheresse Gate, a double medieval tower located between Rue des Serruriers and Place Hardy in Laval. As viewed from the square, it is the right-hand tower that belongs to the Rousseau family. This gate, surrounded by thickets, gets its name (which means "woodchopping") from the woodcutters who used to pass through it on the way to the forest. It was part of the fortified ramparts constructed by the lords of Laval. Place Hardy is also the location of the Church of the Trinity, which soon becomes a cathedral. The square was named after René Hardy de Lévaré, who in 1707, as mayor, cleared the site and turned it into a livestock marketplace. Laval was also the birthplace of the famous French surgeon Ambroise Paré, who was born there around 1509. A statue of him was put up in the town-hall square on July 29, 1840.

1845   February 7
The death of Henri Rousseau's paternal grandfather. Rousseau's father has launched a series of maneuvers in the family business and in real estate leading to his bankruptcy.

1846   September 26
Birth of Jules Rousseau, younger brother of Henri.

The Dungeon, the Old Bridge, and the Mayenne in Laval. (Steel engraving)

The old château of Laval, around 1860.

Henriette Guyard, Rousseau's aunt.

Henri Rousseau with his father.

December 26
Death in Mans of Colonel Jean-Pierre Guyard, Knight of Saint-Louis and bearer of a medal from the Legion of Honor. His decorations are piously preserved by Henri Rousseau's mother, who tells the boy about her father's military feats.

1849   September 17
Henri Rousseau begins elementary school at the Laval *lycée*, which is directed by its founder, the Abbé Jules Dours. Rousseau's schoolmate is Victor Boissel, the future mayor of Laval who, in 1898, refuses to buy the painter's **Sleeping Gypsy.** Anselme Jarry, the father of Alfred Jarry, attends a higher grade in the same school.

1852   July 31
The Rousseau family home is auctioned off. Henri's father has become a salesman of wine and brandy.

1854
Julien Rousseau, ruined financially, obtains a tobacco concession in Couptrain, near Pré-en-Pail, thanks to the military background of his father-in-law.

1860
Henri Rousseau finishes the school year with certificates of merit in singing and drawing. Having little motivation for his studies, he does not get very far in school. (In 1895, he writes about himself: "Given his parents' lack of fortune, he was obliged to follow a different career from that to which his tastes summoned him." This will be a leitmotif until his death: his regret that his parents didn't understand his calling and didn't give him an artistic education.)

1862   January 7
Marriage in Angers of Henri Rousseau's sister Anatolie to Louis Rozé, commercial agent. The Rousseau family lives on Rue de la Madeleine. Julien has gone back to being an ironmonger.

1863   March 7
Henri Rousseau is exempted from military service. He works for a lawyer at 6 Rue de la Haute-du-Mail, Angers. He robs his employer, Monsieur Fillon, of ten francs and some stamps worth one franc. He also "embezzles five francs plus four francs' worth of stamps from Monsieur Constant Gaisnon," a general agent. These thefts are committed with the complicity of two young friends, fifteen and fourteen years of age.
December 1
Pressured by his parents, he joins the French army for seven years. When he is put into the 51st Line Infantry Regiment, his file notes that he is 1.65 meters tall (5'7") and has black eyes and dark-chestnut hair and eyelashes.

1864   February 11
The soldier Rousseau is taken to the jail in Angers at the demand of the examining magistrate.
February 20
The Tribunal of Angers condemns Rousseau to one month's imprisonment. He is detained at Angers, then transferred to the prison at Nantes, from which he is released on March 20.

1867
The two battalions of his regiment that were sent to Mexico in support of Em-

14 - ANGERS. — Le Château - Les Douves. - Le Bout du Monde.
La Promenade du « Bout du Monde » est particulièrement appréciée des
Angevins et des Touristes pour sa situation unique. De sa pointe extrême
qui domine la Ville, on découvre le magnifique panorama d'Angers et la
Maine qui coule au bas du Château. P. C.

ANGERS. — Vue générale.

50. ANGERS - Vue sur la Maine, prise du Château - L. V., phot.

98. - ANGERS
Statue du Roi René et le Château - L. V., phot.

Au Bon Marché department store, 1872.
Close relatives of Clémence Boitard.

Clémence Boitard,
his first wife.

peror Maximilian return to Angers on the night of April 7. Henri Rousseau did not go off with them, but he listens to their tales. (During the last few years of his life, he tells people that he discovered for himself the exoticism of Mexico.) Remaining in France during his military service, he participates in various maneuvers in the west and is a member of the band of the 51st.

1868   February 6
Henri Rousseau's father dies in Angers, 22 Quai de Ligny. Since Rousseau is now an eldest son supporting a widow, he asks to be released from the army. He moves to 25 Rue Rousselet, in the Seventh Arrondissement of Paris. (This is the same apartment house where the Norman writer Barbey d'Aurevilly dies in 1889.) Rousseau falls madly in love with his landlady's daughter Jeanne-Désirée-Clémence Boitard. Clémence was born on June 4, 1850, at 1 Rue de la Surintendance in Saint-Germain-en-Laye. Her mother, Barbe-Jeanne-Caroline Deurbergue (whose father came from Prague), is a seamstress and has taught Clémence to sew. Her father, François-Félix Boitard, a cabinet merchant who ruined himself gambling, died on October 4, 1867, at 26 Rue Bertrand in the Seventh Arrondissement. Henri Rousseau finds a job with a bailiff named Radez on Rue Berger near Les Halles. After obtaining permission from his mother in Angers, Henri Rousseau becomes engaged to Clémence Boitard.

1869   August 14
Henri Rousseau marries Clémence Boitard at the district hall of the Seventh Arrondissement and at the Church of Foreign Missions on Rue du Bac. The bridegroom's witnesses are his younger brother, Jules Rousseau, and a friend of the Rousseau family, Monsieur Gabory. Clémence's witnesses are a cousin, Paul-Clément Piella, residing at 97 Rue de Sèvres, and an uncle, André-César-Alexandre Lemaire de Beaumarchais, inspector of indirect contributions, retired,

Alphonse de Neuville: The Last Cartridges.

A barricade of the Commune.

residing at 13 Rue Saint-Romain, in the same neighborhood.

1870 May 20
Birth of Henri-Anatole-Clément Rousseau, their eldest child.
July 14
Mobilization edict.
July 19
Baptism of Henri-Anatole.
Napoleon III declares war on Prussia.
July 20
Henri Rousseau reports at Dreux as a reservist for his regiment, several units of which are to fight against the Germans: on August 16 at Rezonville and on August 18 at Saint-Privat. (Private Second Class Henri Rousseau, who remains in Dreux, tells Guillaume Apollinaire in 1908 that he was a courageous sergeant and helped save the population from the risks of civil war.) Rousseau writes his wife, asking her to light a candle at Notre-Dame-des-Victoires.
September 15
Rousseau is "sent home as the eldest son of a widow." He finds his wife and his son at 135 Rue de Sèvres, in a modest apartment house near Boulevard des Invalides. (The house is demolished in 1975.)

1871 January 17
Death of little Henri-Anatole at his grandmother Boitard's home on Rue Rousselet.

Henri Rousseau can't stand participating in the bailiff's seizures of the property of poor people, and he looks for another job. A relative of his wife's offers to recommend him to the Paris Customs Office.

The recipient of a Good Conduct Certificate from his regiment on September 15—it doesn't mention his imprisonment—he applies for a job at the Paris Customs Office and is accepted as a supernumerary employee on December 8. (According to the certificate, he is 1.63 meters tall—5'6"—and his left ear has been cut off.)

1872 February 1
Henri Rousseau starts working for the Customs Office; this will cause him to be erroneously nicknamed the Douanier, "customs officer," especially by Alfred Jarry, author of *Ubu Roi*. (Rousseau's service and guard duty at the gates of Paris and on the quays of the Seine inspired several of his paintings and drawings: **The Customs House; View of the Port of Saint-Nicolas; Longshoremen; View of**

The Gate of Vanves, Paris, Fourteenth Arrondissement.

Point-du-Jour; Myself. Landscape Portrait; Waiting. . . .)
July 5
Birth of Antonine-Louise Rousseau.

The Douanier Rousseau begins to paint. He is aided by his wife, Clémence, who, to augment the family budget, designs sewing patterns. (On Sundays, they go to the Luxembourg Gardens, the Bois de Boulogne, and Saint-Germain-en-Laye, where they visit close relatives of Clémence's as well as the Hippodrome of Longchamp.)

The old apartment house, 135 Rue de Sèvres.

Good Conduct Certificate for Henri Rousseau.

The head of the Statue of Liberty on the Champ-de-Mars in 1878.

The painter Bouguereau.

The painter Gérôme at home.

The painter Clément. (Self-portrait)

1874   January 27
Birth of Julia-Clémence Rousseau, who dies on February 18.

1876   June 11
Birth of Julia Rousseau.

Clémence, consumptive after a cold she caught while leaving the theater, places her daughter Julia with a wetnurse, Madame Raynal, in Malakoff, so that the baby can benefit from the pure country air. (The Douanier Rousseau subsequently paints several views of Malakoff.)

1877   January
Rousseau paints and dates a small war scene set in a snow-covered village.

1878   May-October
Rousseau visits the World's Fair and is struck by its allegories.

1879   April 27
Birth of Henri-Anatole Rousseau.
       August 10
Baptism of the child at the Church of Saint Francis Xavier. The godfather, who has come up from the provinces, is Rousseau's uncle Jules Rousseau, and the godmother his widowed aunt Anatolie Rozé. This child is also placed with the wetnurse in Malakoff.

The Douanier Rousseau paints and dates a rustic landscape with a water mill and a horse-drawn wagon.

1882   September 2
Birth of a child.

The painter Félix Clément, winner of the first Grand Prize of Rome, in 1856, and former director of the School of Fine Arts in Lyon, takes up residence at 137 Rue de Sèvres. The Douanier Rousseau makes his acquaintance and meets other painters in Clément's home. He gets well-meaning advice from him and from the painter Gérôme ("If I have kept my naïveté, it is because Monsieur Gérôme, who was a professor at the School of Fine Arts, and Monsieur Clément, director of the School of Lyon, always told me to keep it," Rousseau says by way of an excuse, toward the end of his life, to the art critic André Dupont. In his dealings with Clément, the Douanier regrets not having had an education, and he writes in 1907, "If my parents had known that I was gifted in painting, as our dear, departed Clément himself told them . . . I ought to be the greatest and richest painter in France today.")

Little by little, Rousseau gives up practicing his religion, even becoming anticlerical, which deeply shocks his mother and forces his wife and children to maintain the utmost discretion: they attend catechism in secret.
       November 4
Le Monde Illustré, in its supplement, publishes a large foldout reproducing the panorama of *The Battle of Champigny* by Alphonse de Neuville and Edouard Detaille. Rousseau traces out the central engraving by Fortuné Méaulle (who was born in Angers on April 11, 1844). Rousseau's painting, 28 × 49.5 cm., the size of the actual engraving, is acquired by Dr. Girardin in 1917 and bequeathed to the Museum of Modern Art, Paris, in 1953.

1884   September 23
Thanks to Clément's recommendation to Armand Fallières, the Minister of Public Instruction, the Douanier Rousseau obtains a copyist's card giving him access "on every day of study" to the galleries of the Louvre, the Luxembourg, Versailles, and Saint-Germain. He visits these museums attentively "to raise himself to beauty." He also visits the Cluny Museum, which in 1882 acquired the tapestries of *The Lady with the Unicorn,* the themes and techniques of which will mark Rousseau's *oeuvre.* The "Sunday painter" becomes an "artistic painter"; and, with the indulgence of his superiors in the Customs Office, he tries to get "easier work," in order to work more assiduously on his painting.

1885   March-April
Rousseau is impressed by the major Delacroix exhibit at the Paris School of Fine Arts, particularly by his wild animals.
       May 9-June 21
Rousseau "debuts" in art by showing for the first time two canvases of which he is very proud: **Italian Dance** and **A Sunset.** He exhibits these works with the "dissidents" of the "group of Independents" after trying to enter them at the Salon of French Arts, otherwise known as the Salon. (Rousseau has gotten into the habit of going to the Salon, where he envies the glory and talent of certain great academic painters.) In the school notebook in which he pastes all his press clippings (sent by Argus, to which he has subscribed), he writes: "These two canvases were shown at the Salon. One was perforated by a penknife, but I was refused any recompense, so I showed them again at the group of the so-called *refusés,* which exhibited during the month of June." He also notes his two addresses: 135 Rue de Sèvres and 18 bis Impasse du Maine, where he rented a studio in a small "artists' section."

The theme of **Italian Dance** is indicated by the caption that the painter inscribed in the frame of the painting:

Copyist's pass for the French national museums.

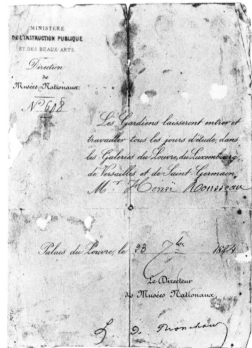

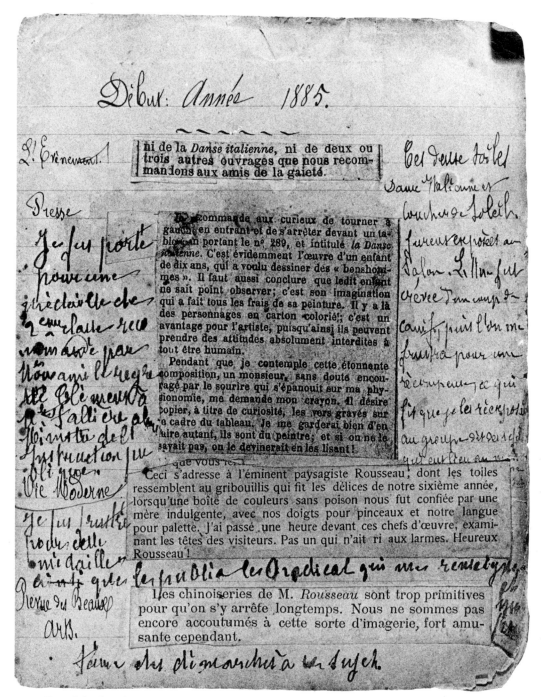

The first page of Rousseau's scrapbook for press clippings.

Pissarro, seeing these paintings, admires "the naïveté of the drawing, the quality of this art, the precision of the hues and the richness of the tones." Art critics try to ridicule Rousseau. "I don't know whether the stroke of thunder was captured with the help of an instantaneous photographic apparatus, but this lightning is wretchedly fixed, superbly wooden," writes Robert Bernier.

1887   March 25–May 3
At the third Salon of the Independents, in the Pavilion of the City of Paris on the Champs-Elysées, Rousseau shows three paintings: **View of Quai d'Orsay (Autumn); A Poor Devil;** and **View of an Avenue in the Tuileries (Spring).**

Journalists speak of his "naïveté," his "sincerity," recalling the Italian primitives, Giotto. In *L'Estafette:* "Don't forget **The Poor Devil** and **Quai d'Orsay,** highly original paintings by Monsieur Henri Rousseau."

Having transmitted several appreciations by critics to the Counsel General of the City of Paris, the Douanier Rousseau asks him in vain for "a subsidy to continue his studies of paintings."

1888   February 2
The death in Algiers of the painter Félix Clément, "for whom I must preserve a great deal of esteem and gratitude despite his having passed away; for he always gave me good advice," writes Rousseau in his scrapbook.

March 22–May 3
In the fourth Salon of the Independents, on the Champs-Elysées, Rousseau enters, along with five canvases, five drawings (nos. 579–83).

Odilon Redon sees **The Departure; After the Feast; View of Ile-Saint-Louis from the Port of Saint-Nicolas (Evening)** (actually a view of Ile de la Cité), and **Dinner on the Grass.** Redon supposedly admires "the genius of this naturalist painter who sometimes rises to classical beauty." The comment in *Cri du Peuple* stresses that Rousseau is a "profound draftsman." Gustave Geoffroy, in contrast, feels that these works are stupefy-

One fine Sunday in spring,
The season when nature recovers her splendor,
See these rustic peasants,
Inspired by a sweet gaiety from their hearts,
Dancing on the greening lawn
In order to forget long, rude labors.

Journalists and art critics made fun of him. L. Beaumont, in *La Vie Moderne* (May 16), wrote that "his paintings resemble the daubings that were our delight when we were six.... I spent an hour in front of these masterpieces, scrutinizing the faces of the visitors. There wasn't one who didn't laugh till tears came. Happy Rousseau!"

March 28
Henri Rousseau receives a diploma from the French Literary and Musical Academy for his composition "Clémence: Waltz with an Introduction for Violin or Mandolin," which he has dedicated to his wife and played at the Salle Beethoven.

1886   August 20–September 21
Encouraged by Signac, one of the founders of the Salon of the Independents, Rousseau shows four paintings at this second salon, in a temporary structure near the Carousel in the Tuileries. These four canvases are: **A Stroke of Lightning on the Left Bank of the Seine, over Vanves; View of Point-du-Jour, Sunset; A Carnival Evening;** and **Waiting.**

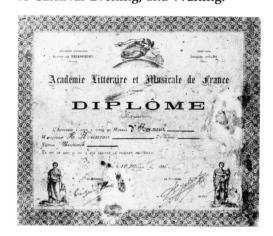

The World's Fair of 1899.
View from the Bridge of Grenelle.

The presentation of ceramics
and porcelains from the various French regions.

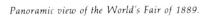

Panoramic view of the World's Fair of 1889.

A path in Montsouris Park.

The Brisemiche Pool in Chaville.

ingly comical.

May 7

Tubercular for several years, Clémence Rousseau dies at 4:00 P.M. at 135 Rue de Sèvres. Her funeral takes place on May 10 at the Church of Saint Francis Xavier. The Douanier Rousseau is grief-stricken. "My poor wife left this earth, which is so arid for some people, after twenty years of a pure, sacred union of living only for one another as even our parents said themselves, how happy this made us mutually. Ah, yes! Those twenty years were the happiness of my life," Rousseau was to write from Santé Prison on December 19, 1907. He has also lost seven children in their infancy. He has kept the two who remained, Julia and Henri, but paid little attention to them.

1889   May 5–October 31

In a visit to the World's Fair, the Douanier discovers the Mexican palace, its aloes and sisals, and the pavilions of African and Asian colonies. The fair gave him the idea of writing a *vaudeville*, a light comedy, in three acts and ten scenes: *A Visit to the World's Fair of 1889*. It tells of a decent Breton family who visit Paris—the Invalides, the Louvre, the Botanical Garden, Place de la République, and the World's Fair. Their servant girl exclaims, "Ah, what bliss! I go see that great fair, with the Eiffel Tower, the Trickyderrière, the Negroes, the Redskins. . . ." (This comedy is published in 1947 by Tzara and performed for the first time in 1968 at the Theater Festival of Nancy by the Czechoslovakian Troupe of the Naïve Theater of Liberec).

September 2–October 4

At the fifth Salon of the Independents, in the hall of the Society of Horticulture, at 84 Boulevard Saint-Germain, the Douanier Rousseau exhibited only three paintings: **To My Father, Portrait of Mademoiselle Lepallier; A Suicide;** and **Portrait of Madame G.**

Le Journal des Artistes writes, "Monsieur H. Rousseau is a primitive, absolutely himself, who, in a portrait of a girl, manages to wipe away life and make a

The title page of Rousseau's farce.

The first page of the manuscript.

The end of the farce.

springtime landscape dismal." *L'Evénement* writes, "I've never seen anything more grotesque than Monsieur Rousseau's **Suicide** and his portraits and Monsieur Van Gogh's *Starry Night.*"

1890   March 19–April 27

At the sixth Salon of the Independents, in the Pavilion of the City of Paris on the Champs-Elysées, Rousseau presents **Myself, Landscape Portrait; View of Issy, Springtime Effect After the Storm; View of Billancourt and Bas-Meudon, Mist Effect; Portrait of M.B.; My First by Julia Rousseau, Born in Paris; Pen-and-Ink Drawing; Pencil-and-Pen Drawing; Two Pen-and-Ink Drawings** (nos. 667–68). Paul Gauguin is supposed to have stopped at these paintings and said, "This is truth . . . the future. *This* is painting! This is the only thing we can look at here." The reviews by journalists are as severe as ever, except the one in the *Avenir National*: "Monsieur H. Rousseau is one of the hard-and-fast members of the Society of Independents. Since the last exhibition, he has made real and visible progress as a colorist, including *plein-air.*"

The Douanier Rousseau, setting himself on the bank of the Seine in **Myself,** later claims to be "the inventor of the landscape portrait." He has painted two first names on the palette in his self-portrait: Clémence and Marie. In regard to this painting, the journalist in *XIXe Siècle* writes, "The artist, out of excessive modesty no doubt, has painted himself the size of a midget, with an oversized head, loaded with thought perhaps." **My First by Julia Rousseau, Born in Paris** is really a painting by his daughter, which he presents along with his own works.

"We are in the midst of the Independents," French President Carnot is told by General Brugère, his chief of staff, as they pass by the Douanier. Rousseau boasted about this comment, which he took as a compliment.

April 4

Death at twenty-seven of the Douanier's niece, Marie Rozé, a music teacher at the

Frank Salisbury: Self-portrait, for "my friend Henri Rousseau," 1891.

Oratory of Angers, who has the reputation of a saint. (Rousseau's family is quite musical; his cousin Laure Béguin is a piano teacher in Paris.)

December 24

Death of the Douanier's mother, Eléonore Rousseau, in the home of her daughter Anatolie Rozé, in Angers. Toward the end of his life, Rousseau tells his friend the German art critic Wilhelm Uhde that his mother was "very pious and spent more money than she should have on cakes for clergymen."

1891   March 19–April 27

At the seventh Salon of the Independents, on the Champs-Elysées, Rousseau produces his first exotic painting: **Surprised!** It is accompanied by six other canvases: **View of the Bois de Boulogne, Springtime; View of the Municipality of Malakoff; View of the Footbridge of Passy; Portrait of M.B.; Portrait of M.L.; Group of the M. Family.**

The tiger surprised by the storm in the jungle is praised, despite the general mirth the painting provokes, by the young Swiss painter Félix Vallotton, in *La Gazette de Lausanne:* "This is the alpha and omega of painting." In an article entitled "The Naïfs," the critic of *Le National* waxes ironic: "A simple customs man or employee of the Customs Office, whose fiscal occupations cannot extinguish his artistic instincts. His is the purest success of this exhibit. . . . You have no idea of how he paints." Argus sends Rousseau a clipping: "Contest of the City of Paris. Silver Medal to Henri Rousseau for his paintings." The Douanier then adds "Medal Winner" to his calling cards, even though the laureate was a different painter with the same name.

1892   March 17–April 27

Inspired by the announcement of the celebration of the centennial of the Republic on September 22, and hoping to obtain a commission from the government at last, Rousseau exhibits an allegorical painting at the eighth Salon of the Independents, on the Champs-Elysées, **One Centennial of Independence. The People Dance Around Two Republics, That of 1792 and That of 1892, Holding Hands and Singing: "Auprès de ma blonde, qu'il fait bon, fait bon dormir."** This painting is accompanied by five others: **Portrait of Mademoiselle Jeanne (Belonging to M.B.); Portrait of Madame L.; View of the Gate of Bas-Meudon After Rain; View of the Bridge of Grenelle (Trocadéro); Longshoreman (Belonging to My Friend Claude Goubot).** Claude Goubot is secretary of the Society of Independent Artists.

Rousseau is still being mocked, and *Le Journal des Débats* speaks of "the ineffable Henri Rousseau, so naïve in himself."

The **Centennial of Independence** was partly inspired by an engraving by Fortuné Méaulle after a watercolor by Meyer; the engraving appeared in the illustrated supplement to *Le Petit Journal* of April 11, 1891, under the title *The Feasts of Andorra. The Farandole.*

"At the Pavilion of the City, there is a customs inspector who with a touching good grace exhibits portraits and compositions that a man at a shooting gallery would regard as attractive targets," writes Arsène Alexandre in *Paris,* on March 18.

"The unexpected note was supplied first by Monsieur Henri Rousseau, whose seven canvases attract the crowd. Visitors halt especially in front of a **Centennial of Independence** depicting the people dancing around the two republics. . . . Monsieur Rousseau is one of the personalities of the Salon of the Independents, and we are happy to note the real progress he has made since last year. A little more effort, and soon we will see him at the Champ-de-Mars," writes Henry Morrel in *Le Petit Moniteur Universel,* on March 20, 1892. And Reverchons, in *La Revue des Beaux-Arts et des Lettres,* writes on April 2, "When one pauses in front of Monsieur Rousseau's painting, only one idea comes to mind: the public is not yet on a level with this genre!"

1893   March 17–April 27

Rousseau perseveres in his allegories with two paintings at the ninth Salon of the Independents, on the Champs-Elysées: **The Last of the 51st (After Long Struggles, the Regiment Was Completely Decimated, the Poor Mutilated Soldier Remains to Save the Standard Under Which Our Forebears Conquered So Much Glory;** and **Liberty (Oh, Liberty, Always Be the Guide of All Those Who, Through Their Labor, Wish to Help the Glory and Grandeur of France). Liberty** may be the painting now entitled **The French Republic.** Rousseau also presents **View of Vanves After Rain; View of Ile Saint-Louis During the Night of the Burning of the Omnibus Depot, Quai de l'Estrapade;** and **Portrait of M.B.**

"Yum, yum!" writes one critic. And *Le Petit Parisien:* "The ridiculous also has its part . . . for instance, this astonishing painting, which looks like the work of an urchin imitating the draftsmen of popu-

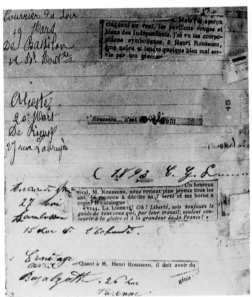

Pages of a notebook of Rousseau's (1891–93).

lar images that depict a standard-bearer with a wooden leg."

The **Portrait of M.B.** shows the policeman Frumence Biche, who died the preceding year; he was the husband of Marie Foucher, ex-housekeeper of Charles Marot, architect of the National Palaces, who lived at the Louvre, which is where the Douanier met her. Smitten with Marie, Rousseau did this portrait of her deceased husband after a photograph in order to console her in her widowhood. But all she gives him is an enduring and helpful friendship.

The Douanier Rousseau moves to 44 Avenue du Maine in the Fourteenth Arrondissement with his children and his mistress, Gabrielle, the daughter of an officer, whom his children detest.

March 29

The Counsel General of the Seine decides to hold a contest to decorate the town hall of Bagnolet.

Rousseau paints **The Carmagnole,** a replica of **The Centennial of Independence,** minus the lanterns and the male choir.

November 6

The sketches of the competitors are exhibited at the Pavilion of Liberal Arts on the Champ-de-Mars.

November 10

The contest jury, made up of three painters, Puvis de Chavannes, Merson (with whom the Douanier is slightly acquainted), and Roll (to whom we owe a *Republic* and a *Centennial Festival of the Revolution of 1789*), does not award the prize to Rousseau. Louis Béroud is one of the chosen painters. (The Douanier sees one of Béroud's paintings, *Nude Woman Reclining,* at the Salon of 1906; it inspires the central theme of **The Dream.**)

High altar of the Church of Saint Francis Xavier, Paris.

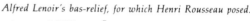

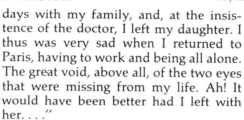

Alfred Lenoir's bas-relief, for which Henri Rousseau posed.

December 1

The Douanier Rousseau retires as an "ambulant clerk, first class," with an annual pension of 1,019 francs. This sum is insufficient for living and painting, so he often pays his bills with his paintings or with portraits of his creditors' children, or by exchanging his works for a monetary "loan." Some of these canvases were destroyed, but others occasionally resurface.

1894

Julia Rousseau, humiliated by the mockeries of the public, upset by her father's bohemian life and the intrusion of his "models," and badly nourished, writes to her aunt Anatolie Rozé, pouring out her distress. The aunt offers to take her in at 4 Rue Voltaire in Angers. The Douanier Rousseau is then "alone" with his son Henri. Having no sense of the passing of time, Rousseau later complains: "After my wife's death . . . I could spend a few

UNE BOMBE AU CAFE TERMINUS
Arrestation de l'assassin

A Bomb of the Café Terminus.
In Le Petit Journal (February 1894).

days with my family, and, at the insistence of the doctor, I left my daughter. I thus was very sad when I returned to Paris, having to work and being all alone. The great void, above all, of the two eyes that were missing from my life. Ah! It would have been better had I left with her. . . ."

April 6–May 27

The tenth Salon of the Independents is moved to the Palace of Liberal Arts on the Champ-de-Mars. Henri Rousseau sends four paintings there: **War. It Passes, Terrifying, Leaving Despair, Tears, and Ruin Everywhere; Decorative Panel; Portrait of a Child; Portrait of M.J.**

War, subsequently also called **The Ride of Discord,** is described by the critic for *Le Petit Journal:* "A symbolic painting that depicts War mounted on an apocalyptic beast." The critic for *La Plume* speaks of "the painter's inspired unawareness."

At this exhibition, Alfred Jarry meets the Douanier Rousseau, who knew Jarry's father in their home town, Laval. The poet is excited by Rousseau's work and discusses **War** in *L'Art Littéraire,* then in the series titled "Les Essais d'art libre."

April 12

At the Galerie Georges Petit, the Douanier sees an exhibit of paintings by one of the founding members of the Independents, Louis Sérendat de Belzim. Rousseau considers the work very good.

May 23

Consecration of the high altar of the Church of Saint Francis Xavier, on Boulevard des Invalides. The bas-relief by Alfred Lenoir depicts the dying Jesuit saint—modeled by the Douanier.

June 26

Rousseau writes to Jarry (who visits Laval, and then goes to Pont-Aven with Gauguin) to tell him that he, Rousseau, has prepared the canvas for Jarry's portrait, and that he is planning to move from 78 Boulevard de Port-Royal. Rousseau also wishes Jarry "good health to the knights of the palette."

1895 January
Publication of the second issue of *L'Ymagier,* a periodical illustrated with popular engravings and drawings by the Pont-Aven painters; the review was founded by Jarry and Rémy de Gourmont the previous year. It includes the Douanier's lithograph on the same theme as **War.** The lithograph, printed on red Japanese

Paul Gauguin: Self-Portrait, 1893.

Cazals: Portrait of Alfred Jarry. In André Breton's collection.

257

vellum, is even closer than the painting to the photographic source in *Le Courrier Français* (October 27, 1889). *L'Ymagier* offers the painting and the lithograph for sale. Jarry also tries to get *Le Mercure de France* to write about Rousseau.

January 23
Henri Rousseau takes back several of his paintings that the art dealer Ambroise Vollard took on consignment but has failed to sell.

March
A long laudatory article by Louis Roy on Rousseau's **War** comes out in *Le Mercure de France.* "Monsieur Rousseau has gone through what all innovators have experienced. He proceeds all by himself, he has the merit—rare today—of being absolutely personal. He is moving toward a new art. . . ."

April 9–May 26
Ten paintings by the Douanier at the eleventh Salon of the Independents, on the Champ-de-Mars: **Portrait of Madame A.J.; Portrait of Madame L.; Portrait of M.B.; Portrait of a Child; View of the Footbridge of Passy; View from an Arch of the Bridge of Sèvres; View of Saint-Cloud from the Heights of Bellevue; View of the Tip of Ile du Bas-Meudon; View of the Quai de l'Arsenal; View of Park Montsouris.**

The critics advise readers to go and see the "laughable" paintings. *Le XIXe Siècle* alludes to Rousseau's "Japanizing portraits in which the heads are deliberately larger than the bodies."

"Finally," writes a friend of Jarry's in *L'Idée Moderne*, "we come to H. Rousseau, who is also an innovator, since *L'Ymagier* is publishing his works. . . . He is primitive because he cannot be otherwise. Look at his portrait of a poet (Monsieur Alfred Jarry), the length of whose hair has caused the catalogue to list the painting as *Portrait of Madame A.J.* The poet, dressed in black, is seated. Around him are the animals he likes best: the owl and the chameleon. The chameleon's tongue, on his ear, was mistaken by one critic for a penholder."

July 10
On Jarry's advice, the Douanier com-

First page of the autobiographical note written by the Douanier.

Handwritten document for Vollard.

poses an autobiographical note for the publishers Coutance and Gérard, who plan to put out the second volume of *Portraits of the Next Century:* "It was only in the year 1885 that he made his debut in Art," writes Rousseau, "after many vexations, alone, with no other master than nature, and some advice from Gérôme and Clément. . . . It was after many harsh ordeals that he managed to become known by the many artists around him. He perfected himself more and more in the original genre that he adopted and he is now becoming one of our best realistic painters. . . . He has been a member of the Independents for a long time now, feeling that all freedom to produce must be left to the initiator, whose mind rises to the beautiful and the good. He will never forget the members of the press who have managed to understand him and who have supported him in moments of discouragement and who will have helped him to become what he must be."

December 28
Death of Le Tensorer, husband of Rousseau's mistress, Joséphine, née Nourry; she was born on February 15, 1852, in Saint-Germain-en-Caux, to a shoemaker and a laundress.

1896 April 1–May 31
At the twelfth Salon of the Independents, on the Champ-de-Mars, the Douanier shows ten paintings: **Portrait of Madame M.; A Philosopher; Portraits of Children; Portrait of Mademoiselle M.; View of the Canal of Charenton at Sunset; View of the Place Known as Dahomey at Quai d'Alfortville; View of the Heights of Bellevue; View of the Fortifications on Boulevard Gouvion-Saint-Cyr; View of the Bois de Boulogne; View of the Bridge of Sèvres and Saint-Cloud.**

The journalists speak of the painter's "chinoiserie," his "mirth-provoking conception of nature and art," "his childlike genre," his painting "done to provide a good laugh for his contemporaries," "his crude, barbaric imagery." *La Vie Artistique*, however, affirms that "his landscapes are not without polish and reveal some sort of contact with Oriental miniature."

His painting of **The Philosopher** was accompanied by this caption:

Like the great philosopher Diogenes
Although not living in a barrel
I am the Wandering Jew on earth
Fearing neither squall nor water,
Trotting along, smoking my old
    pipe,
Proudly braving the lightning, the
    thunder,
To earn a modest sum

3074 — Bois de VINCENNES. Embarcadère du Lac Daumesnil. ND Phot.

Landing dock at Lake Daumesnil, Vincennes.

Despite the rain wetting the earth
I carry on my back and with no replica
The advertisement for the independent newspaper *L'Eclair.*

The Douanier Rousseau moves
again, to a more economical apartment at
14 Avenue du Maine: he has serious
money problems.
September 17
Rousseau is obliged to sign an acknowl-
edgment of indebtedness to his art-supply dealer, Paul Foinet, whose shop is
located at 54 Rue Notre-Dame-des-
Champs, Sixth Arrondissement.

1897   February 25
Death of the painter's son, Henri-Anatole Rousseau, an engraver, just eighteen
years old. He succumbs to tuberculosis at
the Hospital for Sick Children. Rousseau
sinks further into debt.

April 2–May 31
Rousseau's grief and problems do not
prevent him from taking nine paintings
to the thirteenth Salon of the Independents, on the Champ-de-Mars: **The
Sleeping Gypsy; Portraits of Monsieur
and Madame E.F.; Portrait of Mademoiselle V.B.; Portraits of Children; View of
the Railroad from Lyon to Charenton;
View of the Seine Bank at Alfortville
and the Pont d'Ivry; View of the Chair
Factory and the Seine Quay at Alfortville; Bouquet of Wild Flowers; Portrait
of Mademoiselle M.**

The Sleeping Gypsy, the theme for
which comes from a Louis Matout painting that Rousseau saw at the Luxembourg Museum, carries this comment:
"The feline, although ferocious, is reluctant to leap upon its prey, who, worn out,
has fallen into a profound sleep."

Le Mercure de France states, "Monsieur Rousseau, who persists, does not
even manage to elicit a smile from us."
Other critics, however, find Rousseau's
work "mirth-provoking." In *La Revue
Blanche,* Thadée Natanson notes, "One
must, above all, speak of Monsieur Henri

Rousseau, whose fierce naïveté achieves
something of a style and whose stubborn
and ingenuous simplicity has the glory of
making us think of primitive works, with
no other motive than good will."
May 10
Henri Rousseau futilely asks the City of
Paris to buy his **Sleeping Gypsy.** (The
painting is eventually acquired by the
Museum of Modern Art, New York,
which still owns it.)
July 2
Rousseau paints the Cathedral of Mantes-
la-Jolie.
August
Evicted from his place on 78 Boulevard
de Port-Royal, Jarry is generously put up
by Rousseau, who is no less impover-
ished than the poet. The Douanier later
tells Jarry's friend Léon-Paul Fargue,
"We have four great writers: Monsieur
Octave Mirbeau, Monsieur Jarry, Mon-
sieur Fargue, and Monsieur Prudent-
Dervillers."

1898   February 18
A contest is held for the artistic decoration of the banquet room of the town hall
of Vincennes. The artists must be inspired solely by views of the surroundings of Vincennes, which the Douanier
later paints. However, he is not chosen in
the judging on June 21. (He subsequently
also does a small wooden sculpture of
Rochet's statue of General Daumesnil in
front of the town hall.)
April 18–June 12
Rousseau shows a second exotic canvas
at the fourteenth Salon of the Independents, which is now housed in the Palais
de Glace on the Champs-Elysées: **The
Struggle for Life.** He also adds a portrait
and three landscapes: **View of Rue
Louis-Blanc in Alfortville; View of the
Bois de Boulogne (Autumn); View of
the Banks of the Marne (Summer).**

The journalists outdo one another
denouncing this "laughable success,"
these "daubings," these "insanities,"
these "imbecilic and innocent jokes."
However, the editor of *Le Journal des Arts*
evinces some intuition: "His gentle ani-

Jarry biking away from his Corbeil home.

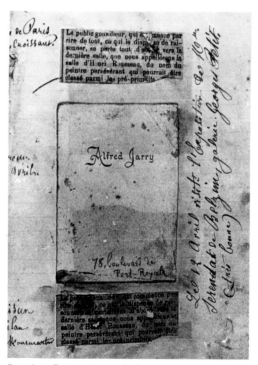

*Page from Rousseau's scrapbook
with Jarry's calling card.*

mals must be quite wild to devour one
another amid trees coming from [shops
providing cactuses and other tropical
plants as garden ornaments]." Frantz
Jourdain, who eventually founds the
Salon d'Automne, writes in *Le Jour,*
"When looking at these bizarre lucubrations, I can only feel a mixture of pity
and sadness."

The Douanier's calling card at
the time that he changed apartments.

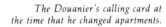

June
The painter rents one of the studios at 3
Rue Vercingétorix (almost across from
number 6, where Paul Gauguin stayed
after returning from Tahiti late in 1893),
in the middle of a paved courtyard nicknamed the Courtyard of Miracles. This
group of glass studios devoid of any
comforts were constructed with materials from the World's Fair of 1889. (They
are eventually destroyed during the development of the Maine-Montparnasse
area.)

July 10
Rousseau writes to the mayor of Laval:
"Being your compatriot, having become
an artist by himself, and desirous of having his native town possess one of his
works and have a souvenir of one of its
children." He hopes to sell the mayor
The Sleeping Gypsy for between eighteen hundred and two thousand francs.

July 18
When the mayor of Laval turns down his
offer, Rousseau wonders whether he can
find the wherewithal to pay for his canvases, which he continues to purchase
from Paul Foinet.

An antique dealer on Rue Servan-

Letter to the mayor of Laval,
offering to sell him **The Sleeping Gypsy.**

The studios at 3 Rue Vercingétorix before they were demolished.

New calling card for 3 Rue Vercingétorix.

The Fashoda meeting.

doni, near Saint-Sulpice, agrees to try to sell Rousseau's works. He introduces the Douanier to the Coucy family on Rue de Varenne, so that the painter can give lessons to the young son at Rue Vercingétorix. Rousseau also decorates shopwindows, including those of a charcoal dealer in exchange for coal. Some bad painters play a hoax on him, announcing that he has been made a knight of the Legion of Honor by President Félix Faure. When Rousseau learns at the police station that he is the victim of a prank, he bursts into tears.

Wearing his heart on his sleeve, he tries to help "the poor people" in his neighborhood, Plaisance, by recommending them to his Freemason brother Victor Pannelier, who owns a large shop for artistic photography on Avenue du Maine and is municipal councilor of the Fourteenth Arrondissement.

His faithful friend Marie Biche, a produce vendor on Place Médicis near the Luxembourg Gardens, sometimes invites him over for a bowl of soup in her home on Rue de la Sorbonne.

Rousseau is friends with the painter Mérodack-Jeanneau, who was born in Angers and who used to have a studio at 3 Rue Vercingétorix. The Douanier receives visits from his acquaintances the Sârses and Rose-Croix-du-Temples. With them he takes part in spiritist séances.

1899 January 5

The painter, in an effort to be a complete artist, finishes a play in five acts and nineteen scenes, which he destines for the Théâtre du Châtelet: *The Vengeance of a Russian Orphan*. This drama, which he hopes will win him great success and substantial income, is eventually published by Tristan Tzara in 1947, and premieres on July 7, 1948, at the Théâtre de l'Oeuvre. This first production is done by the Center of Dramatic Art Training in an adaptation by René Dupuy. It runs again, during the 1948–49 season, at the Studio des Champs-Elysées. The play is a great success on September 19, 1966, at Montreuil Gate, the Théâtre de l'Occi-

Cover of the manuscript of
The Vengeance of a Russian Orphan.

Start of second act.

End of manuscript and signature.

dent, directed by Jean Rougerie, with Elisabeth Wiener playing the part of Sophie, the orphan.

June 21
Rousseau writes a long love letter to Joséphine Nourry, widow of Le Tensorer, trying to raise her beyond organized religion, toward the Spirit above everything else.

September 2
Henri Rousseau marries Joséphine-Rosalie at the district hall of the Fifteenth Arrondissement and at the Church of Notre-Dame-des-Champs: although he has become a Freemason, he makes the concession of a church marriage. The bridegroom's witnesses are the young seamstress Marie Touchet and Joséphine's older brother, Jérôme Nourry, a day laborer residing in Boulogne-sur-Seine. The bride's witnesses are Jérôme Nourry's wife, née Marie Jouet, a laundress, and Jérôme and Joséphine's brother Victor-Aimable Nourry, a shop clerk, residing, like Joséphine, at 30 Avenue de Maine.

The Douanier Rousseau does not show anything at the fifteenth Salon of the Independents, which takes place in a warehouse on Rue du Colisée, the Hôtel Poilly, with few participating artists. Rousseau paints an allegory of his two marriages, **The Present and the Past,** which is accompanied by these verses:

> Separated from one another
> From those whom they loved
> Both of them unite once again
> While remaining faithful to their
>   thoughts.

This painting is subsequently shown at the Salon of the Independents in 1907 under the title **Philosophic Thought.**

1900 February 15

Marriage in Angers of the Douanier's daughter, Julia-Clémence Rousseau, an embroideress, to Marie-Lucien-Jean-Baptiste-Alphonse Bernard, a commercial representative. (Monsieur Bernard dies on July 23, 1941. Julia dies in Cherbourg, Rue Loysel, on August 5, 1956.)

A photograph of the Eiffel Tower that belonged to the Douanier Rousseau.

Catalogue of the Centennial Exhibition of French Art.

The hothouses at the World's Fair of 1900.

Rue Vercingétorix.

Postcard sent by Rousseau to his granddaughter.

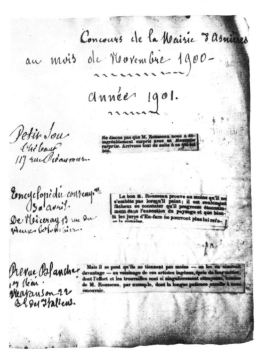

Page from Rousseau's scrapbook of press clippings.

February 18

The Douanier signs an IOU for fifty francs to his friend Marie Biche.

He visits the World's Fair of 1900 and the Centennial Retrospective of French Art, where he especially admires L. Gérôme's *Innocence*, which ultimately inspires the theme of his painting **Happy Quartet**. Rousseau orders a series of photographs of the fair and the Eiffel Tower.

April 1

A contest is proposed for the artistic decoration of the banquet room of the town hall of Asnières; the artists' compositions must be inspired exclusively by views of the surrounding region. The works will be shown starting on December 15 in the salons of the town hall.

November

The Douanier concentrates on the contest for the town hall of Asnières.

December 5

Opening of the sixteenth Salon of the Independents, on Rue du Colisée. Since the Douanier is on the committee, he does not exhibit. Only about fifty painters participate.

December 24

The jury of the Asnières contest sends back the Douanier's projects, which he eventually shows at the Salon of the Independents of 1902.

1901   January

The Douanier Rousseau and his wife leave Rue Vercingétorix and move to 36 Rue Gassendi, between Avenue du Maine and the Montparnasse cemetery. Joséphine opens a small stationery store here and tries to sell her husband's paintings.

February 20

Birth in Angers of Jeanne Bernard, the Douanier's granddaughter. Rousseau visits her several times, sends her color postcards, and feels a great affection for this child, who resembles him. (She becomes a piano techer in Cherbourg and an organist at Notre-Dame-du-Voeu.) Later on, speaking of his paintings, he tells his daughter, Julia, "You'll have one for more than a hundred thousand francs some day." The Bernards live first at 4 Rue des Arènes, then, from 1905 on, at 22 Place Saint-Maurice. During the next few years, Monsieur Bernard visits the Douanier regularly in Paris.

April 19–May 21

At the seventeenth Salon of the Independents, in the big hothouses of the World's Fair of 1900, at Cours-la-Reine, the Douanier shows seven paintings: **Unpleasant Surprise; In the Springtime; Portrait of M.M.; Road to the Fort of Vincennes; Lake Daumesnil (Effect of Storm); Lake Daumesnil (Sunset); View of the Forest of Vincennes, to the Right of the Road to Paris.**

Unpleasant Surprise depicts a naked woman surprised by a bear killed from the back by a hunter lying in wait. Rousseau was inspired by a drawing by Alphonse de Neuville in *Le Tour du Monde* called *A Surprise.*

" 'It's curious,' Renoir once said to me," according to the art dealer Ambroise Vollard, " 'how repulsed people are when they find painterly qualities in a painting. One painter who must make their flesh creep more than any other is the Douanier Rousseau! That scene from prehistoric times, and, right in the middle, a hunter in a department-store suit, carrying a rifle . . . But can't we enjoy a painting only in terms of harmonious colors? Do we have to understand the subject? And what a lovely tone in this Rousseau painting! Do you recall a nude woman facing the hunter? I'm certain that even Ingres wouldn't have disliked that!' "

In *La Revue Blanche*, Thadée Natanson evokes "those ingenuous artists" smitten with their profession, whose effort and discoveries are so singularly attractive, such as Monsieur Rousseau, whose long patience succeeds in moving us." The chronicler for *La Plume* feels that Henri Rousseau "alone deserves the worthy title of Independent." He adds, "One senses a magnificent awareness here, a sincerity that no vexation stops, a patient and continuous will power."

November 6

The painter's debt to Paul Foinet, who asks for the money in a statement of account, now amounts to 614 francs and 80 centimes.

1902   January 9

The Douanier agrees to pay Foinet in monthly installments of ten francs.

February

Henri Rousseau gets involved in politics through his friend the municipal councilor Victor Pannelier, joining a committee in support of the candidacy of Adolphe Messimy as Radical Socialist deputy for the first district against the Nationalist incumbent, Giron. Messimy wins the election in late April.

March 28–May 5

At the eighteenth Salon of the Independents, at Cours-la-Reine, Rousseau exhibits nine paintings and some drawings: **Happy Quartet** (for which he asks two thousand francs, a rather high price compared with the others); **Portrait of a Child; Portrait of Mademoiselle L.;**

Photographic portrait of his granddaughter.

View of the Bridge of Asnières (Sunset); View of the Quai d'Asnières; View from Alfortville; A Corner of Bellevue (Evening); A Corner of the Quai de Saint-Cloud; Bouquet of Flowers. According to the journalist for *Le Petit Parisien*, Monsieur Rousseau's works "bring us back to the childhood of art." Reviewers still use phrases like "high buffoonery," "eccentricity," "people burst into guffaws."

November

Henri-Julien Rousseau offers to teach on a volunteer basis at the Philotechnical Association, founded in 1848 and recognized as having public usefulness in 1879. On Sunday mornings, at 132 Rue d'Alésia, Rousseau gives courses in painting on faïence and porcelain, watercolors and pastels. His students are adult men from the Plaisance neighborhood.

1903   March 14

Death of Joséphine, the Douanier's second wife, at the age of fifty-one, at 36 Rue Gassendi. The funeral service is performed free of charge at the Church of Saint-Pierre de Montrouge on Monday the 16th, and the deceased is buried at the Bagneux graveyard.

March 19–April 25

At the nineteenth Salon of the Independents, at Cours-la-Reine, Rousseau exhibits eight paintings: **Isolé; To Celebrate the Baby; View of Paris from the Quai d'Alfortville (Sunset); Bouquet of Flowers; Banks of the Marne (Nogent); Banks of the Marne (Charenton); View of the Bois de Boulogne; Corner of the Quai d'Ivry.**

"We encounter," writes *Le Petit Parisien*, "the dreadful specimens of the primitive art of the Douanier Rousseau, who shows us, in his **Isolée** [*sic;* the French title is actually **Isolé**, indicating a man, not a woman], a woman in red, sitting, with a handkerchief in her hand, weeping for an absent man, in a framework of ultragreen foliage." Charles Morice writes in *Le Mercure de France:* "Even when foolish, true naïveté has a vestige of charm. Monsieur Henri Rousseau manages not to anger us. At least this sort of stupidity is not tiring. . . ."

June 28

Three pupils of the Douanier Rousseau

*Photograph of Rousseau's **Scouts Attacked by a Tiger,** with a caption by the painter indicating it was in the 1908 Salon.*

receive awards at the Philotechnical Association's distribution of prizes.

July 24
During the statutory assembly of the Philotechnical Association, Rousseau is named professor. (He will use this title in order to give private lessons to the children of his neighbors and to a few adults.)

October 31–December 6
First exhibition of the Salon d'Automne, at the Petit Palais on the Champs-Elysées. Alfred Jarry gives a lecture on art here and praises the Douanier.

November 8
Opening session at the Sorbonne of the courses of the Philotechnical Association. The Douanier Rousseau also gives a course on miniatures.

1904 February 20–March 24
At the twentieth Salon of the Independents, at Cours-la-Reine, the Douanier shows four paintings: **Scouts Attacked by a Tiger; Portrait of a Little Girl; Portraits of Children; Flowers.**

Le Petit Parisien denounces "these works of art which one suffers in silence.... The dreadful compositions of Monsieur Rousseau." *L'Evénement* describes the enormous throng: "Amid the brouhaha, one hears only one sentence: 'Where are the Rousseaus?' Rousseau is a master in his genre, a celebrity, whose reputation is as great in certain taverns as that of Roybet, Carolus Duran, or Bouguereau." (**Scouts Attacked by a Tiger** was inspired by Delacroix's *Tiger Hunt*.)

December 20
A bailiff comes, in vain, to demand the payment of the debt due Rousseau's art-supply dealer, Paul Foinet, and Foinet's son-in-law, Lucien Lefebvre. On December 29, Rousseau is ordered by the justice of the peace of the Fourteenth Arrondissement to pay them two hundred francs in monthly installments of ten francs. (Rousseau has sometimes left paintings as collateral with Paul Foinet, and Madame Foinet has scraped the paintings off some of the canvases so as to reuse them.)

1905 April 17
At the fourteenth Salon of the National Society of Fine Arts, at the Grand Palais, the Douanier's daughter, Julia Bernard, shows a decorative tapestry panel depicting peaches and chrysanthemums (no. 2435). Rousseau, a bit jealous that

From the catalogue of the Salon d'Automne of 1905.

she has been admitted to the Salon, tells her, "You ought to make tapestries of my paintings; you'd turn a nice profit!"

A painter with the same name as the Douanier is decorated by the Minister of Education. The yearbook of the Philotechnical Association mistakenly attributes this honor to the Douanier, who allows others to believe that he is indeed the beneficiary.

March 19–April 30
At the twenty-first Salon of the Independents, at Cours-la-Reine, Rousseau shows four paintings: **A Country Wedding; Portrait of M.G.; Portrait of M.C.; Avenue de Breteuil.**

Wedding is based on a photograph. There are few reactions in the press. *La Rénovation Esthétique*, speaking of pictorial anarchy, alludes to the "embryonic intelligence" of the Douanier Rousseau. Three young painters who greatly admire the Douanier are also exhibited at this Salon; they will soon buy a lot of his paintings and try to get others to appreciate him. These painters are Ardengo Soffici, an Italian; Serge Jastrebzoff (alias

Serge Férat), a Russian; and Robert Delaunay, who eventually falls in love with Wilhelm Uhde's wife, Sonia Terk, and marries her in 1910.

August 19
Death of the academic painter Bouguereau. Rousseau feels "a profound emotion." (He has sometimes asked his paint dealers for colors like "the flesh color of Monsieur Bouguereau.")

Rousseau has left Rue Gassendi and moved to 44 Rue Daguerre, where he has found a studio that is just a shack. Thanks to a mutual "friend," he makes friends with a family of Breton stonecutters, the Papouins, and becomes the godfather of their daughter Marthe. (He goes to Brittany with them in 1907 and paints **Girl in Pink,** a portrait of their daughter Charlotte, to whom he gives lessons in the rudiments of music.)

October 16
Henri Rousseau writes to the under-state-secretary at the School of Fine Arts, Paris, asking him to have the government buy **The Hungry Lion.** After "very harsh setbacks," he writes, "I need to get back

Henri Rousseau (left),
with his friends and neighbors
during a reception
he gave in his studio.

on my feet and undertake other important paintings; always with the intention of making myself worthy as a Frenchman who wishes to do honor to his country." He also reminds the under-state-secretary that a report by his deputy Messimy ought to allow him to obtain "the palms of an officer of the Academy," and that he has composed several musical works, "one of which has been published and circulated."

October 16–November 20
The Douanier Rousseau participates in the third Salon d'Automne (his first), at the Grand Palais on the Champs-Elysées. Rousseau exhibits three paintings: **The Hungry Lion Leaps upon the Antelope, Devours It, the Panther Anxiously Awaits the Moment When She Too Can Have Her Share. Birds of Prey Have Each Torn Out a Piece of Flesh from the Poor Creature Emitting a Cry! Sunset; Landscape on the Banks of the Oise (Territory of Champoval); Landscape on the Banks of the Oise (Villa Mathilde) Territory of Champoval.**

The Hungry Lion was inspired by an engraving, *The Black Panther*, in *Le Musée des Familles*, August 1842. Writing about Rousseau's painting, *Le Gaulois* said, "An old Oriental theme that passed down from the Chaldeans to the Persians and that was not ignored by our Middle Ages." *Le Soleil* said, "And here he is with his naïveté, his manner of seeing, which comes from the Japanese painters, and now he is turning into a decorator. Ah! That tiger clutching an antelope in its claws—what success I predict!" *L'Evénement*: "The painter of this canvas, one of the hits of the Salon d'Automne, is obviously both sincere and an Independent; heaven granted him a special mentality, that of the primitive artists who drew aurochs' profiles on the rocks of caves. Let us hope that he does not start a school. . . ."

For the first time, one of Rousseau's paintings is reproduced in the press. In its November 4 issue, *L'Illustration* reproduces **The Hungry Lion** (next to Cézanne's *Bathers* and Matisse's *The Woman with the Hat*), with this commentary: "A former customs inspector now retired, Monsieur Henri Rousseau, whom past Salons of the Independents celebrated for his miraculous naïveté and his unlearned gaucheness, has been received with pious respect by the Salon d'Automne, where the painting reproduced here occupies a place of honor." In *Gil Blas*, Louis Vauxcelles also discussed the painting: "Monsieur Rousseau has the rigid mentality of the Byzantine mosaicists and the Bayeux tapestry makers; it is unfortunate that his technique is not equal to his candor." Charles Morice in *Le Mercure de France*, although very severe, acknowledges that "There are even decorative qualities in this painting, which looks like the color enlargement of a wood engraving."

Elie Faure, in his preface to the exhibition catalogue, seems to be speaking for the Douanier: "Science will never provide the certainty that men of imagination can draw from the bosom of art. . . . Listen to these primitives. They have swooped down on the crowd in order to explore its abysses in a flash of lightning. . . . Art is the intellectual trace of vanished generations, the soil-clogged fossil that allows new civilizations to reconstruct the organisms swallowed up by the darkness of history and to make the footprints left by the human spirit on the face of the earth radiate in our increased awareness."

1906
Henri Rousseau moves again. This time he rents a studio from the metal founder Armand Quéval, on the second floor of 2 bis Rue Perrel, between Rue Vercingétorix and the Montparnasse railroad line. (The apartment house has been torn down, but a commemorative stone marks its site.)

March 17–April 30
Rousseau sends five works to the twenty-second Salon of the Independents, at Cours-la-Reine: **Liberty Invit-**

The entrance to the studio at 2 bis Rue Perrel.

Berthe Delaunay, Countess de Rose,
mother of Robert Delaunay, in her studio, circa 1905.

Photographic portrait of Robert Delaunay.

ing Artists to Take Part in the Twenty-second Exhibition of Independent Artists; View of the Banks of the Oise; Portrait of M.F.; Portrait of Monsieur Steven; Portrait of Madame Steven. The Portrait of M.F., subsequently known as Portrait of Pierre Loti, is actually a picture of Edmond Frank, whom the Douanier painted in Frank's home at the "Castle of Mist" on Rue Giardon in Montmartre. Georges Courteline purchased it, along with Liberty Inviting Artists, for his Museum of Horrors.

Vlaminick, in his Portraits avant décès, reports, "A laughing public held its sides in front of Henri Rousseau's canvases. He, serene, draped in an old overcoat, was overcome with bliss.... He could not doubt for even an instant that this laughter was aimed at him."

Guillaume Apollinaire asks Jarry to introduce him to the Douanier. The author of Ubu Roi promises him "a mirific expedition at Rousseau's."

March 31
Vollard buys The Hungry Lion from the Douanier for two hundred francs.

May 28
Rousseau has himself photographed standing and holding a violin in his studio, with Wedding and Liberty on the walls. The Douanier dedicates this photo to his daughter.

June 24
At the Philotechnical Association's distribution of prizes, two of the Douanier's students are honored, receiving a prize and a certificate of distinction.

October 5–November 15
Rousseau presents only one painting at the fourth Salon d'Automne, at the Grand Palais on the Champs-Elysées: Joyous Jokesters. In the catalogue preface, Roger Marx writes, "We must realize that these inventors, so arbitrarily labeled as revolutionaries, do not in any wise believe in spontaneous generation; far from proclaiming themselves autodidacts, they claim kinship with masters to whom they love to pay homage." The exhibition is accompanied by a major retrospective of the works of Gauguin and

Gustave Courbet.

The painter Harry Bloomfield does a portrait of the Douanier Rousseau painting in his studio, near his bed, his violin, and his painting The Present and the Past.

1907   March 19–April 30
At the twenty-third Salon of the Independents, at Cours-la-Reine, Rousseau exhibits six paintings: The Representatives of Foreign Powers Coming to Salute the Republic as a Sign of Peace; The Little Cherry Pickers; Philosophical Thought; Banks of the Marne; View of Brittany; View of Alfortville.

View of Brittany is an interpretation of an engraving by Pirodon based on Camille Bernier's painting done in Bannalec. Rousseau does two versions.

He hopes that the French government will buy The Representatives of Foreign Powers; then he offers it to the art dealer Vollard on December 14, 1909. Ultimately, it is owned by Picasso.

"At no comedy, in no circus have I heard people laughing as they laugh in front of Rousseau's painting The Sovereigns," reports German art critic Wilhelm Uhde in his book on Rousseau. "However, from time to time, one sees a few young people contemplating these paintings with a very serious and meditative air." One such young man is Ardengo Soffici, who is struck by "the poetic candor emanating from his paintings despite the infantilism of forms and expression." This is also the case with Robert Delaunay.

Le Soleil resoundingly condemns the Douanier Rousseau: "It's no use seeking any thought in the good Douanier, any striving toward truth, toward the reality of form, an aspiration so touching in the old Cézanne, who is passionate about colors. Rousseau paints buffoons like a schoolboy." And in Le Figaro, Arsène Alexandre recommends "the fine portraits painted by Monsieur Bloomfield, for instance, that of the once famous Douanier Rousseau, who nearly became head of a school like Cézanne." Wilhelm

Uhde grows very fond of the Plaisance painter, becoming his devoted friend, generous buyer, and first biographer (1911).

September 30–October 22
Rousseau exhibits at the Salon d'Automne for the last time. This is the fifth Salon, and again it takes place at the Grand Palais on the Champs-Elysées. Its president, Frantz Jourdain, who hates the Douanier's work, relegates it to a spot behind a curtain in a section for decorative arts. Rousseau, starting to dislike Jourdain, sits on a chair and looks at his four paintings: The Snake Charmer (Belonging to M.D.); Landscape (Environs of Asnières); Exotic Landscape; Exotic Landscape. The Charmer was commis-

Max Weber at home, 7 Rue Belloni, Paris (1907–09).

sioned by Robert Delaunay's mother, who told Rousseau about her voyage to India. (The theme of the painting was actually inspired by Lévy-Dhurmer's painting *In Paradise*, which Rousseau admired at the Salon of 1897. The spoonbill and the snakes are taken from an album published by Galeries Lafayette, *Wild Beasts: Approximately 200 Amusing Illustrations Drawn from the Life of Animals, with an Instructive Text*. The album has 196 pages of photographs by Meisenbach, Riffarth and Co. of animals in the menagerie of the Jardin des Plantes. Rousseau traces these photos, reproduces them with a pantograph, or is inspired by them in his exotic paintings. From time to time, he goes to the Jardin des Plantes. He likes to see the menagerie and the hothouses, entranced as he is by their atmosphere. He also loves to go on walks in Montsouris Park and the Luxembourg Gardens.)

Apollinaire composes a comic poem about this Salon, describing the reciprocal animosity between Frantz Jourdain and Rousseau. The poet concludes, "For a long time, we pitied unhappy Rousseau and noted the profound differences between toll gates and the plastic arts." In *Le Figaro*, Arsène Alexandre writes, "The poor and naïve customs inspector, whom people tried to tout as a great man two years ago, is now relegated to the basement. . . ."

At the retrospective of Cézanne's paintings, Rousseau is furious that the works shown are incomplete, and he exclaims, "You know, I could complete all these paintings!"

At a reception given by Delaunay's mother, Rousseau meets the American painter Max Weber.

October

Louis Sauvaget, a twenty-seven-year-old swindler whom the painter met in the orchestra of the Club of the Fifth Arrondissement several years earlier, comes to him and complains about having been victimized by powerful bankers. Sauvaget asks Rousseau to help him recover the money they owe him. He manages to convince the Douanier, who agrees to be his accomplice in a scheme to misappropriate money from the Banque de France in Melun by using forged documents. The scheme nets them twenty-one thousand francs. Rousseau gets only a small part of this amount and spends his share mainly on lottery tickets to benefit tubercular children in Ormesson. The scam is discovered by the bank.

December 2

The police report sent to Monsieur Boucher, examining magistrate at the Tribunal, indicates that the painter has "an irregular life style," "no visible

Letter to the examining magistrate Boucher.

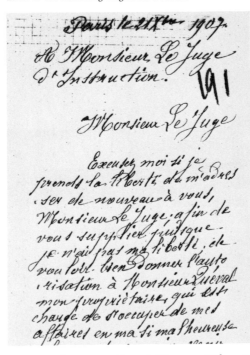

means of support," and "does a little oil painting, but his works have no value." At sixty-three, he looks only fifty, has a rather thick mustache, faces straight ahead when he walks, looks sickly with his pale complexion and several reddish spots, and now wears his hair short (he used to wear it long). Taken into custody, Rousseau is placed in Santé Prison that very same evening.

December 5

The Douanier, from prison, writes a long letter to the judge, trying to obtain his indulgence. Rousseau claims that he was taken in by Sauvaget. "People have always reproached me for having too weak a character and being too good; and it is certain that if I hadn't helped unfortunates as I have done, I would be well off today." Rousseau proves to the magistrate that he is a very well known painter; he begs the magistrate to set him free so that he can give his Sunday class at the Philotechnical Association and he promises him a present "which will not be something to complain about." The next day, Rousseau writes the judge again: "If you will have the kindness to grant me my liberty, then I will do a beautiful portrait of you in the composition and size of your choosing."

The press carries on about the arrest and the scam. The investigation continues; Sauvaget exonerates the Douanier, who keeps sending desperate letters to the judge, on December 6, 13, 19, and 21.

December 22

The Douanier writes a long letter asking his "Very Dear Brother," Pannelier, to intervene in his favor.

The municipal councilor, a member

of the Council General of the Seine and knight of the Legion of Honor, recommends Rousseau to the judge by transmitting this letter to him.

December 28

Rousseau writes to the judge again to obtain his freedom.

December 31

Judge Boucher signs an order of provisional release, which the painter asked for so that he could "do his painting of two meters square for the Salon, for which I need at least two months, given the composition."

1908   March 19–May 2

Delighted to be taking part in the twenty-fourth Salon of the Independents, at Cours-la-Reine, Rousseau exhibits **Fight Between Tiger and Buffalo; Soccer Players; Portrait of a Child; Landscape (Belonging to Mademoiselle Vel)**. **Fight Between Tiger and Buffalo** is a very large painting inspired by a Pirodon engraving that appeared in *L'Art* (March 1906) and was based on Charles Verlat's painting *Royal Tiger Attacking a Buffalo*. **Soccer Players** is inspired by a popular color print.

While Guillaume Apollinaire is discovering the "utterly French grace of Mademoiselle Marie Laurencin, who vibrates in gladness," as he wrote in *La Revue des Lettres et des Arts*, the poet finds that Monsieur Rousseau's exhibition is "both touching and amusing," and that this "self-taught artist has undeniably natural qualities." The journalist for *Le Soleil* notes that "the Douanier Rousseau is a bit worn out, but he is sought after, cited, and draws crowds." *Le Matin* comments ironically, "To crown our joys, we have the divine Rousseau, who this time gives us a fight between a buffalo and a panther, the latter sporting as many stripes as the soccer players hanging not so far away. Go on, you vain, ironical pack, hold your tongues, do not blaspheme, Henri Rousseau is a modern Giotto. . . ."

La République Française writes, "This dramatic scene takes place in India, of course: against green-painted tinware, a dried cat skin is stretched out, while a horn emerges from a dusky conglomeration. All this in the midst of a metallic arborescence . . ." Rousseau later paints a replica of this work; the reduced version is now at the Leningrad Hermitage, the earlier version at the Cleveland Museum in Ohio.

Henri Rousseau prints a prospectus, announcing his mixed courses for children and young people, as well as those for adults, at his studio on Rue Perrel: "Nude Painting, Live Models." He also organizes artistic evenings at his place,

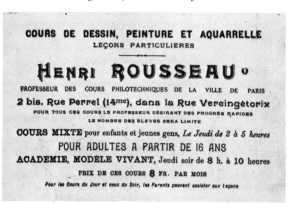

The Bateau-Lavoir in Montmartre.

inviting pupils, neighbors, and shop-keepers to meet with young artists, writers, and poets. He edits small programs of songs and musical pieces. The group drinks, sings, plays music. The painter arranges contests for his pupils, who sometimes put on skits for him.

June 27
At the Philotechnical Association's distribution of prizes, two of the Douanier's pupils win awards.

July 21
Rousseau writes to the "dear poet" Guillaume Apollinaire, telling him to come and see him with "the lady" he has told the painter about. This lady is Apollinaire's mistress, Marie Laurencin, whom he met through Picasso in May 1907. "I will be happy to hear you recite beautiful things as you are accustomed to doing." Rousseau then offers to paint their portrait.

Using a photograph he has had taken, Rousseau paints **Old Juniet's Carriole.** Monsieur Junier, a grocer at 74 Rue

Program for a musical and poetic evening given by the Douanier in his studio.

Vercingétorix, and his wife and children have become friends with Rousseau.

The Salon d'Automne refuses to show the Douanier's canvases. But Uhde decides to organize a one-man show for Rousseau, who dreams of establishing an academy. His paintings are gathered in a location on Rue Notre-Dame-des-Champs, where a merchant displays some of his furniture. No one comes to the exhibit: Uhde has neglected to indicate the address on his invitation.

November 14
The Douanier Rousseau gives a huge party in his studio, during which he plays his own compositions on the violin. His friends from the neighborhood include Apollinaire, Marie Laurencin, Francis Picabia, Utrillo, and Rousseau's lawyer Guilhermet. Apollinaire has introduced the Douanier to Picasso, who will improvise a banquet in Rousseau's honor at his Bateau-Lavoir studio at 13 Rue Ravignan, Montmartre. Picasso in-

vites Georges Braque, Marie Laurencin, Apollinaire, Max Jacob, André Salmon, Leo and Gertrude Stein, and others. A throne is set up for Rousseau under the lanterns, and he starts to play his violin. The merry and extremely alcoholic party ends in disorder.

Apollinaire recites a long poem at Picasso's banquet as a toast to the glory of the Douanier Rousseau. The concluding lines are as follows:

> We are united to celebrate your glory
> Let's drink these wines poured by Picasso
> For this is the time to drink them
> Crying in unison: "Long live Rousseau!"
>
> O glorious painter of the Bounteous Republic
> Your name is the flag of the proud Independents
> And your face, the pride of our era,
> Will be carved in white marble from Mount Pentelicus.
>
> So up! Let's rise and clink our glasses
> And let the purest merriment be reborn;
> Away, black cares, flee, severe brows,
> I drink to my Rousseau. I drink to his health.

"Charming in his weakness, naïveté, and touching vanity," and worn out with excitement, Rousseau is driven home at dawn by the Steins in their car.

"We are the two greatest painters of our time, you in the Egyptian style and I in the modern style," Rousseau has said to Picasso.

December 19
The Douanier organizes a going-away party for his young American friend, the painter Max Weber. He invites Apollinaire and "our friends the Picassos" (the painter and his mistress Fernande Olivier). He also invites a dealer in art objects and African statues, Joseph Brummer, whose portrait he eventually paints. The "Marseillaise," songs of the Second Em-

pire, and folk ditties are played and sung in honor of Max Weber, who has convinced his pupils in the Matisse Academy of Rousseau's genius; the Douanier hopes that Weber will spread the word about him in America.

1909 January 8 and 9
The court judges Sauvaget and Rousseau. The witnesses for the Douanier are his landlord Monsieur Quéval, Municipal Councilor Pannelier, the painter Maximilien Luce, who introduced Rousseau to the Independents and praised his painting. Rousseau's lawyer passes an allegorical painting of his among the jurors; the painting shows the court and the jurors as monkeys among coconut trees. The lawyer also passes around his client's scrapbook of press clippings. All of this arouses bursts of laughter. Guilhermet quotes Rousseau: "If they condemn me, it will be an injustice; but what a loss for art!" The lawyer insists on Rousseau's gullibility and concludes his defense with these words: "Do not condemn a primitive!" Sauvaget is sentenced to five years' hard labor; Rousseau to two years in prison (suspended) plus a fine. The presiding judge tells the painter that he has three days to appeal, and Rousseau replies, "Thank you, Your Honor; I will do a portrait of your lady."

In their stories on the trial, the numerous reporters who have come to cover it emphasize Rousseau's artlessness. His appeal is rejected on February 11. "Thus ended this tragicomedy. Rousseau could have been sent to prison. His habitual naïveté helped him to triumph even over justice," concluded Maurice Garçon in his book *Le Douanier Rousseau: Accusé Naif.*

The Philotechnical Association strikes his name from its list of teachers.

January 20
Rousseau writes to Apollinaire, asking him to avenge the harm done to him. The painter is still short of money and tries to get cash from both Apollinaire and Brummer.

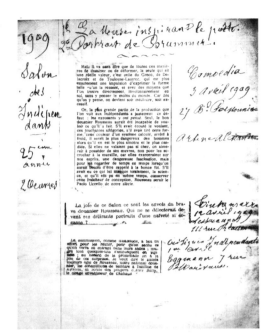

March 25–May 2
At the twenty-fifth Salon of the Independents, which takes place in the hothouses of the Orangerie at the Tuileries, Rousseau presents only two paintings: **The Muse Inspiring the Poet,** which depicts Marie Laurencin in a peplos and Guillaume Apollinaire, and **Landscape Portrait (Belonging to M.B.),** a portrait of Brummer.

In his article in *Le Figaro,* Arsène Alexandre speaks of the Salon's "family of Candides, of which Monsieur Rousseau remains the prototype," and to which he links Marie Laurencin with her *Meeting in the Country.* In order to do a second version of his Apollinaire portrait, Rousseau looks for true poet's narcissi.

He falls in love with a fifty-nine-year-old widow, Léonie; her eighty-nine-year-old father, a retired customs employee, refuses to give her permission to marry some wretched painter. Rousseau gives her presents, which she accepts, but she rejects his advances. He even goes so far as to include her generously in his will, in order to overcome her resistance.

August 5
Art dealer Vollard buys three of Rousseau's paintings for 190 francs: **Unpleasant Surprise; Fight Between Tiger and Buffalo; View of the Luxembourg, Chopin Monument. Joyous Jokesters** is shown at the Izdebsky Salon in Kiev and Odessa.

1910 March
After getting Vollard, Apollinaire, and Uhde to pen testimonials to his talent and good conduct, Rousseau makes vain attempts to convince the father of his dear Léonie to allow her to marry him.

March 17–May 1
Rousseau's final presentation, his swan song, **The Dream,** is shown at the twenty-sixth Salon of the Independents, in a barracks on Cours-la-Reine. The painting bears the following text:

Henri Rousseau in his studio on Rue Perrel and Jeanne Bernard-Rousseau in her parlor at Cherbourg.

Picasso and Fernande Olivier.

*Bill for rented piano,
August 3 to September 3, 1910.*

Yadurgha in a lovely dream,
Having gently fallen asleep,
Hearing the sounds of a musette
Of a well-meaning charmer,
While the moon reflects,
On the flowers, the greening trees
The wild serpents lend an ear
To the gay tunes of the instrument.

Rousseau writes to Apollinaire on March 11, "I've sent my big painting, everyone likes it, I think that you will display all your literary talent and that you will avenge all the insults and affronts I have suffered." On March 18, after evoking Modigliani and Lhote, Apollinaire writes in *L'Intransigeant*, "I believe that this year no one will dare to laugh.... Ask the painters. They are all unanimous; they admire everything, I tell you, even this Louis-Philippe couch lost in the virgin forest, and they are right to do so."

On March 19, the Douanier Rousseau gives a long interview which appears in *Comoedia;* he talks at length about his work.

In *La Phalange*, Léon Werth writes a long article about Rousseau, vaunting the artist's qualities of the heart and postulating that Rousseau is inspired by engravings in books: "And perhaps they have been in his memory for years, since his childhood." Rousseau receives more and more commissions for paintings. Soffici, Vollard, Jastrebzoff and his sister Hélène d'Oettingen, the Delaunays, and Uhde buy paintings from him. He sometimes does these works hastily.

Rousseau suffers from a phlegmon in his leg, but he neglects it. Apollinaire alludes to it in a poem," Memory of the Douanier" (1914):

Wounds on your leg
You showed me those bleeding holes
When we drank a Quinquina
At the Îles Marquises bar on Rue de la Gaieté
One morning balmy with Greenery.

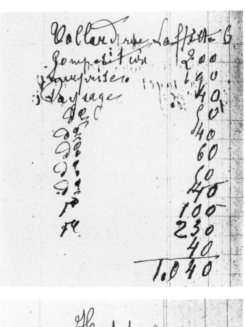

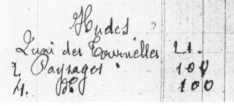

*Notebook list of sales of paintings
to Vollard and Uhde.*

*Julia Bernard-Rousseau and her daughter Jeanne with
Rousseau's sofa, which inspired the sofa in* **The Dream.**

March 22
Vollard pays Rousseau one hundred francs for his **Fight Between a Jaguar and a Horse.**

Several of Rousseau's paintings are shown at the Izdebsky Salon in Saint Petersburg and Riga. During the summer, Rousseau is worried about their not coming back.

June 23
"Before the vacation, [the Douanier] gives a familial, artistic, literary, musical party" in his study; he invites Vollard.

July 2
Rousseau joins the demonstration against the execution of the shoemaker Liabeuf on Boulevard Arago.

July 14
After decorating his studio with French and foreign flags, Rousseau gives a reception celebrating peace and tells Uhde, "When a king wants to wage war, a mother must go to him and order him not to do it."

He hurries to finish a rustic landscape commissioned by Soffici. And he visits Hélène d'Oettingen and Serge Férat at 21 Boulevard Berthier to leave the painting with them, since they are about to visit Italy. He again talks to them about Léonie, whom he wants to marry at all cost.

August 19
Having illustrated his stationery with a *pensée* (a pansy, but also French for "thought"), he sends a final love letter to "his beloved Léonie," to whom all his *pensées* are directed, "in order to convince her to love him, to unite with him": "For your part, be less cold toward me, do not break my heart when I try to caress you, don't be grumpy and don't refuse to respond to my overtures...."

Uhde visits Rousseau and finds him stretched out on his couch, suffering greatly from his bad leg.

When Rousseau visits Delaunay, he limps and complains sorrowfully about his ailment. The neighborhood people say that his trial and his troubles have "given him a turn."

Rousseau is taken to Necker Hospi-

Notice of the death of Henri Rousseau.

tal, where his son died. He sends an urgent message to Uhde, who dashes over. "I found him," writes Uhde, "in a hopeless state. I stayed sitting at the edge of his bed for a long time, with his hand clutching mine.... Unable to take any nourishment, he still had the strength to speak about his last and unfinished work and to regret the delay caused by his malady." Rousseau's daughter comes to see him.

Robert Delaunay also comes to visit him and promises to send Léonie to the hospital. She doesn't come, however. Rousseau apparently becomes delirious, talking about God and the angels and hearing their celestial music. In despair, with only his landlord, Monsieur Quéval, and his landlord's wife for company, Rousseau asks, "But why did Robert break the Eiffel Tower?" Gangrene has claimed his leg. He is operated on. The surgeon tells Rousseau's daughter that the patient has suffered too much excitement.

Robert Delaunay: Eiffel Tower, 1910.

Bill for paints bought from Hardy-Alan.

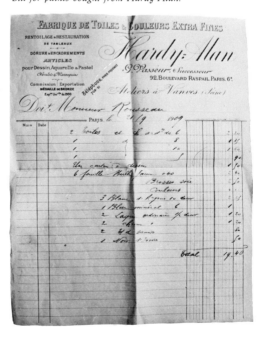

September 2
Death of the Douanier Rousseau from a blood clot at the hospital. Roch Grey (Hélène d'Oettingen) is told at the hospital that Rousseau was alcoholic.

September 4
Funeral service at the Church of Saint-Jean-Baptiste de la Salle, on Rue Dutot. Rousseau is buried in a pauper's grave at the Bagneux graveyard. Only seven people attend the burial, including Paul Signac, representing the Society of Independent Artists. When Rousseau's daughter, Julia Bernard, goes to his studio, she finds a little old man who has often come to share his soup with the artist; the visitor is weeping in front of an unfinished painting. Numerous bills are unpaid; his daughter pays his debts, notably to Hardy-Alan, the painter's art-supply dealer, at 92 Boulevard Raspail.

Le Soleil runs an article about Rousseau on September 6: "We know that he changed from a customs inspector to a painter without knowing how to draw or having any of the notions required by art. This decent man had faith, and he began to cover his canvases.... His entire success (and he was very successful, even famous) was something he owed to his ignorance." On September 16, *Le Mercure de France* announces his decease: "He had enthusiasm, faith in his art as a painter, and also qualities of instinct, spontaneity, qualities lacking in so many triumphant artists at the Salons. Unhappily, he lacked taste, measure, everything constituting talent...."

October 16
Le Mercure de France publishes the translation of a long article that Soffici finished just before learning, in Italy, about the Douanier's death. The article appeared first in *La Voce*. It is a very significant homage to the Douanier Rousseau, whom Soffici compares to Paolo Uccello. In his introduction to this article, Rémy de Gourmont relates that when he met

Photographic portrait of Wilhelm Uhde.

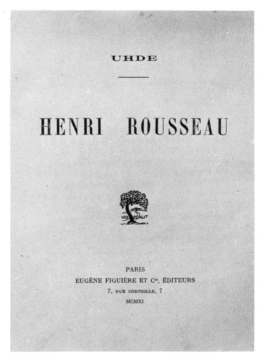

First book on Rousseau, written by Uhde and published in 1911 by Eugène Figuière.

the Douanier, Rousseau was painting grain-crowned figures of Ceres on the ceilings of bakeries.

November 18–December 2
When Max Weber, in New York, learns of Rousseau's death, he organizes a small exhibition of the Douanier's works, including a painted vase, at Alfred Stieglitz's gallery. In the catalogue preface, Weber states, "He was truly naïve and personal.... He passionately loved nature and painted it as he saw it.... His life was simple and pure, it imbues his work."

1911 April 20–June 13
At the Salon of the Independents, a Rousseau retrospective shows forty-four paintings and two photographs. Apollinaire promptly writes in *L'Intransigeant*, "Artistic youth wanted to express the honor in which it holds the works of this poor old angel ... whom one could also call the Master of Plaisance, because of the neighborhood he lived in and because of the grace that makes his paintings so delightful to look at." (The French word *plaisance* means "pleasure.") *L'Evénement* reports that this exhibit provoked the mirth of the public. Rousseau's last friends and a few knowledgeable art lovers hurriedly hunt down his paintings, urging Monsieur Quéval and Madame Bernard to sell them.

September 22
Wilhelm Uhde writes a small book, published by Eugène Figuière, which remains the finest tribute to this still-controversial painter, who, within a few years, becomes so famous, so sought-after by museums and collectors. Eugène Fasquelle publishes the complete edition of *The Gestures and Opinions of Dr. Faustroll, Pataphysician: A Neo-Scientific Novel* by Alfred Jarry. In chapter 32, "How the Painting Was Procured," the author quotes and presents "Monsieur Henri Rousseau, decorative artistic painter, known as the Douanier, decorated and bemedaled."

December 18
At Kandinsky's instigation, several

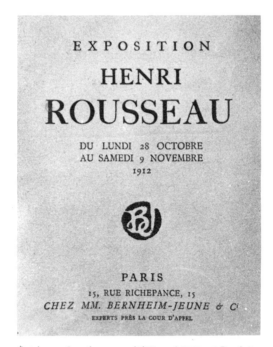

Catalogue of posthumous exhibition of 1912, at Bernheim.

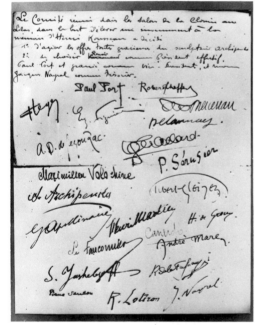

Document announcing the decision to put up a monument to Henri Rousseau.

paintings by the Douanier Rousseau and Robert Delaunay are presented at the first group show of the Blue Rider.

1912
Robert Delaunay, Uhde, and the metal founder Armand Quéval have collected money from friends to buy a plot for thirty years at the Bagneux graveyard. Rousseau's coffin is transferred to his tomb on Saturday, March 2. Henry Kahnweiler, Picasso, Marie Laurencin, Raoul Dufy, Apollinaire, Delaunay, Albert-Léon Gleizes, Jean Metzinger, and others were among the seventy-five contributors. A tombstone is placed on the grave; in 1913, Brancusi and Ortiz de Zarate carve Apollinaire's epitaph on the tombstone:

We greet you
Gentle Rousseau, you hear us
Delaunay his wife Monsieur Quéval
    and I
Let our baggage pass free through heaven's gate
We'll bring you brushes, paints, and canvases
So that you can devote your sacred leisures
In the Real light to painting, as you did my portrait,
Painting the Face of the stars.
    Guillaume Apollinaire

October 28–November 9
Exhibition of twenty-seven paintings and two drawings at the Bernheim-Jeune gallery, 15 Rue Richepance. Uhde writes a preface for the small catalogue. "The paintings were all found to be very beautiful and all at once everyone was convinced that Rousseau was a great painter. It was no longer compromising to show interest in his paintings. The best collections were enriched with Rousseaus and art dealers tried to acquire them," says Uhde. At the first Autumn Salon in Berlin: a retrospective tribute to the Douanier Rousseau.

1914 January 15
Guillaume Apollinaire devotes issue number 20 of *Les Soirées de Paris* to the Douanier Rousseau.

1927 January 15
Basler, Salmon, Soupault, and Zervos write monographs on Rousseau.

1936
Jacques Doucet offers Rousseau's **Snake Charmer** to the Louvre; the painting enters this museum the following year.

1937
An Association of the Friends of Henri Rousseau is created on September 21, 1937, during the Exhibition of the Popular Masters of Reality at 11 Rue Royale in Paris. This exhibition includes twenty-one paintings by the Douanier Rousseau. The Association of the Friends of Henri Rousseau is officially recognized on October 12. Albert Sarraut is its chairman, Adolphe Beck, mayor of Laval, one of its first members, and Maximilien Gauthier its secretary general.

1941
An entrepreneur of traveling shows asks the Prefect of the Seine permission to buy the Douanier's skull, to exhibit it at fairs.

1944 December 22–January 21, 1945
Exhibition at the Museum of Modern Art of the City of Paris commemorating the centennial of Henri Rousseau's birth. In his brief preface to the catalogue of twenty-one paintings, Paul Eluard concludes: "What he saw was love, and he will always make our eyes widen in wonder."

1947 March 31
A small street leading to Montsouris Park in the Fourteenth Arrondissement is named Rue de Douanier-Rousseau by a municipal decree.
    May
Tristan Tzara writes a preface to the Geneva edition (published by Pierre Cailler) of Rousseau's comedy *A Visit to the World's Fair of 1889* and his drama *The Vengeance of a Russian Orphan*. Still unpublished is *L'Etudiant en goguette*, a play in two acts and three scenes. (The manuscripts were lent by Rousseau's daughter

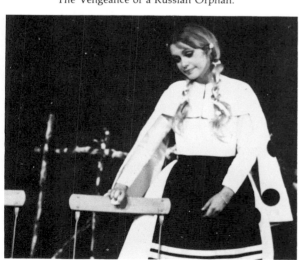

Elisabeth Wiener in
The Vengeance of a Russian Orphan.

Tomb of the Douanier Rousseau in Laval.

to Robert Delaunay along with other mementos, notably the scrapbooks in which the Douanier pasted and commented on the press clippings about his works, and some photographs. These

Commemorative plaque on the birthplace of Henri Rousseau, Beucheresse Gate.

documents were then sold to Tristan Tzara by Sonia Delaunay.)
    October 12
A commemorative plaque is placed on the house in which Rousseau was born, the Beucheresse Gate. His remains are transferred to the Parc de la Perrine, behind the old Laval museum, after their exhumation at the Bagneux graveyard on February 7.

1961
The Galerie Charpentier, 76 Faubourg Saint-Honoré, Paris, organizes a huge retrospective of eighty works to commemorate the fiftieth anniversary of Rousseau's death.

1967 June
Opening of the Henri Rousseau Museum in Laval, with the hanging of **The Harvest at the Castle.** Unfortunately, this museum, which is devoted to "naïve" painters, no longer bears Rousseau's name.

Harry Bloomfield: Portrait of the Douanier Rousseau in His Studio, *1907.*

Robert Delaunay: Posthumous Portrait of Henri-Julien Rousseau.

Selected Bibliography

ADHÉMAR, Jean, and FRÈREBEAU, Mariel. *Max Ernst: Estampes et livres illustrés.* Paris: Bibliothèque nationale, 1975.

ALEXANDRE, Arsène. "Le Salon des Indépendants." *Comoedia* (April 3, 1909).

———. "La Vie and l'oeuvre d'Henri Rousseau, peintre et ancien employé de l'Octroi." *Comoedia* (March 19, 1910).

ALLEY, Ronald. *Portrait of a Primitive: The Art of Henri Rousseau.* Oxford: Phaidon, 1978.

APOLLINAIRE, Guillaume. *Les Peintres cubistes.* Paris: Figuière, 1913.

———. In *Les Soirées de Paris*, no. 20 (January 15, 1914).

———. *Il y a.* Paris: Albert Messein, 1925.

———. *Chroniques d'art* (1902–1918). Compiled by Breunig. Paris: Gallimard, 1960.

———. *Catalogue de l'Exposition de la Bibliothèque nationale.* Edited by Jean Adhémar, Lise Dubief, and Gérard Willemetz. Paris, 1969.

———. *Apollinaire on Art: Essays and Reviews, 1902–1918.* London, 1972.

BARSKAIA, Anna-Grigorievna. *La Peinture française: Seconde moitié du XIXe, début du XXe siècle, Musée de l'Ermitage, Leningrad.* Leningrad: Editions d'Art Aurore, 1975.

BARTHES, Roland. *La Chambre claire. Notes sur la photographie.* Paris: Gallimard-Seuil, Cahiers du Cinéma, 1980. In English: *Camera Lucida: Notes on Photography.* New York: Hill & Wang, 1981.

BASLER, Adolphe. *Henri Rousseau (sa vie—son oeuvre).* Paris: Librairie de France, 1927.

———. *Henri Rousseau.* Les peintres français modernes, no. 34. Paris: Gallimard, 1929.

BAUDELAIRE, Charles. *Oeuvres complètes.* Paris: Gallimard, Bibliothèque de la Pléiade, 1954.

BAZIN, Germain. "La Guerre du Douanier Rousseau." *Bulletin des Musées de France* (April 1946).

———. *Le Message de l'absolu: De l'aube au crépuscule des images.* Paris: Hachette, 1964.

BÉHAR, Henri. *Le Théâtre dada et surréaliste.* Paris: Gallimard, 1979.

BERNARDIN DE SAINT-PIERRE. *Paul et Virginie.* Paris: Alcide Picard et Kann.

BERNARD-ROUSSEAU, Jeanne. "La Petite-fille de Rousseau raconte la vie de son grand-père." *Arts* (October 17, 1947).

———. "Révélé par Jeanne, sa petite-fille, le secret du Douanier Rousseau." *Elle* (February 10, 1961).

BERTRAM, Anthony. *Henri Rousseau.* London: The Studio, 1936.

BIHALJI-MERIN, Oto. "Le Monde des Naïfs," preface to the Exhibition of the National Museum of Modern Art, Paris (October 14–December 6, 1964).

———. *Die Kunst der Naiven.* Catalogue, Das Kunsthaus, Zurich (January 30–March 31, 1975).

———. *Modern Primitives.* London: Thames and Hudson, 1978.

———. *Les Peintres naïfs.* Cologne: Delpire–Du Mont Schauberg.

BOITARD. *Le Jardin des Plantes: Description et moeurs des mammifères de la ménagerie et du Muséum d'histoire naturelle.* Paris: Dubochet, 1845.

BOURET, Jean. Preface to *Catalogue de l'Exposition du cinquantenaire de la mort du Douanier Rousseau.* Paris: Galerie Charpentier, 1961.

———. *Henri Rousseau.* Neuchâtel: Ides et Calendes, 1961.

———. *Henri Rousseau.* London: Oldbourne, 1961, and New York: Burns and MacEachern, 1961.

BOYELDIEU D'AUVIGNY, Louise. *Mont-Jouy, ou Erreurs et repentir.* Paris: Louis Janet. (Book awarded at Madame Piquet's boarding school to Clémence Boitard for first prize in French on September 3, 1863.)

BRASSAÏ. *Conversations avec Picasso.* Paris: Gallimard, 1964. In English: *Picasso and Company.* New York: Doubleday, 1966, and London: Thames & Hudson, 1966.

BRAUNER, Victor. *Cahiers de dessin: "Conglomeros."* Paris: Alexandre Iolas, 1968.

———. *Victor Brauner.* Catalogue of the Exhibition at the National Museum of Modern Art, Paris, 1972. Texts by Jean Leymarie and Dominique Bozo.

BRETON, André. *Flagrant délit.* Paris: Thésée, 1949.

———. *Le Surréalisme et la peinture: Henri Rousseau sculpteur?* Paris: Gallimard, 1965.

BRYEN, Camille, and GHEERBRANT, Alain. *Anthologie de la peinture naturelle.* Paris: K, éditeur, 1949.

CABANNE, Pierre. "Le Procès en mystification d'un naïf de génie." *Arts* (February 15–21, 1961).

CANNING, Kate. *Le Tigre du Douanier Rousseau.* Paris: Jean-Pierre Delarge, 1979.

CASTELOT, André. *Maximilien et Charlotte: La Tragédie de l'ambition.* Paris: Librairie académique Perrin, 1977.

CERTIGNY, Henry. *La Vérité sur le Douanier Rousseau.* Paris: Plon, 1961.

———. *La Vérité sur le Douanier Rousseau: Addenda no. 1.* Paris: Plon, 1966.

———. *La Vérité sur le Douanier Rousseau: Addenda no. 2.* Lausanne/Paris: La Bibliothèque des Arts, 1971.

———. *Le Douanier Rousseau et Frumence Biche.* Lausanne/Paris: La Bibliothèque des Arts, 1973.

———. "Aspects inconnus du Douanier Rousseau," *Galerie des Arts*, no. 57 (October 1968).

———. "Une source inconnue du Douanier Rousseau." *L'Oeil*, no. 291 (October 1979).

———. "Le Douanier Rousseau et la source du Centenaire de l'Indépendance." *L'Oeil*, no. 309 (April 1981).

CHAMSON, André. *Collection Girardin.* Paris: Petit Palais, 1954.

CHANTEREAU, René. *Rousseau.* Médicines et Peintures. Laboratoire Chantereau.

CHASSÉ, Charles. "D'Ubu-Roi au Douanier Rousseau." *La Nouvelle Revue Critique* (1947).

CHASSEGUET-SMIRGEL, Janine. *Pour une psychanalyse de l'art et de la créativité.* Paris: Payot, 1971.

CHATEAUBRIAND, François René de. *Atala, René, Les Abencérages, suivis du Voyage en Amérique.* Paris: Firmin-Didot, 1857.

CHETWYND, Tom. *Le Dictionnaire des rêves: La "Clé des songes" interprétée par la psychanalyse.* Paris: Seghers, 1975.

CHIBA, Kusano and Tomiyama: *Rousseau.* The Book of Great Masters, no. 27. Tokyo: The Zanho Press. Published by Shogakukan, Japan. 1980.

CHRIST, Yvan. *Les Métamorphoses de la banlieue parisienne.* Paris: André Balland, 1969.

CLAIRVAL, Henri de. *Daumesnil.* Paris: Librairie académique Perrin, 1970.

CLANCIER, Anne. *Entretiens sur l'art et la psychanalyse.* Décades du Centre culturel international de Cerisy-la-Salle. Paris/The Hague: Mouton, 1968.

———. *Psychanalyse et critique littéraire.* Toulouse: Privat, Nouvelle Recherche, 1973.

COOPER, Douglas. *Rousseau.* Paris: Braun, 1951.

———. *The Courtauld Collection.* London: University of London, the Athlone Press, 1954.

COQUIOT, Gustave. *Les Indépendants 1884–1920.* Paris: Ollendorff, 1920.

———. *Vagabondages à travers la peinture et les paysages, les bêtes et les hommes.* Paris: Ollendorff, 1921.

COUANIER DE LAUNAY. *Histoire de Laval.* Laval: Librairie Cantin, 1979.

COURTHION, Pierre. *Henri Rousseau le Douanier.* Geneva: Editions d'Art Albert Skira, 1944.

———. *Henri Rousseau.* Paris: Fernand Hazan, 1956.

———. *Paris des temps nouveaux.* Geneva: Editions d'Art Albert Skira, 1957.

———. "Henri Rousseau." *L'Oeil*, no. 46 (October 1958).

COUTURIER, Marie-Alain. *Dieu et l'art dans une vie.* Paris: Le Cerf, 1956.

CRESPELLE, J. P. *Montparnasse vivant.* Paris: Hachette, 1962.

DANE, Marie-Claude. *L'Ecole de Paris dans le XVe arrondissement 1885–1940.* Catalogue of the exhibition of the town-hall annex of the XVth arrondissement (April 23–May

A dried flower in Rousseau's Larousse; his name does not yet appear here.

20, 1979). (Marie-Claude Dane confirms her discovery of the iconographic source of **The Battle of Champigny**.)

DASNOY, Albert. *Exégèse de la peinture naïve.* Brussels: Laconti, 1970.

DELAUNAY, Robert. "Henri Rousseau le Douanier." *L'Amour de l'Art*, no. 7 (November 1920).

——. "Mon ami Henri Rousseau." *Les Lettres Françaises* (August/September 1952).

——. *Les Cahiers inédits de Robert Delaunay: Du cubisme à l'art abstrait.* Paris: S.E.V.P.E.N., 1957.

DELAUNAY, Sonia. "Images inédites du Douanier." *Les Lettres Françaises* (August 1, 1952).

——. *Nous irons jusqu'au soleil.* Paris: Robert Laffont, 1978.

——. *Sonia et Robert Delaunay.* Catalogue of the Sonia Delaunay Donation, Bibliothèque nationale, Paris (1977).

DESCARGUES, Pierre. *Le Douanier Rousseau.* Geneva: Editions d'Art Albert Skira, 1972.

DOLTO, Françoise. *Psychanalyse et pédiatrie.* Paris: Le Seuil, 1971.

DRACOULIDÈS, N. N. *Psychanalyse de l'artiste et de son oeuvre.* Geneva: Editions du Mont-Blanc, 1952.

DUCHARTRE, Pierre-Louis, and SAULNIER, René. *L'Imagerie populaire.* Paris: Librairie de France, 1925.

EHRENZWEIG, Anton. *L'Ordre caché de l'art.* Paris: N.R.F./Gallimard, 1974.

ELGAR, Frank. *Rousseau.* Paris: Fernand Hazan, 1980.

ELUARD, Paul. Preface to the Exhibition Organized to Commemorate the Centennial of the Birth of Henri Rousseau, Museum of Modern Art of the City of Paris (December 22, 1944–January 21, 1945).

ERLANDE-BRANDENBURG, Alain. *La Dame à la Licorne.* Paris: Réunion des Musées nationaux, 1978.

——. *Le Musée de Cluny.* Paris: Réunion des Musées nationaux, 1979.

FAURE, Elie. *Histoire de l'art moderne*, vol. 2. Paris: Le Livre de poche, 1965.

FELLION, Gaston. "Le Douanier Rousseau et le mythe de la peinture naïve." *The Lion*, no. 294 (July 1980).

FERNANDEZ, Dominique. *L'Arbre jusqu'aux racines: Psychanalyse et création.* Paris: Grasset, 1972.

FLEURET, Fernand. *La Boîte à perruque.* Paris: Les Ecrivains associés, 1935.

FORGES, Marie-Thérèse de. "Une Source du Douanier Rousseau." *Art de France*, no. 4 (1964).

——. *Collection Jean Walter—Paul Guillaume.* Catalogue, Orangerie of the Tuileries. Paris: Réunion des Musées nationaux, 1966.

——. *Donation Picasso.* Catalogue of the Exhibition of the Personal Collection of Picasso. Paris: Réunion des Musées nationaux, 1978.

FRANK, Edmond. Letter concerning *Portrait of Pierre Loti* to the director of the Galerie Charpentier, August 20, 1952.

FREUD, Sigmund. *The Interpretation of Dreams.* New York: Modern Library, 1950.

——. *The Joke and Its Relation to the Unconscious.* Translated by James Strachey. New York: Norton, 1963.

——. *Leonardo da Vinci and a Memory of His Childhood.* Translated by Alan Tyson. New York: Norton, 1965.

FRIEDMAN, Michel. *Les Secrets du Facteur Cheval.* Paris: Jean-Claude Simoën, 1977.

GALERIES LAFAYETTE. *Bêtes sauvages: Environ 200 illustrations amusantes de la vie des animaux avec texte instructif.* Special publication of the Grands Magasins "Aux Galeries Lafayette," Rue Lafayette, Boulevard Haussmann, Chaussée d'Antin (Opera), Paris. Photographs by Meisenbach, Riffarth, and Co.

GARÇON, Maurice. *Le Douanier Rousseau: Accusé Naïf*. Paris: Quatre Chemins, Editard, 1953.

GAUTHIER, Maximilien. *Les Maîtres populaires de la réalité: Henri Rousseau*. Le musée de Grenoble, 1937.

———. *Henri Rousseau*. Paris: Les Gémeaux, 1949.

———. *Rousseau*. Paris: Flammarion, 1956.

———. Preface to the Wildenstein Exhibition, New York (April 17–May 25, 1963).

GEORGES-MICHEL, Michel. *De Renoir à Picasso: Les Peintres que j'ai connus*. Paris: Arthème Fayard, 1954.

GILOT, Françoise, and LAKE, Carlton. *Vivre avec Picasso*. Paris: Calmann-Lévy, 1965. In English: *Life with Picasso*. New York: McGraw-Hill, 1973.

GOLDWATER, Robert J. *Primitivism in Modern Painting*. London and New York: Harper and Brothers, 1938.

GORDON, Jan. *Modern French Painters*. New York: Dodd, Mead, 1923.

GOURMONT, Rémy de. In *Le Mercure de France* (October 16, 1910).

———. In *La France* (December 1, 1912).

———. *Le Puits de vérité*. Paris: Messein, 1922.

GREY, Roch. "Souvenirs de Rousseau." *Les Soirées de Paris* (January 15, 1914).

———. *Henri Rousseau*. Rome: Valori Plastici, 1922.

———. *Henri Rousseau*. Catalogue, Galerie René Drouin. Paris: Editions Tel, 1943.

GUILHERMET, Georges. *Souvenirs d'un avocat de la Belle Epoque*. Paris: Editions Universelles, 1953.

HIRET, René: "Nos grands hommes de Laval et notre lycée." In *Annuaire 1958–1959*. Association of Graduates of the Laval Lycée, 81st year. Laval, 1959.

HOOG, Michel: "La Direction des Beaux-Arts et les Fauves, 1903–1905." *Art de France*, no. 3 (1963).

———. "La Ville de Paris de Robert Delaunay: Sources et développement." *La Revue du Louvre*, no. 1 (1965).

———. *Robert Delaunay*. Catalogue of the Exhibition at the Orangerie of the Tuileries (May 25–August 30, 1976). Paris: Editions des Musées nationaux, 1976.

———. *Robert Delaunay*. Paris: Flammarion, 1976, and New York: Crown, 1977.

HUYGHE, René. *La Peinture d'instinct*. Histoire de l'art contemporain. Paris: Alcan, 1935.

JAKOVSKY, Anatole. *Gentil Rousseau* . . . Catalogue of The Jubilee Exhibition of the Birth of Henri Rousseau, Museum of Modern Art of the City of Paris (December 22, 1944–January 21, 1945).

———. *La Peinture naïve*. Paris: Jacques Damase, 1949.

———. *Les Peintres naïfs*. Paris: La Bibliothèque des Arts, 1956.

———. *Die naive Malerei in Frankreich*. Zurich: Diogenes Verlag, 1957.

———. *La Peinture naïve française du Douanier Rousseau à nos jours*. Paris: Maison de la pensée française, 1960.

———. "Le Douanier et les contrebandiers." *Jardin des Arts*, no. 79 (June 1961).

———. "Le Douanier Rousseau savait-il peindre?" *Médecine de France*, no. 218 (1971).

———. *Lexique universel des peintres naïfs*. Basel: Basilius Presse, 1976.

———. *Naive Painting*. London: Phaidon, 1979.

JARRY, Alfred. In *Minutes d'Art*, nos. 5 and 6.

———. In *L'Art Littéraire* (May–June 1894).

———. In *Les Indépendants*. Les Essais d'art libre. (June–July 1894).

———. In *L'Ymagier*, no. 2 (January 1895). (See Rousseau lithograph on p. 102.)

———. *Gestes et opinions du docteur Faustroll, pataphysicien* (chap. 23: "Comment on se procura de la toile"). Paris: Librairie Stock, 1923.

———. *Oeuvres complètes*. Paris: Gallimard, Bibliothèque de la Pléiade, 1972.

JONES, Ernest. *Hamlet and Oedipus*. New York: Norton, 1976.

JUNG, Carl Gustav. *Man and His Symbols. The Roots of the Conscious*. New York: Doubleday, 1969.

KAHNWEILER, Daniel-Henry. *Confessions esthétiques*. Paris: Gallimard, 1963.

KAPFERER, Simone. "Adieux de Paris aux cendres du Douanier Rousseau." *Arts* (February 15, 1947).

KAUFMANN, Pierre. *Psychanalyse et théorie de la culture: Qu'est-ce que c'est la vie de l'esprit?* Paris: Denoël-Gonthier, 1974.

KOFMAN, Sarah. *L'Enfance de l'art: Une Interprétation de l'esthétique freudienne*. Paris: Petite Bibliothèque Payot, 1970.

KOLLE, Helmut. *Henri Rousseau*. Leipzig: Klinkhardt und Biermann, 1922.

KOUZNETSOVA, Irina. *La Peinture française au musée Pouchkine*. Leningrad: Editions d'Art Aurore, 1980.

LABROSSE, André. In *Montmartre*, no. 1 (1961).

LACAMBRE, Geneviève; LACLOTTE, Michel; and ROHAN-CHABOT, Jacqueline de. *Le Musée du Luxembourg en 1874: Peintures*. Catalogue. Paris: Editions des Musées nationaux, 1974.

LARKIN, David: *Rousseau*. Paris: Editions du Chêne, 1975, and New York: Ballantine, 1975.

LE BASSER, Francis: *Musée Henri Rousseau. Les Naïfs. Vieux Château de Laval*. Supplement, "ABC Décor," with texts by Jakovsky, Certigny (*La Moisson au Château*), and Bordeaux-Le-Pecq.

LE DIBERDER, Yves. "Rousseau s'inspirait-il des photos et des gravures?" *Arts* (December 26, 1947).

LEFRANC. "L'Art et l'agio." *Commune*, third year, no. 33 (May 1936).

LEONARD, Sandra E. *Henri Rousseau and Max Weber*. New York: Richard L. Feigen, 1970.

LE PICHON, Yann. "Les Sources de Rousseau révélées." *Arts*, no. 809 (February 15–21, 1961).

———. *Robert Demachy, photographe: Quelques Instantanés de sa vie*. Paris: Société française de photographie et de contrejour, 1980.

———. *Bernard Conte*. Paris: Junes et fils, 1981.

LHOTE, André. "Exposition Henri Rousseau." *Nouvelle Revue Française* (November 1, 1923).

———. "L'Art populaire." *Nouvelle Revue Française* (August 1929).

LO DUCA. *Henri Rousseau dit le Douanier*. Paris: Editions du Chêne, 1951.

LONZI, C. *Rousseau*. Chefs-d'oeuvre de l'art: Grands Peintres, no. 43. Paris: Hachette, 1967.

MALRAUX, André. *Psychologie de l'art: la monnaie de l'absolu*. Geneva: Editions l'Art Albert Skira, 1950. In English: *Psychology of Art*. Translated by Stuart Gilbert. New York: Pantheon, 1951.

———. *Les Voix du Silence*. La Galerie de la Pléiade. Paris: Gallimard, 1951. In English: *Voices of Silence: Man and His Art*. Translated by Stuart Gilbert. Princeton: Princeton University Press, 1978.

———. *La Tête d'obsidienne*. Paris: Gallimard, 1974.

———. *L'Homme précaire et la littérature*. Paris: Gallimard, 1977.

MARITAIN, Jacques. *L'Intuition créatrice dans l'art et la poésie*. Paris: Desclée de Brouwer, 1966. In English: *Creative Intuition in Art and Poetry*. New York: New American Library, 1955.

MARREY, Bernard. *Les Grands Magasins*. Paris: Picard, 1976.

MILNER, Marion. *L'Inconscient et la peinture*. Le Fil rouge. Paris: Presses Universitaires de France, 1976.

MIYAGAWA, Atsushi. *Rousseau*. L'Art moderne du monde, no. 10. Tokyo: The Zauho Press. Published by Shueisha, Japan, 1971.

MORARIU, Modest. *Henri Rousseau le Douanier*. Bucharest: Editions Meridiane, 1975; Paris: Editions Beaulieu, 1975.

NACENTA, Raymond. Preface to *Catalogue de l'Exposition du cinquantenaire de la mort du Douanier Rousseau*. Paris: Galerie Charpentier, 1961.

———. *Les Naïfs*. Paris: Nouvelles éditions françaises, 1961.

———. "Primitifs d'aujourd'hui," preface to the Catalogue of the Exhibition of the Galerie Charpentier (1964).

———. *Ecoles de Paris*. Paris: Ides et Calendes.

OLIVIER, Fernande. *Picasso et ses amis*. Paris:

Stock, 1933.

PASSERON, René: *Histoire de la peinture surréaliste*. Paris: Le Livre de poche, 1968.

PAYRO, Julio E. *Rousseau el Aduanero*. Buenos Aires: Poseidon, 1944.

PEDRAZZINI, Marie-Charlotte. "Le legs fabuleux de Mme Walter." *Paris-Match* (January 29, 1966).

PERRUCHOT, Henri. *Le Douanier Rousseau*. Témoins du XXe siècle. Paris: Editions universitaires, 1957.

PLANCHENAULT, René: *L'Apocalypse d'Angers*. Caisse nationale des monuments historiques et des sites. Paris, 1966.

PROUST, Marcel. *A la recherche du temps perdu*. Paris: Gallimard, Bibliothèque de la Pléiade, 1954. In English: *Remembrance of Things Past*. Translated by C. K. Scott Moncrieff, Terence Kilmartin, and Andreas Mayor. New York: Random House, 1981, and London: Chatto and Windus, 1981.

RABOFF, Ernest. *Henri Rousseau: L'art pour les enfants*. Geneva: Bradley Smith, 1971. In English: *Henri Rousseau*. New York: Doubleday, 1970.

RAYNAL, Maurice. "Le Banquet Rousseau." *Les Soirées de Paris*, no. 20. (January 15, 1914).

REYER, Georges. "Un Photographe retrouve le Douanier Rousseau." *Paris-Match* (April 16, 1960).

RICH, Daniel Catton. *Henri Rousseau*. New York: The Museum of Modern Art, 1946.

RIMBAUD, Arthur. *Oeuvres complètes*. Paris: Gallimard, Bibliothèque de la Pléiade, 1946. In English: *Complete Works*. Translated by Paul Schmidt. New York: Harper & Row, 1976.

ROUSSEAU, Henri (le Douanier): *Une Visite à l'Exposition de 1889*. Farce in three acts and ten scenes, with two illustrations. Preface by Tristan Tzara. Geneva: Pierre Cailler, 1947. (Excerpted in *Bulletin de la Vie Artistique*, no. 8 [April 15, 1922] and no. 9 [May 1, 1922].)

———. *La Vengeance d'une orpheline russe*. Drama in five acts and nineteen scenes, with two illustrations. Geneva: Pierre Cailler, 1947. (Excerpted by Tristan Tzara in *Orbes*, nos. 2 and 4 [1929–33].)

———. *L'Etudiant en goguette*. Unpublished manuscript.

———. "Clémence: Valse avec introduction pour violon ou mandoline." Paris: L. Barbarin.

———. Scrapbooks of newspaper clippings and account book. Manuscripts of the farce and the drama (Tristan Tzara Collection).

———. Catalogues of the Salon of The Independents and the Salon d'Automne.

ROY, Louis: "Un Isolé: Henri Rousseau." *Le Mercure de France* (March 1895).

SALMON, André. *Propos d'atelier*. Paris: Crès, 1922.

———. *Henri Rousseau dit le Douanier*. Peintres et Sculpteurs. Paris: Crès, 1927.

———. *Henri Rousseau*. Paris: Aimery Somogy, 1962.

———. *Rousseau (Henri, Julien, Félix) dit le Douanier*. Dictionnaire Bénézit, vol. 9. Paris, 1976.

SALONS. Catalogues of the Salon, the Salon of the Independents and Salon d'Automne, and the Panorama-Salons.

SARTRE, Jean-Paul. *L'Imaginaire. Psychologie phénoménologique de l'imagination*. Paris: N.R.F./Gallimard, 1940. In English: *Psychology of Imagination*. New York: Lyle Stuart, 1980.

SÉRULLAZ, Maurice. *Dessins français de l'Art Institute de Chicago de Watteau à Picasso*. Catalogue (October 15, 1976–January 17, 1977). Paris: Editions des Musées nationaux.

SHATTUCK, Roger. *The Banquet Years*. London: Jonathan Cape, 1959, and New York: Random House, 1968.

———. *Les Primitifs de l'avant-garde*. Paris: Flammarion, 1974.

SINOIR, Emile. *Histoire du lycée de Laval*.

SOFFICI, Ardengo. In *La Voce* (September 15, 1910).

———. "La France jugée à l'étranger: Le Peintre Henri Rousseau." *Le Mercure de France* (October 16, 1910).

———. *Trenta artisti moderni italiani e stranieri*. Florence: Vallecchi, 1950.

SOUPAULT, Philippe. "La Légende du Douanier Rousseau." *L'Amour de l'Art*, vol. 7, no. 10 (October 1926).

———. *Henri Rousseau le Douanier*. Paris: Editions des Quatre Chemins, 1927.

———. *Henri Rousseau le Douanier*. Geneva: Editions d'Art Albert Skira, 1949.

STEIN, Gertrude: *The Autobiography of Alice B. Toklas*. New York: Harcourt, Brace, 1933.

STERNBERG, Jacques, and Chapelo, Pierre. *Le Tour du monde en 300 gravures. Redécouvertes*. Paris: Editions Planète, 1972.

SZITTYA, Emil. *Henri Rousseau*. Hamburg: Asmus Verlag, 1924.

THARAUD, Jérôme, and Tharaud, Jean. *Le Gentil Douanier et un artiste maudit*. Paris: Les Cahiers libres, 1929.

TILLIETTE, Xavier. "Inspection du Douanier." *Etudes* (May 1961).

TROHEL, Jules. "Origines mayennaises du Douanier Rousseau: Notes et documents artistiques." *Le Mercure de France*, no. 723 (August 1, 1928).

———. "Alfred Jarry et les huissiers." *Le Mercure de France* (July 1, 1934).

TZARA, Tristan. Preface to *Une Visite à l'Exposition de 1889*. Geneva: Pierre Cailler, 1947.

———. *Henri Rousseau*. Catalogue, Sidney Janis Gallery, New York (November 5–December 22, 1951).

———. "Le rôle du temps et de l'espace dans l'oeuvre du Douanier Rousseau." *Art de France*, no. 2 (1962).

UHDE, Wilhelm. *Henri Rousseau*. Paris: Eugène Figuière, 1911.

———. Preface to *L'Exposition Henri Rousseau*. Catalogue (October 28–November 9, 1912). Paris: Bernheim-Jeune, 1912.

———. *Henri Rousseau*. Berlin and Dresden: Rudolf Kaemmerer, 1923.

———. *Rousseau (Le Douanier)*. Lausanne: Jean Marguerat, 1948.

———. *Cinq Maîtres primitifs*. Paris: Librairie Palmes, Philippe Baudy, 1949. In English: *Five Primitive Masters*. New York, 1949.

VACHON, Marius. *Eugène Delacroix à l'Ecole des Beaux-Arts (March-April 1885)*. Paris: Ludovic Baschet, 1885.

VALLIER, Dora. *Henri Rousseau*. Paris: Flammarion, 1961; New York: Harry N. Abrams, 1964; and London: Thames & Hudson, 1964.

———. "L'Emploi du pantographe dans l'oeuvre du Douanier Rousseau." *Revue de l'Art*, no. 7 (1970).

———. *Tout l'oeuvre peint de Henri Rousseau*. Paris: Flammarion, 1970.

———. *Henri Rousseau*. Paris: Flammarion, 1979, and New York: Crown, 1979.

VALLOTTON, Félix. In *Le Journal Suisse* (March 25, 1891).

VIATTE, Germain. "Lettres inédites à Ambroise Vollard." *Art de France*, no. 2 (1962).

VIERNY, Dina. *Le Monde merveilleux des Naïfs: Hommage à Wilhelm Uhde*. Paris: Dina Vierny, 1974.

VOLLARD, Ambroise. *Souvenirs d'un marchand de tableaux*. Paris: Albin Michel, 1927.

WALDBERG, Patrick. *L'Art immédiat*. Paris: Séraphine, Galerie d'art de tradition populaire, 1968.

WARNOD, André. *Les Berceaux de la jeune peinture: Ecole de Paris, Montmartre, Montparnasse*. Paris: Albin Michel, 1925.

WARNOD, Jeanine. *Le Bateau-Lavoir*. Paris: Les Presses de la connaissance, 1975.

———. *La Ruche et Montparnasse*. Geneva, Paris: Weber, 1978.

WEBER, Max. "Rousseau as I Knew Him." *Art News*, vol. 41 (February 15, 1942).

WERNER, Alfred. *Henri Rousseau*. Amsterdam: Harry N. Abrams, 1956.

WILENSKI, R. H. *Douanier Rousseau*. London: Faber and Faber, 1953.

———. *Modern French Painters*. New York: Reynal and Hitchcock, 1963.

WYSS, Johann. *Swiss Family Robinson*. New York: Dell, 1960.

ZERVOS, Christian. *Henri Rousseau*. Paris: Editions Cahiers d'art, 1927.

———. *Histoire de l'art contemporain*. Paris: Editions Cahiers d'art, 1938.

Sources of Illustrations

The works not entered in the present list are in personal collections. Unless otherwise indicated, all the paintings listed here are painted in oil on canvas. I have assigned identification numbers to the works, going in this order: top, left to right; bottom, left to right.

The dimensions are given in centimeters: height by width. The location of the signature is indicated as follows. S: signed; D: dated; b.r.: bottom right; b.l.: bottom left; t.r.: top right; t.l.: top left.

Pages

34 1. *Henri Rousseau as Orchestra Conductor.* 46 × 29.5. S.b.r.: Henri J. Rousseau. Private collection.
4. *The Promenade—Bois de Vincennes.* 44 × 54. S.b.l.: Henri Rousseau. Private collection, Pratteln, Switzerland. Photo: W. Dietrich.

35 *A Carnival Evening.* 116.5 × 89.5 S.b.r.: H. Rousseau. Museum of Art, Philadelphia. Louis E. Stern Collection.

36 1. *Happy Quartet.* 94 × 57. S.b.r.: H. Rousseau. Collection of Mr. and Mrs. John Hay Whitney, New York.
2. *The Acacias.* Pencil drawing. Private collection, D.R.

37 *The Rendezvous in the Forest.* 92 × 73. S.b.r.: Henri Rousseau. National Gallery of Art, Washington, D.C. Gift of the W. Averell Harriman Foundation in memory of Marie N. Harriman.

38 1. *The Wedding Party in the Photographer's Studio.* 85 × 122. S.D.b.l.: D. A. J. Dagnan-Bouveret, Paris 1878–1879. Musée des Beaux-Arts, Lyon. Photo: Bulloz.
2. Photo: Miltos Toscas.

39 *The Wedding—A Country Wedding.* 163 × 114. S.b.r.: Henri Julien Rousseau. Musée de l'Orangerie, Paris. J. Walter—P. Guillaume Collection. Photo: Musées Nationaux.

40 1. *The Present and the Past.* 85 × 47.5. S.D.b.r.: Henri Rousseau. The Barnes Foundation, Merion, Pennsylvania.
4. *The Environs of Batignolles.* 25 × 29. Oil on cardboard. Title in pencil on back, in painter's hand. Private collection.

41 1. *The Artist Painting His Wife.* 56.5 × 66. Collection of Madame Nina Kandinsky, Neuilly-sur-Seine. Photo: Snark International.

42 1. Sculpture by Robert Tatin. Photo: Lapad-Viollet.
2. *Portrait of the Artist with a lamp.* 24 × 19. Musée du Louvre, Paris. Donation Picasso. Photo: Musées nationaux.
3. *Self-Portrait.* S.b.r.: H. Rousseau. Private collection D. R.
4. *Portrait of Clémence.* Oil on wood. Private collection. D. R.

43 1. *Portrait of Rousseau's Second Wife with a Lamp.* 22.5 × 17.5. Musée du Louvre, Paris. Donation Picasso. Photo: Musées Nationaux.
3. *Portrait of Monsieur Steven.* 41 × 33. S.b.r.: H. Rousseau. Private collection, New York.
4. *Portrait of Madame Steven.* 45.5 × 35.5. S.b.r.: H. Rousseau. Private collection, New York.

44 Self-portrait in pen and ink after the photograph on p. 26.

52 *Portrait of a Baby.* Tzara Collection.

53 *The Abandoned Child in the Countryside near the Bridge of Saint-Cloud. Stroller and the Child.* 54 × 38. S.b.r.: H. Rousseau. Museum of Fine Arts, Dallas. Anonymous gift.

54 *Mother and Child.* 24 × 18. S.b.l.: H. Rousseau. Collection of Mrs. Joy Weber. With

the permission of Richard L. Feigen and Co.
2. *Girl Knitting.* 17.5 × 13.5. Pencil drawing. Private collection, Switzerland. Photo: G. Howald.

55 1. *View of the Fortifications—Landscape of Fortifications.* 38 × 46. S.b.r.: Henri Rousseau. Private collection, Switzerland.
2. Photo: Atget (C.N.M.H.S.) © SPADEM 1981.

56–57 *Old Juniet's Carriole.* 97 × 129. S.D.b.l.: Henri J. Rousseau 1908. Musée de l'Orangerie, Paris. J. Walter—P. Guillaume Collection. Photo: Musées Nationaux.

58 *Old Juniet's Carriole.* Photo: Musées Nationaux.
3. James Johnson Sweeney Collection.
4. *View of Montsouris Park—Promenade in Montsouris Park.* 46.5 × 38.5. S.b.l.: H. Rousseau. Pushkin Museum, Moscow.

59 1. *Promenade to the Manor.* 33 × 41. S.b.r.: Henri Rousseau. Private collection, France.
2. Sketch for *View of Malakoff.* 19 × 28. Oil on paper. S.b.r.: H. Rousseau. On the back: "Presented to my friend Weber December 2, 1908 / Paris 2 Xbre / his friend H. Rousseau." *View of Malakoff. Environs of Paris.* Collection of Mrs. Joy Weber, New York. With the permission of Richard L. Feigen and Co.
3. *View of Malakoff.* 46 × 55. S.D.b.r.: Henri Rousseau 1908. Private collection, Switzerland. Photo: G. Howald.

60 *Montsouris Park, the Kiosk—View of Montsouris Park.* 65 × 80. S.b.l.: Henri Rousseau. The Barnes Foundation, Merion, Pennsylvania.
3. *The Baby's Baptismal Celebration—The Family.* 46 × 55. S.b.l.: Henri Rousseau. The Barnes Foundation, Merion, Pennsylvania.

61 *Portrait of a Child—The Child of the Rocks.* 55 × 45. S.b.r.: H. Rousseau. National Gallery of Art, Washington, D.C. Chester Dale Collection.

62 1. *Portrait of a Child—The Child with the Doll.* 67 × 52. S.b.r.: H. J. Rousseau. Musée de l'Orangerie, Paris. J. Walter—P. Guillaume Collection. Photo: Musées Nationaux.
2. *Portrait of Maya.* P. Picasso. 73 × 60. D.b.l.: 16.1.38. Musée Picasso. Photo: Giraudon. © SPADEM 1981.

63 *Portrait of a Child—To Celebrate Baby—Child with Punchinello.* 100 × 81. S.b.r.: Henri Rousseau. Kunstverein, Winterthur.

64 Photo: Miltos Toscas. Plaster medallion recreated for the tomb of Henri Rousseau.

72 *The Douanier Rousseau Rising Toward Glory and Entering Posterity—Homage to Henri Rousseau.* 100 × 56. S.b.r.: R. Rimbert. Foundation Wildenstein. Photo: M. Beck.
3. *The City of Paris* (detail). 267 × 406. S.D.b.l.: R. Delaunay 1910-11-12. Musée national d'Art moderne, France. © ADAGP 1981.
4. *Carousel Bridge.* Photo: Bibliothèque historique de la Ville de Paris.

73 *Myself. Landscape Portrait.* 143 × 110.

S.D.b.l.: Henri Rousseau, 1890. National Gallery, Prague.

74 *Sergeant Frumence Biche.* 92 × 73. S.b.r.: H. Rousseau. Private collection.
4. Photo: *Paris-Match*, Garofalo.

75 *The Muse Inspiring the Poet.* 131 × 97. S.D.b.r.: H. Rousseau 1909. Pushkin Museum, Moscow.

76 Photo: Bulloz.
2. *Portrait of Guillaume Apollinaire and Marie Laurencin with Poet's Narcissus—The Muse Inspiring the Poet.* 146 × 97. S.D.b.r.: Henri Rousseau 1909. Kunstmuseum, Basel. Photo: H. Hintz.

77 2. *Apollinaire and His Friends.* 130 × 194. S.D.t.r.: Marie Laurencin 1909. *Musée national d'Art moderne, Paris.* Photo: Musées nationaux © A.D.A.G.P. 1981.
3. *Saint-Germain-des-Prés—Patrix.* S.b.r.: Emile Binnet. Photo: Snark International.

78 1. *Portrait of Pierre Loti.* 61 × 50. S.b.r.: H. Rousseau. Kunsthaus, Zurich.
3. Photo: Nadar. Bibliothèque Nationale, Paris © SPADEM 1981.

79 1. Photo: Bibl. Nat. Paris.
2. *Landscape Portrait (Belonging to M.B.)—Portrait of Monsieur Brummer.* 117 × 87. S.D.b.l.: H. Rousseau 1909. Private collection, Switzerland. Photo: H. Hinz.
3. *The Leisures, or Homage to Louis David.* 154 × 185. S.D.b.r.: 48-49 F. Léger. Musée national d'Art moderne, Paris. Photo: Musées Nationaux. © SPADEM 1981.

80 1. Photo: Bulloz.
2. *Portrait of a Child—The Girl.* 61 × 46. Philadelphia (Pennsylvania) Museum of Art. Gift of Mr. and Mrs. R. Sturgis Ingersoll.
3. *Portrait of a Woman.* 160 × 105. Musée du Louvre, Paris. Donation Picasso. Photo: Musées Nationaux.
5. Photo: Brassaï.

81 *Portrait of a Woman.* 198 × 115. S.b.l.: Henri Rousseau. Musée d'Orsay, Paris. Photo: G. Perron.

82 2. Sirot-Angel Collection.

83 *Promenade in the Forest of Saint Germain—Promenade.* 70 × 60.5. S.b.l.: H. Rousseau. Kunsthaus, Zurich.

94 2. *Old Tower of Avranches.* 55.5 × 46. S.b.l.: H. Rousseau, with title "Old Tower of Avranches." Private collection.
3. *Overall View of Vanves, to the Left of the Gate of This Name, September 1909—View of the Fortifications.* 31 × 41. S.b.l.: H. Rousseau. Hermitage Museum, Leningrad.
5. Photo: Atget (C.N.M.H.S.). © SPADEM 1981.

95 *The Customs House.* 37.5 × 32.5. S.b.r.: H. Rousseau. The Courtauld Institute, London.

96 1. *Strollers in a Park.* 46 × 55. S.b.l.: H. Rousseau. Musée de l'Orangerie, Paris. J. Walter—G. Guillaume Collection. Photo: Roland.
2. *The Ravine of Presles.* 66 × 51. S.b.r.: Maurice Utrillo. Oil on Wood. Musée d'Art

moderne de la Ville de Paris. Photo: Bulloz. © SPADEM 1981.

97 *View from an Arch of the Bridge of Sèvres.* S.b.r.: H. Rousseau. Private collection. Photo: Roland.

98 1. *Landscape with a Dirigible—Quai d'Ivry.* 46 × 54.5. S.b.l.: Henri Rousseau. Bridgestone Gallery, Tokyo.

99 1. *View of the Bridge at Sèvres and Saint-Cloud with Airplane, Balloon, and Dirigible.* 80 × 102. S.D.b.l.: Henri Rousseau 1908. Pushkin Museum, Moscow.

100–101 *View of Point-du-Jour. Sunset—Viaduct of Auteuil.* 85 × 115. S.b.l.: Henri Rousseau. Collection of P. Rival, Vidauban. Photo: H. Donner.

102 1. Photo: Lapi-Viollet.
2. *The Bridge of Grenelle Under Snow.* 19 × 74. S.b.l.: H. Rousseau. Private collection, Paris.
3. Photo: Roger-Viollet.

103 *View of the Footbridge of Passy.* 38 × 45. S.b.r.: H. Rousseau. Collection of Morton R. Goldsmith, Scarsdale, New York.

104–105 1. Photo: Bibl. Nat. Paris.
2. *View of Ile Saint-Louis from the Port of Saint-Nicolas, Evening.* 46 × 55. S.b.l.: Henri Rousseau. Collection of Mr. and Mrs. Paul Mellon, Upperville, Virginia.

106 *The Washerwomen of Melun.* Henri Rousseau. Private Collection. D.R.

107 *Notre-Dame Seen from Port Henri-IV.* 33 × 40. S.D.b.r.: H. Rousseau 1909. The Phillips Collection, Washington, D.C.
3. *The Seine in Paris.* 65 × 81. S. A. Marquet 1934. Musée de l'Annonciade, S. Tropez. Photo: Musées Nationaux. © ADAGP 1981.

108 1. *View of the Luxembourg, Chopin Monument.* 38 × 47. S.D.b.r.: H. Rousseau 1909. Hermitage Museum, Leningrad.

109 2. *The Avenue, Park of Saint-Cloud.* 46 × 37.5. S.b.r.: H. Rousseau. Städtische Galerie. Frankfurt/Main, West Germany.

110 1. *Landscape in Buttes-Chaumont.* 46 × 38. S.b.r.: H. Rousseau. Private collection. Photo: Roland.
2. Viollet Collection.

111 *Soccer Players.* 100.5 × 80.5. S.D.b.r.: Henri Rousseau 1908. The Solomon R. Guggenheim Museum, New York. Photo: Robert E. Mates.

112 1. *View of Saint-Cloud from the Heights of Bellevue.* 21 × 27. S.b.l.: Henri Rousseau. Private collection, Switzerland. Photo: G. Howald.
2. *Lakeside Village.* Lucien Vieillard 1969. D.R.

113 *The Stone Quarry.* 47.5 × 55.5. S.b.l.: H. Rousseau. Private collection, New York. Published by Ides et Calendes, Neuchâtel.

114 1. *The Water Mill.* S.b.r.: H. Rousseau. Photo: Roger-Viollet.
2. *View of a Park—River and Countryside.* 25 × 20.7. Pen-and-ink drawing. S.b.l.: Henri Rousseau. The Art Institute, Chicago. Mr. and Mrs. Henry C. Woods Collection.

115 *The River.* S.b.r.: H. Rousseau. Photo: Roger-Viollet.

116 1. *Banks of the Marne.* 48 × 64. S.b.r.: Henri Rousseau. Private collection. Photo: H. Hinz.
2. *The Pond.* 25 × 33. Private collection.

117 1. *The Fisherman.* 36 × 47. S.b.r.: Henri Rousseau. Collection of Michael Bakwin, New York.
2. *Landscape on the Banks of the Oise (Villa Mathilde. Territory of Champoval).* Henri Rousseau. Collection of Mrs. Joy Weber.

118 1. *Landscape with Water Mill and Cart.* 32.5 × 55.5. S.D.b.r.: H. Rousseau, 1879. Museum of Fine Arts, Göteborg.

119 1. *The Tollgate—The Barrier.* 36 × 48. S.b.l.: Henri Rousseau. G. Renand Collection, Paris.

120 1. *Suburb. View of the Chair Factory and the Seine Quay at Alfortville.* 73 × 93. S.b.r.: Henri Rousseau. Musée de l'Orangerie, Paris. J. Walter—P. Guillaume Collection. Photo: Musées Nationaux.

121 1. *Banks of the Marne (Charenton). The Alfort Mill.* 37 × 45. S.b.l.: Henri Rousseau. Private collection. Published by Ides et Calendes, Neuchâtel.
3. Sketch for *The Alfort Mill.* 25 × 30.5. S.b.l.: H. Rousseau. Private collection.

122 1. *The Cliff.* 22 × 35. S.b.l.: Henri Rousseau. Musée de l'Orangerie, Paris. J. Walter—P. Guillaume Collection. Photo: Musées Nationaux.
2. *The Cliff with Boats.* S.b.r. G. Courbet. Private collection. Photo: Bulloz.

123 1. *The D'Entrecasteaux in a Tempest—The Boat in the Tempest.* 54 × 65. S.b.l.: Henri Rousseau. Musée de l'Orangerie, Paris. J. Walter—P. Guillaume Collection. Photo: Musées Nationaux.

124 1. *Landscape with Farm and Cow.* 38 × 55. S.b.r.: Henri Rousseau. Private collection.
2. *Rainy Morning.* Henri Rousseau. Private collection.
3. *Country Road.* S.b.l.: H. Rousseau. Private collection. Photo: Roger-Viollet.

125 *The Forest Road.* 44 × 62. Henri Rousseau. Private collection.

126 *The Shepherd—The Goatherd.* 40 × 53.5. S.b.r.: H. Rousseau. Collection of James Thrall Soby, New Canaan, Connecticut.

127 1. *View of Brittany—Summer.* 40 × 52. S.b.r.: Henri Rousseau. Private collection.
3. *The Pasture.* 47 × 55. S.b.r.: H. Rousseau. Bridgestone Museum of Art, Tokyo.

128 *The Peasant Woman in the Meadow—Landscape with Flock.* 51 × 66. S.b.r.: Henri Julien Rousseau. Philadelphia (Pennsylvania) Museum of Art. Louise and Walter Arensberg Collection.
2. Sketch for *View of the Surroundings of Paris. Township of Bagneux.* S.b.l. and r.: H. Rousseau. Private collection.

129 1. *The Haystacks—Paths in the Forest.* 38 × 46.5. S.b.r.: H. Rousseau. Private collection, Switzerland.
2. *View of the Surroundings of Paris. Township of Bagneux.* On the back: *View of the Surroundings of Paris, Township of Bagneux,* 1909. H. Rousseau. 33 × 46. S.b.l.: Henri Rousseau. Private collection.

130–31 2. *Lady in the Exotic Forest.* 99 × 81. S.b.r.: Henri Rousseau. The Barnes Foundation, Merion, Pennsylvania.

131 *Lady with Umbrella in the Exotic Forest.* 74 × 60. S.b.l.: Henri Rousseau. Private collection.

143 2. *The Elephant or Light Bay Horse.* Tapestry of material woven at the Manufactory of the Gobelins after a cartoon by van der Eckhout. Collection du Mobilier National, Paris. Photo: Hachette.

144–45 1. *Surprised! Tropical Storm with Tiger.* 130 × 162. S.D.b.l.: Henri Rousseau 1891. The National Gallery, London. Photo: E. T. Archive.

145 2. *Encounter Between a Lion and a Tiger.* 24 × 32. S.b.r.: E. Delacroix. National Gallery, Prague. Photo: Giraudon.
3. *Copy of Encounter Between a Lion and a Tiger by Delacroix—Tiger Attacking a Lion,* around 1885. Oil on wood. (Painting by Delacroix formerly owned by the Galerie Bernheim and now in the Museum of Prague. Guaranteed by H. Certigny, who has reproduced it as no. 23 in *La Vérité sur le Douanier Rousseau.* Guaranteed by R. Trillat, graphological expert. Guaranteed by A. Jabovsky, who

Paris.

has reproduced it in an article [*Médicine de France,* no. 218].) S.b.r.: after E. D. Henri Rousseau.

146 *Fight Between a Tiger and a Bull—Fight Between Tiger and Buffalo.* 46 × 55. S.b.l.: Henri Rousseau. Hermitage Museum, Leningrad.

147 1. *Fight Between Tiger and Buffalo.* 172 × 191.5. S.D.b.r.: Henri Rousseau 1908. Museum of Art, Cleveland. Gift of Hanna Fund.

148 1. *Scouts Attacked by a Tiger.* 130 × 162. S.b.r.: Henri Rousseau. The Barnes Foundation, Merion, Pennsylvania.

149 1. *Fight Between a Jaguar and a Horse—Horse Attacked by a Jaguar.* 90 × 116. S.b.r.: Henri Rousseau. Pushkin Museum, Moscow.
2. *Lion Attacking a White Horse.* T. Géricault. Musée de Louvre, Paris. Photo: Giraudon.

150 1. *Lion's Head.* 15.5 × 20. S.b.l.: H. Rousseau. Oil on panel. Private collection.

151 1. *The Lion Hunter.* 44 × 55. S.b.l.: H. Rousseau. Private collection. Photo: M. Coen.
3. *Lion Reclining.* S.b.r.: H. Rousseau. Private collection. Photo: Roger-Viollet.

152–53 2. *The Hungry Lion.* 200 × 300. S.b.r.: Henri Rousseau. Private collection, Switzerland. Photo: H. Hinz.
3. *Joie de Vivre.* M. Ernst. 60 × 73. Galerie Beyeler, Basel. © SPADEM 1981.

154–55 *The Lion's Meal.* 113.5 × 160. S.b.r.: Henri Rousseau. The Metropolitan Museum of Art, New York. Samuel A. Lewisohn Legacy, 1951.

156–57 *Negro Attacked by a Jaguar—Virgin Forest at Sunset.* 114 × 162.5. S.b.r.: Henri Rousseau. Kunstmuseum, Basel.

158–59 1. *The Port of Algiers.* 37 × 59.5. S.D.b.l.: H. Rousseau. G. Renand Collection, Paris. Photo: G. Perron.

159 1. *The Tiger Hunt.* 38 × 46. S.b.r.: H. Rousseau. Columbus (Ohio) Museum of Art. Gift of Ferdinand Howald.

160 1. *Head of Virginia Deer.* 32 × 41.5. S.b.r.: Henri Rousseau. Oil on wood. Private collection.
2. *The Owl.* 24.5 × 15. S.b.r.: H. R. Oil on wood. Private collection.
4. *Piece of Game.* T. Géricault (detail). 59.5 × 72.5. Museum of Fine Arts and Archeology, Besançon.

161 1. *The Waterfall.* 116 × 150. S.D.b.r.: Henri Rousseau 1910. The Art Institute of Chicago. Helen Birch Bartlett Memorial Collection, 1962.

163 1. *Exotic Landscape.* 130 × 162. S.D.b.r.: Henri Rousseau 1910. The Norton Simon Foundation, Pasadena.

164 1. *Zizi.* 21.5 × 14.5 S.b.r.: Henri Rousseau. G. Renand Collection, Paris. Photo: G. Perron.
3. *Smell* (detail). Photo: Giraudon.

165 1. *Tropical Forest with Monkeys.* 129.5 × 160. S.D.b.r.: Henri Rousseau 1910. Collection of Mr. and Mrs. John Hay Whitney, New York.

166 1. *The Gibbon Apes—Jungle with Two Monkeys.* 63 × 48. S.b.l.: Henri Rousseau. Collection of Mr. and Mrs. Charles S. Payson, New York.
4. *Joyous Jokesters.* 146 × 114. S.b.l.: Henri Julien Rousseau. Philadelphia (Pennsylvania) Museum of Art. Louise and Walter C. Arensberg Collection.

167 1. *Monkeys in the Virgin Forest.* 114 × 162. S.b.r.: Henri Rousseau. Private collection, Tokyo.

168 1. *Wader.* 34.5 × 21. G. Renand Collection, Paris. Photo: G. Perron.

168–69 *The Flamingos.* 113 × 162. S.b.l.: Henri Rousseau. Collection of Mr. and Mrs. Charles S. Payson, New York.

283

This work,
which owes its layout to Pierre Chapelot,
its technical production to Claude Chapuis,
and its iconography to Catherine Feroldi,
was set in Palatino
by American–Stratford Graphic Services, Inc.
It was engraved by Actual,
under the direction of René Béguelin,
printed by Weber, Switzerland,
and bound by Brun, at Malesherbes, France.

This edition published 1982
by Phaidon Press Limited
Littlegate House, St. Ebbe's Street
Oxford, OX1 1SQ
English translation copyright © 1982
by Viking Penguin Inc.

Originally published in French under the title
Le Monde du Douanier Rousseau
Copyright © 1981 by Editions Robert Laffont

BRITISH LIBRARY CATALOGUING IN PUBLICATION DATA
Le Pichon, Yann
    Henri Rousseau.
    1. Rousseau, Henri
    2. Painters–France–Biography
    I. Title   II. Le monde du Douanier Rousseau.
    English
    759.4'092   ND553.R67

ISBN 0-7148-2256-6